West Palm Beach, Florida, March 1981

"The most wrongest thing you ever did was f--- me. People fear me. . . . You're only alive today, my friend, because Don's wife walked in. Not because we stopped. You wasn't supposed to walk away no more. . . ."

I lay in my bed holding the telephone receiver at arm's length, listening to Tommy Agro scream at the top of his lungs. My head ached. My broken ribs burned like kindling. And my nose, splayed across my face, was split down the middle. Attached to the telephone was a tape recorder, hooked up courtesy of the FBI office in West Palm Beach, Florida. It didn't take me long to get Tommy Agro to confess that he and two of his New York sluggers had flown to Palm Beach County to beat me to death. To make an example of me.

Two months earlier, on January 19, 1981, Tommy Agro had summoned me to Don Ritz's pizzeria on Singer Island. He was there with two of his crew, Paul Principe and Frank Russo. They used lead pipes and a baseball bat, and the last thing I remember was Agro himself drawing back his leg and digging his dainty little alligator loafer deep into my ribs. . . .

So I joined forces with the FBI, something to this day I can't believe I did. . . .

But after a while, working with the feds, I started to enjoy myself. I was getting my revenge. On the Mafia. Nothing ever tasted as sweet.

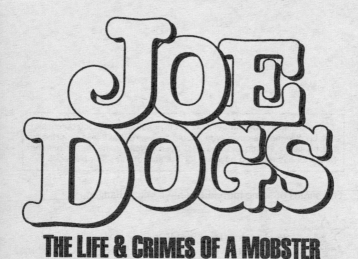

THE LIFE & CRIMES OF A MOBSTER

Joseph "Joe Dogs" Iannuzzi

POCKET **STAR** BOOKS

New York London Toronto Sydney Tokyo Singapore

The names of some individuals have been changed.

 A Pocket Star Book published by
POCKET BOOKS, a division of Simon & Schuster Inc.
1230 Avenue of the Americas, New York, NY 10020

ISBN: 0-671-79753-0

First Pocket Books printing July 1995

10 9 8 7 6 5 4 3 2 1

POCKET STAR BOOKS and colophon are registered
trademarks of Simon & Schuster Inc.

Cover art by Darryl Zudeck

Printed in the U.S.A.

For Francie

The Players

THE GAMBINO *FAMIGLIA*

Carlo "Don Carlo" Gambino   Boss of the Gambino Family, the nation's most powerful Mafia Family, until his death in 1976

Paul "Big Paulie" Castellano   Succeeded Carlo Gambino as boss in 1976; held position until murdered in 1985

Joseph N. Gallo   Longtime *consigliere* of Gambino Family; archenemy of Joe "Joe Dogs" Iannuzzi

Aniello "Neil" Dellacroce   mentor of John Gotti, rival of Paul Castellano; Gambino Family underboss to both Carlo Gambino and Castellano

Joseph "Piney" Armone   New York–based Gambino Family capo

Thomas "T.A." Agro   Gambino Family soldier; member of Joe "Piney" Armone's crew; ran Southeast Florida for Gambino Family; Joe Iannuzzi's boss and mentor

Robert "Skinny Bobby" DeSimone
Louie Esposito
}   Gambino Family associates; Florida–based members of Tommy Agro's crew

Paul Principe
Frank Russo
}   Gambino Family associates; New York–based sluggers of Tommy Agro's crew

Andrew "Fat Andy" Ruggiano Miami–based Gambino Family capo

Gerald Alicino
Frank "Fingers" Abbandando } Members of Fat Andy Ruggiano's crew
Salvatore Reale
Ronald "Stone" Pearlman

THE COLOMBO *FAMIGLIA*

Carmine "the Snake" Persico Boss of the Colombo Crime Family

Gennaro "Gerry Lang" Langello Colombo Crime Family underboss

Dominic "Donny Shacks" Montemarano Colombo Crime Family capo

Dominick "Little Dom" Cataldo Colombo Crime Family soldier and hit man; sometime partner of Joe Iannuzzi

Ralphie } New York–based members of Little Dom
Billy Ray } Cataldo's crew

Nick "Jiggs" Forlano Miami–based Colombo Family capo

John "Johnny Irish" Matera Fort Lauderdale–based Colombo soldier who succeeded Jiggs Forlano as capo upon Forlano's death

Tony Black Florida–based Colombo soldier

Thomas Farese Fort Lauderdale–based Colombo soldier and drug dealer

Robert "Bobby Anthony" Amelia Colombo Family associate; small-time drug dealer

Freddie "Freddie Campo" Campagnuolo Palm Beach–based bookmaker and Colombo Family associate

Robbie member of Freddie Campo Campagnuolo's crew

Prologue

West Palm Beach, Florida, March 1981

"I GOT PEOPLE THAT WILL EAT THE FUCKING EYES OUT of your fucking head! You dumb bastard! And they're as loyal as a motherfucker. With balls the size of cows. All I have to do is tell them to load up, be in this place at this time, and they'll walk in and blast everybody. No fuckin' hesitation. No nothin'. And don't look for nothin' beside it. No questions asked. They'll blow you up. You think you got something going? You got nothing going.

"You think I'm easy? You think I'm where I'm at today because I'm easy? What I've done you haven't dreamt of, my friend. Why do you think people fear me? Because I was a hard-on, you fuckin' moron? You think I got where I was because I was a jerkoff in the street? You're easy, you motherfucker. The most wrongest thing you ever did was fuck me. People fear me, you dumb fuck. You're only alive today, my friend, because Don's wife walked in. Not because we stopped. You wasn't supposed to walk away no more. And I'm gonna even enlighten you more better than that, while you're having these fuckin' hallucinations. I missed you three times. I was there looking for you two other times before this, you dumb motherfucker."

I lay in my bed holding the telephone receiver at arm's length, listening to Tommy Agro scream at the top of his lungs. My head ached. My broken ribs burned like kindling. And my nose, splayed across my face, was split

1

down the middle. Attached to the telephone was a tape recorder, hooked up courtesy of the FBI office in West Palm Beach, Florida. It didn't take me long to get Tommy Agro to confess that he and two of his New York sluggers had flown to Palm Beach County to beat me to death. To make an example of me.

Two months earlier, on January 19, 1981, Tommy Agro had summoned me to Don Ritz's Pizzeria on Singer Island. He was there with two of his crew, Paul Principe and Frank Russo. They used lead pipes and a baseball bat, and the last thing I remember was Agro himself drawing back his leg and digging his dainty little alligator loafer deep into my ribs.

Tommy ran a crew for the Gambino Family, out of New York. He didn't usually leave jobs unfinished. I knew, because I was his right hand in Florida. But Don Ritz's wife walked in and spooked him just as he was about to chop off *my* right hand. Mafia symbolism.

So as Agro raged on, I smiled. Eight weeks later it still hurt to smile through my swollen face, but I couldn't help it. His verbal rampage lasted a good fifteen minutes. I had one thought: I've got him, and this will be the end. But it was only the beginning.

That tape ultimately was the start of an eighteen-month investigation that incarcerated—or made dead—a slew of wiseguys, lieutenants, capos, and bosses in the Gambino and Colombo Mafia Families from Miami to New York.

I'd awakened two days after the beating in St. Mary's Hospital. A priest. My mother and sister, who must have flown in from New York, told me he'd given me the last rites. Extreme Unction, my mother called it. My wife, Bunny, was there, and my girlfriend, Donna, standing next to one of my daughters. My first thought was What did I do? I didn't deserve this. Then I saw the feds back by the door. Special Agents Larry Doss and Gunnar Askeland of the FBI.

Tommy'd called that day, too. The first voice I'd heard coming out of a coma. "You'd better get me my money! Don't you get it in your dopey fuckin' head you're gonna disappear. You fucked up all Florida! Now you're where you belong. By yourself. Like a dog. I gave you the right name. Joe Dogs!'' Pretty much the same rant he'd go on two months later. But I didn't have a tape recorder that day.

Jesus! I was angry. Not because of the unbelievable pain caused by the split nose, the busted ribs, or the grapefruit-sized hematoma on my temple. Not because my teeth had been knocked out and my left ear partially severed. I was mad because my mentor, my close friend, my *compare*, did this to me because I was a lousy three months late on my juice payments. I was furious.

So I joined forces with the FBI, something that to this day I can't believe I did. I was forced to do it. I was a vegetable and I was in shock and I was to suffer from double vision for more than a year. And at first I hated myself for what I'd become.

But after a while, working with the feds, I started to enjoy myself. I was getting my revenge. On the Mafia. Nothing ever tasted as sweet.

PART
ONE

Making
My
Bones

1
Night Raiders

"JOEY, COME HERE," MY MOTHER YELLED. "COME AND eat your oatmeal and get cleaned up. You're going with your father. It's Saturday."

I dropped whatever I was doing in the backyard of my parents' suburban two-family home in Port Chester, New York, and hurried into the house. I loved going with my dad on Saturdays, because everybody looked up to him. He was the local bookie. He was also in charge of the local numbers game, the "policy racket" they called it. Even in this little town twenty-five miles north of New York City there was plenty of action to be had.

We'd make the rounds of luncheonettes, restaurants, bars, even rich people's homes. And people would give me money because I was Joe Iannuzzi's kid. I remember going to a mansion and meeting the black guy who played Rochester in the old Jack Benny shows. I don't know if he lived there or worked there, but he gave me two silver dollars. He'd hit the number that day.

And then there was Tom Mix, the old movie cowboy. My dad would drive up to his ranch in Harrison, New

York, a beautiful place. I posed for a picture with him, me sitting on a horse. He gave me a silver dollar, too. It was cowboys and Indians, because we also had to stop by the local Indian reservation. They loved to bet. But they only gave me Indian head pennies.

My old man would take me to a restaurant and I got to eat anything I wanted. The people used to call him "Cheecha." I didn't know why they called him that. I was seven years old. And the apple hadn't fallen very far from the tree.

"Your grandmother had to bail you out, you bastard. You're just like your father, a no-good bum. You're making my life miserable." I had to take this from my mother. She had just sprung me from jail.

My first pinch. April 1945. I was fourteen years old. We had a gang. Called ourselves the "Night Raiders." We even had business cards printed. We'd break into a joint, rob it, and leave our cards, which read, "Compliments of the Night Raiders."

We were dumb kids making a living. My mother and father were divorced by then. Thank God. My old man would have broken my neck. My mother just yelled. About being embarrassed. "You're making it rotten for me and Eddie."

Eddie was the Irish guy she was dating. Later, after my father died, she married him. Eddie and I never got along. We'd have fistfights. I guess I was jealous because Eddie was going out with my mother and he treated my sisters better than he treated me.

"Fuck Eddie," I said to her. "I don't care how rotten I make it for that bum."

"Watch how you talk. You're going to be a gangster. Just like your father. He was a louse."

Then my mother shipped me off to live with my grandmother.

I went through the usual baloney a kid from a broken marriage goes through. Ran away from home, came back, ran away again. Finally I joined the army. That pleased my mother. I was now someone else's responsibility.

8

In the army I was disciplined. I had to take orders. It was the best thing that ever happened to me. I joined the boxing team and learned to use my fists. I was decorated in Korea. I took a Chinese bayonet in the thigh. But once I received that honorable discharge I was right back out on the streets. Along the way I got married, had two little girls, got divorced, got married again, had another little girl, and settled down with a family—Sheryl, Debbie, Stephanie, and my wife, Bunny.

Well, I guess settling down isn't how most people would look at it.

2
Joe Diner

"JOEY, DID YOU DO ALL THE FIGURING ON THE BETS FOR last week?"

"Yeah, Hook, here they are." It was 1966. I was thirty-five years old, living in Glen Cove, Long Island, and working in a diner. I was also connected to two bookmakers named Hook and Zabie. I never kidded myself, even after Korea, about trying to make an honest living. I'd been a bad kid, always looking for an edge. It remained my single most solid attribute. Wiseguys just don't happen. They're made. After the war I'd set about making myself.

I'd moved to Yonkers, New York, but got run out of town after some trouble with the local bookmakers and shylocks. Since my wife, Bunny, and her people lived on Long Island, Glen Cove is where I bounced.

Hook and Zabie were associates—not made members —of the Colombo Mafia Family, paying rent to Buster Aloi, a Colombo capo. I was doing their "sheet writing" over the phone. That is, I took the bets.

"We had a good week, Hook," I told him. "We even beat Chubby."

Chubby, a Queens bookmaker who laid off some of his horse bets with us, was also a big bettor himself. When he called, he was good for $10,000 to $15,000 a day. And he only bet hot horses. Chubby always knew when the fix was in. He killed us.

"We beat Chubby for forty-eight thousand and some-odd," I told Hook. "And we beat six runners and the eight strays that called in. Our only loss is to the old man, Vito. Vito wins three hundred and change."

Hook smiled and shook his head. "That Vito is a weekly bill, like rent. Thank God he don't bet that much!"

I was doing good, pulling in about $250 a week from the diner, another $300 writing the afternoon track sheet, and another $300 sheet writing the trotters at night.

Then I took a pinch. The cops busted down my door and arrested me for bookmaking and possession of gambling paraphernalia. Misdemeanors, a bullshit pinch. But they lifted a couple thousand out of my pocket, collections for Hook, and swiped another $400 out of my wife's purse that she was saving for Christmas. Hook and Zabie paid her back the next day.

I was now unemployed. For one week. After that I worked the phones from a friend of my wife's house. She was a German girl. Good-looking woman. Hook and Zabie paid her phone and rent, so she was happy.

"Joe, you have an emergency phone call."

The caddy master was careening his golf cart down the thirteenth fairway. I was a golf fanatic; good at it, too. I had an eight handicap. The caddy master breathlessly informed me that the hospital was on the phone. Bunny had delivered a baby boy. Joseph Iannuzzi III. It was November 26, 1967. I rushed to the hospital—six or seven hours later. After all, my partners and I had to celebrate in the clubhouse first.

My *compare*—my godfather, my rabbi, the guy who looked after me—at that time was Mike "Midge" Belvedere, a bookmaker in West Babylon, Long Island. Midge was also connected to the Colombo Crime Family. Midge and his wife, Ann, were my son's godparents. Midge was a good-looking guy, a bronze Sicilian with thick, wavy black hair and dark, dark eyes. Almost black. When he stared at you, you felt like knives were going through your head. Midge dressed well and played the gangster role to the hilt.

His wife, Ann, was beautiful. She looked like Elizabeth Taylor, but with a better body. But once she opened her mouth, *marrone,* if you weren't looking at her you'd think a truck driver had joined the conversation.

Once when we were all vacationing in Florida, coming out of a hotel after seeing Sergio Franchi perform, the television actress Joi Lansing pushed through the mob waiting for the valet to bring around their cars. Joi Lansing smiled at Midge and gave him the eye. Ann sidled up to her slowly and said, "If you don't take your fuckin' eyes off my husband, I'll smack you in the face with your own big tit, you fuckin' whore." Ann was beautiful.

So I was managing the Bonton diner in Babylon and doing the figuring for Midge when one day he asks me to take a ride with him to Queens to buy some shoes. But instead of going to Queens, Midge drove to Brooklyn, where he bought four pairs of alligator loafers. I think he spent $800 or $900. While we were heading back to the car, a guy stopped Midge, hugged him, kissed him, and the two began talking and laughing.

"Frankie," Midge said finally, "meet a very close friend of mine, Joe Diner." Everybody had to have a nickname, including Frankie, whom I recognized as "Frankie Five Hundred," one of the biggest bookmakers in New York.

"Hi, Joe," Frankie said, sticking out his hand. "Come and join me for dinner, the both of you. I got to meet with that cocksucker Smitty at the Cypress Gardens restaurant, and I hate that fuckin' bum. But he's my capo, and I have to pay the rent."

Midge tried to talk me into it, but I had to be at work myself that night at the diner, and I couldn't afford to lose the job. I offered to take a cab home to free up Midge to eat with Frankie Five Hundred, and at one point Midge even insisted on paying the fare, handing me thirty dollars. But at the last minute he changed his mind, explaining to Frankie he "had to give the Mrs. a break."

So we said our goodbyes, Midge dropped me off at work, and he went home. Business was slow after dinner, and I was listening to the Yankee game on the radio when a flash bulletin came on.

"Tonight at Cypress Gardens restaurant an unidentified gunman killed three people while they were eating dinner. Police say the weapon used was an automatic. Killed were James "Smitty" D'Angelo, an alleged captain in the Bonanno Crime Family, as well as his brother, Tom, a railroad conductor. Also killed was an alleged numbers kingpin only identified as Frankie Five Hundred. Tune in for more details after the game."

A few days later Midge and I went to Frankie's wake, where I met the Colombo capo Buster Aloi for the first time. Midge went on and on, telling Buster what a lucky charm I was, how if it hadn't been for me he'd probably have gotten whacked, too. Buster just looked at me and nodded.

3

The Promised Land

I LEFT NEW YORK FOR FLORIDA IN 1968. THERE WAS A recession on, money was tight, real tight, and I'd been offered a job down south hanging drywall. Florida was wide open at the time, booming, and in the back of my mind I had the vague idea that it was time for me to go straight. But when I got down there I was flat broke, and the only job available was through an old friend who set me up with a drywall contractor who had "won" the bid to hang drywall on a nursing home construction site, and he hired me even though I didn't even have enough money in my pocket to join the union.

"Look, Joe," he told me, "when the union guy comes around, I'll let you know. Then you go hide. And if for some reason he finds you, I'll have my brother slip you his union card. Fuhgedaboudit, the guy's blind anyway."

The union delegate came around nearly every three days, and eventually the shop steward got wise to me. He was going to squeal, so I went and told my boss.

"Oh yeah, Joe? I'll fix that cocksucker. I'll call you when I need you." Then he laid everyone off, the shop steward last.

That was the law in Florida. If you wanted to replace a shop steward, he had to be the last man laid off. The next day my boss made me the shop steward and hired every worker back—except the old shop steward. I didn't even have a union card, and I was the shop steward! Florida was my kind of place.

I took it upon myself to shake everyone down. I was what you might call a slugger. If a subcontractor wanted to drop off material, they had to pay me off. I shook them down even if they were union. And everybody paid. But mostly it was the non-union suppliers, who were always in a hurry to get unloaded without having to hire union guys and pay union wages to unload. I was pocketing between $600 and $800 a week, off the books, and I loved the job. When that nursing home was finally completed, I hated to see that job go.

In 1969 I bought a house in West Palm Beach. Four-bedroom ranch. Mostly cash. What little mortgage I took I put in my wife's name. Florida was my new home. I was happy being away from New York, and Bunny and the kids loved it. I was making a decent living in the drywall business, and before long I had lots of things going on the side. A little shylocking, a little bookmaking. Sometimes I was hired out just to provide a little muscle. I never minded smacking a guy.

Late in 1970, two years after I'd settled in, I got a call from Louie Esposito, a friend of Midge's as well as a Gambino Family associate. Louie tells me he's bringing eighteen people down from Babylon, New York, for New Year's Eve, and he wants me to find him hotel reservations in Fort Lauderdale.

"Louie, are you nuts?" I asked him. "It's the middle of the season. You know what they're going to want as a deposit?"

"Joey, give them whatever they want, and take off work. I'll pay you a hundred a day every day you take off."

I found all the rooms he needed in the Fort Lauderdale Holiday Inn, and when the gang arrived Louie announced that we were all going to the track the next day.

"What's open?" Louie asked.

"Gulfstream," I told him. "But, Louie, I can't go. I can't afford to miss work."

"Forget it, Joe. You're going. Here's two hundred. You bet with that."

Marrone, I thought to myself, this guy must be sitting pretty fuckin' good.

We went to the track the next day, and Louie is sending me to the window to bet for him. "Who do you like, Joe?" he asked.

I told him I liked this one horse with speed, and that he was a drop-down horse and should go all the way.

"Here's four hundred. Go bet him to win." He handed me eighty five-dollar bills. I looked at him and smiled.

At the window, I bet $410 on the horse to win. I wasn't going to lose all my money! The horse won and paid five to one—$12.60. Louie collected $2,520. I made sixty-three bucks. Hey, this was more than a day's pay back in the early 1970s.

"Did you bet him?" Louie wanted to know. "How much did you bet on him?"

I was too embarrassed to let him know I'd only laid out ten dollars. He must have read it on my face.

"Here, you fuckin' scaredy-cat, here's a hundred," he said, peeling off ten ten-dollar bills. "You picked the horse and you don't even bet it? I don't believe this."

Marrone, another hundred! Then he handed me a hundred five-dollar bills.

14

"Bet the three horse," he said. "And don't bet it all at the same window."

I go and bet, this time throwing on another hundred of my own. The three horse won and paid even money. I got back $200 and Louie took in $1,000. Louie had two more winners that day; I kept feeding those five-dollar bills into the window. When we got back to his hotel room he showed me an enormous suitcase filled with five- and ten-dollar bills. I found out later that the stash was his cut from the big Aqueduct racetrack armored car heist. The guy was a horse thief.

The year was 1972. Louie Esposito was on the lam from another big robbery attempt in New Jersey. He and another guy got a tip that this house had over $2 million in cash stashed in the library room, and this tipster had always been solid with the information.

So Louie and the other guy dressed as Catholic priests and went to the house. They said their car broke down. After the maid let them in, they pulled guns and headed directly to the library, as they knew the layout from the tipster.

Sure enough, when they opened the library door there were stacks of cash lining the bookshelves. But apparently the lady of the house had heard what was going on, and she ran to the front door screaming, "Robbery! Robbery!" Before they could subdue her, the neighbors had heard her screams and called the police.

Louie said that within no more than two minutes there were squad cars all over the place. He and his partner fled into some woods behind the house. Louie hid in the rafters of a construction site all night. The cops caught his partner. Louie told me he was on the lam because he wasn't sure if his partner had given him up.

"But, Louie," I asked him, "what happened to all that money from the Aqueduct heist?"

"Are you kidding, Joey?" A queer look crossed his face. "My share of that was only eight hundred thousand. I went through that in a couple of months. Gee, though, I wish I could have paid off my house. Anyway, I have to find some work until I make another score. You got a job for me?"

I was at one of my construction sites.

"Yeah, sure, Louie, come and work for me and you just hide in one of the rooms on the job. I'm the foreman anyway, so you can stay there and it won't cost you anything. I'll even put you on the payroll."

"Good, Joe, thanks. But I got to get my own place soon. I want to bring my son down here with me. My wife's having trouble with him. He won't listen to anything she says. Fuckin' kid! I give him everything. I can't understand why he's like that."

"Yeah, Lou," I told him. "It's real odd that your kid is like that. I mean, considering that his father is a graduate of Penn State and all. Or is that the state pen?"

Louie looked at me like he didn't get it. That was all right. He was a good thief. He did a lot of payroll and safe jobs plus a couple of real big stick-up robberies. I figured that sometime down the road he'd pay me back.

"Joe, answer the phone," Bunny said. "It's probably for you anyway."

"Hello?"

"Hello. Can I speak to Louie please?"

"Who?"

"Louie! Louie! Tell him it's Tommy A."

"I think you have the wrong number," I said. "There's no Louie here. What area code did you dial? This is Florida, you know."

"Yeah, I know," said the voice at the other end of the line. "My friend Louie gave me this number. He was supposed to be staying with a friend of his named Joe Diner. Is that you?"

"Nah. I don't know what you're talking about. You got the wrong number." I hung up.

Louie was in the backyard, so I went out and told him that I was pretty sure the law knew he was here. "Some guy named Tommy called up and asked for you. I told him he had the wrong number and hung up. You better be careful."

Louie started laughing. "Oh shit, Joey. I forgot to tell

16

you. I told my friend T.A. about you, told him that I was coming to stay here for a while, until the heat died. I hope he calls back.''

Just then the phone rang again, and I ran inside just in time to hear Bunny say, ''Listen, mister, there is nobody here by the name of Louie Esposito.''

I grabbed the phone from her. ''Tommy, I'm sorry. Louie didn't tell me you were going to call. Here he is.''

Louie talked for ten minutes and hung up. ''Joe, T.A. says that what you did with the phone was very good. He commends both you and your lovely wife, and he wants to take you both to dinner. He'll be here tomorrow, and we're going out tomorrow night. You know a good restaurant?''

''Yeah, we can go to my cousin Ozzie's place, Alfredo's. In Boynton Beach.''

''Oh, he'll like it there,'' Bunny chirped in. ''The food is great.''

In the meantime, Louie told me all about T.A., Tommy Agro, so I'd be prepared to not only talk to him but to keep an eye on his mannerisms. T.A., Louie said, had a tendency to flip out occasionally. Break into cold sweats. Start acting real buglike, like Jimmy Cagney in *White Heat*. He sounded like a real challenge to meet.

Louie also said that T.A. was ''almost there''—that he was ''proposed.''

''He'll make it the next time the books open up,'' Louie told me.

I didn't know what he meant. Proposed? Books? What the fuck, I thought, is he getting married or something? But I went along with what Louie was saying, pretending to understand what the hell he was talking about.

''Wow, that's great. Really? The next time the books open, huh?''

I didn't have a clue.

4
Tommy A.

"Hi, Joey, how are you? Louie told me a lot of good things about you."

You'd never know by looking at Tommy Agro, alias T.A., alias Tom Ambrosio, that he was to become the single greatest influence on my life. He was a squat, florid little man, standing five feet three inches on the tip of his toes. On this tiny frame he balanced a set of incongruously large shoulders, with a belly to match. He had a headful of thick, wavy black hair that must have looked beautiful on the horse it came off of. And though he wore elevator shoes to bring him closer to the sky, he was still always the last one to know it was raining.

T.A., a few years older than me, was an immaculate dresser, smooth and sharp. As they say, he was "All Mafia," and his mouth and mannerisms let you know it. Though lacking in any formal education, Tommy was an extremely street-smart person. But if you didn't know him, he could fool you into thinking he was a college grad.

"Hi, Tom, this is my wife, Bunny. Louie told me how close you two are. Please excuse the way I talked to you on the phone, but I had to be careful. You know what I mean."

"Of course, Joey, like I told Louie—you did the right thing. Hello, Bunny. Louie tells me you're a very good cook."

Tommy was accompanied by a tall blond flight attendant, and she was a knockout. Young, dumb, and full of cum, I thought.

So after I had a few Scotches in me, I asked Tommy if he'd mind if I danced with his girl. The music had started, and Phil Tolatta, the manager/maitre d', was singing "Strangers in the Night."

He looked at me screwy for a moment, then he laughed and said, "No, Joey, go right ahead. Sandi, dance with Joey. But be careful, don't hurt him. Because Bunny looks like she'll kill you."

As we were dancing, Sandi told me that I was the first man who had ever asked her to dance in Tommy's company. "Aren't you afraid of him?" she asked. "Everyone else is."

The evening ended great, everyone had a wonderful time, and as we were all saying our goodbyes I invited Tommy and Sandi to be my guest the following night. Tommy quickly agreed.

"I can't make it tomorrow night," Louie said.

"That's okay, Louie," I told him. "I'm old enough to go alone."

I took Tom and Sandi to the Palm Beach Kennel Club for dinner. The club was at the dog track, and I loved gambling on the dogs. I was pretty good at it, too, and Tommy was impressed by the way I picked winners. So impressed, as a matter of fact, that he asked to go again.

After the races, we went back to Alfredo's for dinner, and Tommy and I started to get a little closer in our conversation.

"Joey," he said, "if you know of anyone who wants a loan, you know, they pay the juice every week, you let me know. But they have to be solid. You know what I mean? And you can earn off the money, too."

"How much interest—or juice, as you call it—do you charge?" I asked him.

"Joey, it's all according to how much they want and whatever we can get without having problems. You know what I mean?"

"Yeah, well, I think I might know someone. A guy asked me the other day if I knew a shylock, and I told him no, not here in Florida. But I could tell him about you, and you take it from there. I think he wants five thousand."

"All right, Joey. Listen, you know what you do? If he

mentions it to you again, tell him you know someone, but don't tell him who it is. Tell him it's five points a week. That's two fifty juice a week. But don't go to him and tell him you know somebody. Wait till he asks you again. Believe me, Joey, he will.

"Here's my home phone number," Tommy said, pulling a scrap of paper from his pocket. "Call me if he wants the loan. But you can call me anyway, to say hello, if you want."

I put Tommy's phone number in my wallet, but then took it out again and rewrote the number in code. I wanted to impress him. I wanted to be just like him. I wanted to be in the Mafia next to Tommy. I was ga-ga over the fact that I was doing something for him. Tommy Agro had just become my idol!

Bunny must have noticed that I was acting weird. She squeezed my hand, kissed me on the cheek, and whispered to me to be careful.

I ignored her. I was with Tommy A. I felt strong.

The next night we went to the dog track again, and we won all night. We won enough to pay for dinner and to throw big tips around and still have a couple hundred dollars in winnings left in our pockets.

At the end of the night Tommy gave me my new name. "Joe Diner" had become "Joe Dogs."

5

"When You Eat Alone, You Die Alone"

TWO WEEKS LATER TOMMY WAS BACK DOWN IN FLORida. He'd flown in immediately after I'd called him and told him he'd been right. Lou Masiello, the guy who'd asked me if I knew a shylock, had indeed come back again.

"Lou, you pay Joey here two fifty a week juice,"

Tommy told Masiello at the meet I'd set up. "Try and be prompt with it, as I don't want no trouble."

"Oh, don't worry, Tommy, I wouldn't do anything like that," Masiello protested. "I've borrowed money before. I just got a little tight. I'll probably only need it for a couple of months. And besides, I wouldn't do anything to hurt Joe."

"Look, Lou," said Tommy, balling up his fists. "Let me make myself clear to you. All Joe did was introduce us. He's just doing me a favor by collecting this money for me. It's more convenient that way. I have other guys down here who would gladly come to your home and collect the interest weekly. Do I make myself clear?

"Joe is with me, Lou," T.A. continued. "Do you understand the terminology when I say 'with me'?"

Masiello seemed to indeed understand Tommy's terminology. Myself? I wasn't too sure on the specifics, though I caught the general drift.

As Tommy continued, a fine line of sweat appeared across his forehead. "Lou, it just dawns on me, what the fuck am I explaining these things to you for? You want the loan on these terms, you got it. If not, forget it, and I don't ever want to see you again. *Capisci?*"

"Yeah, Tommy, I understand," Masiello stammered. "I don't want you to be mad at me. I want to be your friend. Honest, Tom."

"Good, Lou, then we're friends. You see Joey every week, and we stay friends, okay? Now shake my hand and take the money and go. I have some business to talk over with Joe."

After Masiello left, I had one brief flash of nerves, wondering what I was getting into. Was this how I wanted to be? Was this the life I wanted to live? I was forty-one, at an age when other guys were settled in, just approaching the peak of their careers. Here I was joining the Mafia. Yes, I decided. Tommy had handled Masiello so professionally. He was so suave and sharp. He not only really told Lou how it was, he told Lou that I was with him! *With him.* I felt great, like King Kong.

"Joey, I have my wife flying down here tomorrow," Tommy said, interrupting my reverie. "I told her all about you and Bunny, and she wants to meet you. Tomorrow night we all go out, but tonight you and me talk. We'll have some drinks. Shoot some shit."

On the way to the bar we stopped at my house to tell Bunny about Tommy's wife, Marian, and our dinner date tomorrow.

"But tonight's boys' night out, honey," I added. "Don't worry, no women."

"There'd better not be," Bunny answered, but she was looking at Tommy. "By the way, Tommy, did you tell your wife about Sandi when you told her about Joe and I?"

Tommy looked at her and laughed. Then he said, "No, darling, and don't you tell her either."

He was no longer laughing.

I took Tommy to the Holiday Inn just down the block from my house, and we went into the lounge and had a few drinks.

"Joey, I want you to relax," T.A. told me. "I know you're trying to impress me, but don't knock yourself out. I'm impressed with you, and I'm impressed with your wife. I like the way you handle yourself. Now here is what I want you to do. Find yourself some more customers like that guy Lou. Expand yourself. Do things. And if you have any problems, call me. I'll help you. But on the other hand, if you do good, don't forget me. Because I have my own *compare,* and I can't forget him.

"In this life," Tommy continued, "when you eat alone, you die alone. Remember this, remember what I'm telling you. You think you knew people before? Forget about them. You belong to an organization now that is the biggest. So when I tell you to expand and do things, always be careful. Don't get hurt.

"If someone gives you a problem and you see you can't handle it, walk away. Never do anything foolish, because it doesn't pay to get pinched for something that can be handled differently. Joey, when you're with me, there is no one in this fuckin' world that can fuck with you. Not even the Pope! I swear on my daughter Kimmy."

I was almost swooning as Tommy lit my cigarette. Hook and Midge and even Louie Esposito, they were nothing compared to Tommy Agro. The guy had—how else can I put it?—class!

We met Marian the next day, and the four of us went to (where else?) the Kennel Club. We won again; I was on a roll. Bunny and Marian got along great, but then everyone got along with Bunny. She was a good lady, and I never went anywhere without her.

"That is one of your detriments," Tommy told me just before he flew back up north. "Joey, don't be bringing your wife along with you all the time. It don't look good."

6
Staking Out the Gold Coast

OVER THE NEXT COUPLE OF YEARS I BECAME TOMMY Agro's top guy in Florida. The state was virgin turf back then, except for Miami, which had a legacy stretching back to Meyer Lansky and Joey Adonis; and the Gold Coast strip between North Miami and Palm Beach was exploding economically. Ripe for the plucking.

I was making a little book. Collecting for union no-show jobs. I had my fingers in some crooked horse races. And I had about eight good shylock victims in the streets. Even Lou Masiello, our first customer, had extended his loan to $12,000 and was paying $600 a week in juice.

People in the Palm Beach County area knew who I was. I was treated with great respect. I was also feared. I could be a son of a bitch, but only to those who didn't toe the line. It was part of the business. I didn't necessarily enjoy it, but if someone owed money and didn't pay,

I knew how to break a leg. Because of all these factors, whenever I walked into a restaurant or a club, I was given the red-carpet treatment.

And I loved it.

If Tommy, who was staking out the Gold Coast for his faction of the Gambino Crime Family, had a problem with something down south, he would call me and tell me to take care of it. Most of the time I could handle it myself. I didn't trust anyone else to do my work.

And along with frequent visits from T.A. himself, I began to meet different members of his crew. One of them was Bobby DeSimone, out of Hollywood, Florida. Bobby was what we called a "babe in the woods," a knockaround whore who will hang with any crew in any Family that will have him. He'd been with a couple of Families up in New York, and they had all chased him. Tommy told me he kept Bobby close to him because he felt "obligated." Obligated for what, he didn't say. I never turned my back on Bobby DeSimone.

Yet for all my tough-guy lifestyle, I was still perilously naive about the Mafia. For one thing, I didn't even know what Cosa Nostra Crime Family I was affiliated with. In 1973, during one of his visits, I finally popped the question to Tommy. I felt like a jerk, but I had to find out. I'd been pretending all along like I knew everything.

"T.A., what's our Family name?"

Bug-eyed, Tommy Agro laughed like hell at my question. Finally he told me that we were with the Gambinos, the largest Mafia Family in the United States, and that the head of the Family was Don Carlo Gambino. He went on to explain to me how the ranks in the Family operated.

There was Don Carlo, who, coincidentally, maintained a winter residence in West Palm. Directly below the Don was, naturally, the underboss. At the time, that was Aniello, or Neil, Dellacroce. Third in command was our *consigliere*, or counselor, Joe N. Gallo. Although in theory the *consigliere* had no official power of his own in the Family and derived his clout solely from the boss, in fact Gallo had several key Family duties to perform, including presiding over Family disputes and sit-downs between capos. He often had to decide who got whacked and who didn't.

The next rung down was occupied by captains, or capos, who each ran their own crew. In these crews were made guys, or buttons, or wiseguys, who had been formally inducted into the Mafia. These crews also included associates, who hoped to make their button when the bosses opened the books. If a captain had more than one wiseguy in his crew, which was usually the case, he appointed one as his lieutenant. Of course, all of the buttons had their own crews, and some members of those crews even had their own crews. It was all kind of confusing at first.

But one thing was for certain. Getting a button was all these guys lived for. It was their badge of honor. You could only get "made" if you were of pure Italian extraction. But that didn't stop capos and soldiers from hiring on Jews, micks, even the occasional spade, as part of a crew.

Tommy, for instance, didn't have his button, and belonged to the crew headed by the longstanding Gambino capo Joe "Piney" Armone, who got his nickname back in the 1930s by shaking down the sidewalk Christmas tree sellers on New York's Lower East Side. But that didn't make me a member of Armone's crew. I owed fealty to Tommy Agro and Tommy Agro alone. What happened over his head had nothing directly to do with me. Or so I thought.

After explaining all this to me, Tommy told me I was to forget everything he just told me. Forget to ever mention it again, he meant.

"Here's how it works," Tommy said. "If you went out and made a score—dope, robbery, extortion, hijack, whatever—and you made a hundred thousand, what would you do? Would you tell me? Or would you keep it to yourself? C'mon, Joey, I want to know."

I hesitated slightly, thinking it over briefly before answering.

"Well, Tom, to be honest with you, if I did something without your knowledge, I would give you a percentage of what I took. Wait, wait, don't interrupt me. I want to explain to you why. Because if for some reason I ran into a problem or had some difficulty, I would have to turn to you for help."

As I was saying this, I reached into my jacket pocket, pulled out an envelope, and slid it across the table.

I continued: "As I feel, you are like my employer, or *compare*. And for that reason, just because I don't have a problem is no reason not to reward you with a little something."

Tommy reached out and opened the envelope. He counted out $10,000, put it in his jacket pocket, and ordered two more drinks.

"What did you do?" he asked.

"Does Macy's tell Gimbels?" I answered. "Remember last year you introduced me to our two friends, Little Dom Cataldo and Little Vic Orena? Well, they were down a few weeks ago, and asked me to help them with a problem. It was no big deal, a cinch really, but I don't want to go into detail. I just figured since you introduced me, you deserve a share."

The waitress delivered our drinks, and Tommy stroked the crack in her ass with one hand while handing her a hundred-dollar tip with the other. Then he gave me a soft, appreciative slap in the face.

"Little Dom told me he needed you for something, and he and Little Vic commended you to me," Tommy said. "But that's all they said. They didn't tell me you earned with them. Dominick is a good man, Joey. He's like me, only with another Family. And little Vic, he's like my *compare*, a capo, with the same Family. They're with the Colombos, Joey."

"Tommy, Tommy, I didn't know. I thought they were with us. Did I do wrong then by going with them?"

"No, Joey, it's all right. They came to me first anyway. Which is the right thing to do. But even if they didn't, you proved yourself by sharing your loaf of bread with me."

Tommy always made me feel good. I didn't understand why people called him the "Fuckin' Maniac" behind his back. He was always calm with me. Although I did wonder about those pills that he was always popping.

7
Little Dom's Boot Hill

PEEKSKILL, NEW YORK, 1973.

"Christ, Joe, I told you to get a thirty-eight. This fuckin' thing is too big. I'm not gonna kill a fuckin' bear, you know."

Little Dom Cataldo and I were scrunched down in the front seat of his car waiting for the carriers to come out of the loan office with the satchel. Dominick had a tip. There was supposed to be between $80,000 and $100,000 in this deal. Little Dom had flown me up from Florida to serve as his wheel man.

"Hey, Dom, cool out. All I could get was a Magnum. Anyways, you told me you just needed it to scare somebody, not to use it."

"Yeah, I know, Joe, but you never can tell."

Little Dom Cataldo, who was trying to make his button in the Colombo Family, stood five feet eight inches tall. He had a nice build and looked a bit like the actor John Garfield. To look at him and talk to him, you'd never believe that the guy had murdered over ten people. "I put him in Boot Hill" was one of Little Dom's favorite expressions. It was not brag, just fact.

In fact, Dominick did have a favorite burial ground. A certain hill along the Taconic State Parkway twenty miles or so north of New York City. He told me he wouldn't trust anyone. If there was someone he had to bury, he would lock them in the trunk of his car and drive to Boot Hill personally, check into a motel, sleep until three or four in the morning, then go out and dig the hole.

"Not deep, Joe, you know, three to three and a half feet. Like that, you know? Then put some lime over the

27

body, cover up, throw some grass seed around, and leave. It takes like an hour, not too long.

"But, Joey, there was this one fat motherfucker, he was a Lucchese guy, the fat pig," Dominick continued, mentioning another New York City–based Mafia Family. "I hated this cocksucker and I finally got his closest guy to drive over to this joint where he was going to meet with this broad. His own guy, Johnny was his name, conned him.

"Anyway, when they get to this place in the parking lot, I walked up and popped him right there in Johnny's car. Johnny says, 'What the fuck am I gonna do with this big fuck now?' So I was thinking. I told Johnny I needed some help with this fat bastard. I tell Johnny to help me throw him in my trunk and we'll get a shovel and pick, and I know a spot upstate that we could bury him.

"Because, Joe," Dom tells me, looking all kinds of sincere, "it's not right that I leave the problem with Johnny. I mean, after all, he got the cocksucker there for me to whack, so it's only right that I help him get rid of the body, because what can he say to his *Famiglia?*

"So we drive to Boot Hill, and it's late when we get there. I show him where to dig, and tell him to dig it deep, 'cause the lime smells. He don't know what I'm talking about, so I tell him I'll be back in a couple of hours, to dig it five or six feet deep.

"I drive down to the motel where I usually stay and had a nap. I told the clerk to give me a call in two hours. When I got back there, it was like four-thirty in the morning, and Johnny must have dug over six feet.

"I drove the car as close as I could to the hole, then John and I carried the fat fuck up and threw him in.

" 'Oh shit, Johnny,' I says. 'I forgot to take his watch off, his ring, and his dough. No sense in burying them.' So Johnny says he would go and get them. He jumps in the hole and I shot him, too. Put the lime in and then the dirt and then the seed. But I had a lot of dirt to spread around, because I had a two-story job there.

"Ha-ha, that's funny, Joey. A two-story job."

Little Dominick Cataldo cracked himself up. Then we saw the carriers leave the building.

"Here they come, Joe. Two of them. You know what to do. Go ahead."

It was cold out. I wore a black leather jacket and a pair of leather police gloves that were lined with lead. I staggered up to the car the carriers were entering, laid on the hood, and made retching sounds like I was going to puke. They stopped, reached for me, and one of them said, "Hey, you fuckin' drunk, get the hell off my car."

Little Dom was covering me. I punched the guy so hard I heard his jaw crack. Dominick shoved the magnum in the other guy's mouth and he passed out. Dom grabbed the satchel and we were out of there. It took a total of thirty seconds.

Dominick was driving, and I wanted to count the money. "No, Joey. Not here. Wait till we stop somewhere."

We drove to Bear Mountain, got a room in a motel, and counted out $143,000. He told me there wouldn't be any investigation over this because it was drug money. It was a wiseguy's money, and he wouldn't do anything, because his captain wasn't in on it. He was fucking his capo, so he would keep quiet.

Dom told me he was giving the tipster $23,000, so we split the remaining $120,000.

"Not bad, huh, Joe? For a few minutes' work?"

"No, pretty good. But hey, Dom, tell me something."

"Yeah, what, Joe?"

"When the guy went down in the hole to get the jewelry and you shot him, did you go down and get it yourself?"

"No, Joe. I don't make mistakes like that. I'm not a mercenary. What I do, I do for a reason. I'll never leave a body, Joe. The law is so intelligent today, they can find a clue easily. The way I do it, it's a lot of work, but I'm clean."

I had another question. "Hey, Dom, how come you asked me to help you here? You got a million guys you could use."

"Because, Joe, I don't want no one to know, not even my captain. I already gave him enough money this year. Are you going to tell Tommy A. about this?"

"I see no reason to," I answered. "Fuhgedaboudit. I'll throw him a bone and tell him I did something down south."

"Yeah, Joe, good. The less people know, the better."

"It's dead," I said.

8

"He Knows I'll Hurt Him"

"JOEY, I'M HERE AT THE APARTMENT DOWN SOUTH," Tommy A. said into the phone. "Don't tell anybody I'm here. Come and cook something for us, willya?"

It was late 1974. I'd been a member of T.A.'s crew for two years now. Tommy was on the lam for an extortion bit he'd done. A horse bettor had owed him a lot of money, and Tommy threatened him. Now they were looking for him. They wanted him to talk to the grand jury. It was amazing how these guys got their information about indictments about to be handed up. Tommy was holing up in his Hollywood apartment, waiting for the heat to blow by.

"Bunny, honey, I'm going out and I don't know when I'll be back." I tried to make it to the door before the same old argument started. I didn't make it.

"Joe, where you going now?" she said. "We used to be so happy when we were broke. But ever since you got involved with Tommy, I don't see you anymore. We used to go everywhere together and do everything together. But the last couple of years it's Tommy this and Tommy that. What's wrong with you?"

"Hey, look, I don't want no shit." I was tired of this fight. "I bought you this house. We have an expensive piece of property. You have your own car, jewelry, money in the bank. What the fuck more do you want from me?

"Oh yeah," I added. "Don't forget the boat!"

Bunny was crying now. "I dread the day Louie Esposito showed up here. We used to be so happy. I hate all those bastards for ruining our lives."

"Okay, honey, listen, I'm sorry," I said. "I'll be back as soon as possible. I just can't tell you where I'm going."

"Okay, Joey. But call me. Please?"

I hated to see Bunny cry. She was always there at my side when I needed her. I'm no good, I'm thinking. I fuck around on her. I was never like this before. She's better off without me. But I do love her.

An hour later I'd forgotten all about the fight.

"Hi, Tom. What's new? Hi, Buzz, Louie, Bobby. How you all doing?"

"C'mon, cook something, you fuckin' suitcase," Tommy yelled. Terms of endearment.

"Okay, but I play every other hand of pinochle, or you fuckin' guys starve."

Every time Tommy came down we would meet at his apartment and play pinochle. I was the worst player. But after all, these guys had all been in prison, so that's all they did every day, play cards. Sitting around the table with Tommy were Louie Esposito, Bobby DeSimone and a guy named Buzzy who I had met on a couple of occasions. He never said his last name. I didn't ask.

DeSimone, the "babe in the woods" to whom Tommy felt "obligated," had done two stretches in the state pen. He was tall, thin, and had a mouth like a motor. "Skinny Bobby," they called him, and his pedigree was bad. Both his brothers were nuts, and aspiring members of the mob. Bobby was a wannabe. His brothers were oughtabes. Buzzy was also a tall guy, and Italian, despite the nickname. He was one good-looking fella. He didn't belong with this motley crew. Buzzy was a drug dealer.

"Here, Tom, this is for you." I handed him an envelope containing $5,000.

He opened it and asked, "What's this from?"

I didn't want to broadcast my business in front of the crew. I told Tommy I'd fill him in later.

DeSimone said, "Well, Joey, if you didn't want to tell

31

Tommy in front of us, why did you give him the money now? Are you trying to make us look bad?"

Tommy wheeled in his chair. "Bobby, go wash your fuckin' mouth out with soap. At least Joey contributes. What do you ever do, you skinny fuck?"

"I was only kidding, T.A.," Bobby answered in that high-pitched whiny voice of his. "I didn't mean no harm."

"Well I wasn't kidding," Tommy screamed. "Keep your fuckin' big mouth closed tight. Buzzy, it's your bid."

"I open," Buzzy said, adding, "and, hey, Tom, that kid Bobby Anthony wants to talk to you about that . . . you know."

It was amazing. We were all together. We were all one crew. And we're all talking in code, like one of us is a cop. That's how we always talked.

"Yeah, okay, Buzz," Tommy said. "Do you know this guy?"

"Yeah," said Buzzy, "he's okay. He just got out. Did a ten-year bit for whacking that cop. Used to work in advertising. He's the one that made up that slogan for Virginia Slims, 'You've Come a Long Way, Baby,' or something like that. He got a million bucks for it."

"Yeah, that's nice," Tommy said. "What's he want with me?"

"I don't know. He's with the Harlem group, you know, Charlie and Jerry."

"Yeah, I know 'em. Tell them to come here next Monday. I hear they're staying in the Diplomat, spending all kinds of money."

"Look, Bobby," Tommy A. was saying to Bobby Amelia, alias Bobby Anthony, a small-time drug dealer with a Harlem crew. "You asked for this meet. You asked for this money. What's my end gonna be as an investor? I want to know."

Bobby Anthony shot a quick glance at his partner. Bobby had introduced him only as Rabbit. "Well, Tom, if you want to invest, then you guys share in the risk. If there's a bust and we lose the dope, then you guys lose your money. But if you want to shylock us the money, then we're responsible. It's as simple as that. But if you invest, I can guarantee you at least ten times your money."

Tommy was cautious. "What, are you nuts? How do I know what you're doing? You guys can say you got ripped off and what the fuck can I do about it? Then we have trouble. I pass. Fuhgedaboudit."

"Well, Tom, here's what we can do." It was the Rabbit speaking. "You be a silent investor, and I'll guarantee personally that you get back a hundred fifty thousand profit in no more than two months' time. If not, we'll pay you your money back, plus five thousand, in two months."

"So you're gonna guarantee the money, huh?" Tommy answered. "And who the fuck are you? You're only sitting here because you're Bobby's partner, and I'm showing him the courtesy to let you in here. So don't go talking like an asshole."

I'm thinking to myself that Bobby Anthony was trying to manipulate Tommy. But I didn't know for sure, so I kept my mouth shut. I liked Bobby. He was a small, thin guy. Nice-looking. And a hell of a lot of fun. I think T.A. was a little jealous of Bobby Anthony.

Finally I broke the tension. "Look, Bobby, let us think it over for a while, and we'll let you know by Thursday. Three days from now. But for an answer right now, fuhgedaboudit. I would have to pass also."

I could tell Tommy admired the way I was talking. By now I felt secure enough to talk like that to these guys. I'd learned a lot. Bobby agreed to meet with us again Thursday, but Rabbit cut in and said he couldn't make it, he had to be in New York.

"Oh gee, what a shame," Tommy said. "Then maybe we should cancel."

Bobby Anthony grinned. He knew what Tommy was doing. He knew his partner was a mope. On the way out Bobby pulled me aside and told me to call him. After they left, Tommy asked us what we thought about the deal.

I answered first. "To be honest, Tom, at first I thought

it sounded like a rip-off. But there's a lot of risk in dope. You have to take your chances by trusting people, or else show your face up front. But I know you wouldn't want to get involved with that, would you?"

"Fuck no," Tommy said. "What, are you crazy? My *compare* told me to make money but don't show my face. Orders from the tall guy, you know who I mean. Not the top guy. You know, the under."

Here we go again with the crazy double-talk. Tommy was referring to his captain, Piney Armone, who took *his* orders from Neil Dellacroce, Carlo Gambino's underboss. Dellacroce was currently locked in a power struggle with Gambino's cousin Paul Castellano, alias "Big Paulie," to succeed the aging Don Carlo.

"Yeah," I said. "I know who you mean."

"Well, he's into this shit big-time, Joey. But not Carlo. The boss is very sick anyway. I don't know who will be the top guy when he goes. My *compare* tells me that he heard rumors that maybe Paulie will. I hope so, because I don't get along too well with Neil. He just has some kind of hard-on for me, so my *compare* told me to stay away from him."

"So what do we do with Bobby and his intelligent partner the Rabbit?" I wanted to know.

"Joey, we'll talk about it later. Let's go pick up the girls."

My date's name was Anna. Tommy's was Tracy. Two young broads. Anna was pretty, about five nine, slim, nice ass and legs, no tits, and dark hair. I was tired of blondes. Tracy was a tiny blonde with big tits and a big ass. Tommy loved them small. We went to the dog track, Biscayne in Miami, and we won again. We let the girls keep the winnings, about $300 apiece.

"See, Joey," Tommy told me at one point during the night. "These girls are nice. I don't go with hookers. I don't pay to get laid."

I thought about the expensive dinner and the $600 from the track, and I told Tommy to stay out of the sun tomorrow. "Your head is getting baked."

The next day we decided to go in on the deal with

Bobby Anthony. Tommy didn't see it as taking much of a chance. "I don't think he'll fuck with me," he said. "He knows I'll hurt him."

We arranged a meet at my house in West Palm, but Tommy didn't want Bobby Anthony coming into the house. He didn't like the fact that I was so friendly with people from all the Families. He wanted me for himself.

"Joey, they just want to make you a rent job," he'd tell me, meaning that anybody could use me for anything anytime they pleased. "You're part of my crew."

Frankly, I think he was a paranoid schizo, not to mention becoming a pain in the ass. I liked a lot of people. I liked Bobby Anthony. Tommy always wanted to know what I was doing and who I was doing it with. Oh, he used to try to couch it, saying things like he had to know everything I was doing because if I got whacked he'd have to retaliate. But I knew he just wanted his piece of the pie.

Bobby Anthony showed up at my house on time, and Tommy made him conduct business on the front stoop. Bobby shot me a glance like Tommy was nuts, but shook it off and went into his spiel.

"Here it is, Tommy. I talked it over with my partner," Bobby began. "I know you don't like Rabbit, but I do, and personal feelings don't come into this. I'm not too crazy about you myself, but business is business. You give us fifteen thousand, and we give you back ten times that in no longer than two months. But if something happens bad with the deal, we pay you back the fifteen thousand plus five thousand juice. That's it. Take it or leave it."

I admired the way Bobby Anthony spoke to Tommy. Not disrespectful, but straight. He showed Tommy that he wasn't afraid of him.

"Give him the money, Joey," Tommy said. "Count it in the car and get outta here."

Bunny cooked dinner that night, and at the table Tommy made contingency plans.

"Joey, if Bobby fucks up, I'll take care of it. I don't want you getting involved. I got to go in for a year on that bookmaking bit, and I need you out here to be my eyes and ears. So you don't do nothing, understand? He fucks up, I'll reach out and take care of it. Gee, Bunny, this is good. Is it what the Jews eat?''

"No, Tommy," Bunny said. "Jewish people don't eat pork."

9

"You See Tommy Coming, You Kill Him. Okay?"

TOMMY AGRO WAS THE KIND OF GUY EVEN HIS BEST friends didn't want to cross. I found out firsthand just what kind of crossed wires this guy had about a week after we did the deal with Bobby Anthony. Bunny and I went to the Diplomat Hotel in Hollywood, Florida. A friend named Jiggs Forlano had called saying he wanted to see me about some business we were doing, so we decided to make an evening of it with our wives. I had called ahead to the Tack Room, and Tony, the maitre d', had, as usual, saved me the front center table.

Nick "Jiggs" Forlano was a retired capo from the Colombo Family, or as retired as a capo can get. He was very low key, very quiet, very deadly. He'd been notorious in his day, and the word on the street was that he'd refused the leadership of the Colombo Family when Joe Colombo got shot back in '71, and instead grubstaked a claim in South Florida. I got along great with him. Jiggs and his lovely wife, Sophie, were waiting for us in the lobby of the Dip when we arrived.

We were sitting in the Tack Room when Bobby Anthony walked in, and I invited him to join us for a drink. When I introduced him to Jiggs and Sophie, Bobby embarrassed me, telling Jiggs how he'd heard what a real killer he'd once been. I felt uneasy but managed a laugh. Jiggs just stared at him, chewing on an unlit cigar.

"Yo, wait a minute, Cap," Bobby said nervously. "I was only kidding. I got a big mouth."

Jiggs nodded in agreement, then broke into a smile. "Okay then, sit down and be quiet before I tell your boss Gerry to spank you." He was referring to Bobby's boss in Harlem.

The next to arrive was Bobby DeSimone with his wife, Betty. I asked him where Tommy was.

"He'll be right here, Joey," DeSimone said. "But he doesn't know you're out tonight. He'll be surprised to see you."

"I tried to call him," I told DeSimone, "but his line was always busy."

"That's no excuse, Joey," said the motormouth. "You know Tommy has two phones." This asshole hated my guts because Tommy and I got along so well.

Moments later Tommy walked in with Louie Esposito's girl, Lily. Louie had flown back to New York on business, and although Lily was the biggest blowjob in Queens, Tommy had decided to escort her. Now that I think of it, that's probably *why* Tommy had decided to escort her.

"Tom, sit down," Jiggs said. The table was packed, but we squeezed in two more.

Tommy looked us over, saw Bobby Anthony and all the others, shook hands with Jiggs, gave Sophie a kiss, and ignored me.

He sat right across from me, and I said, "Hey, buddy, what's wrong? Don't you feel good?"

"Yeah, I feel fine," he answered without looking at me. He had something on his mind, and I didn't like the way he was acting. He put a cigarette in his mouth, I struck a match to light it, and he slapped my hand away and lit it himself.

Ten minutes went by and Tommy put another cigarette in his mouth. I struck another match. He smacked my hand down, harder this time, and said, "I'll light my own cigarettes. Go light your friend's there." He pointed to Bobby Anthony.

Minchia, I thought. My cock! I was pissed off, and a little concerned.

I excused myself from the table, walked into the Celebrity Room, and asked Miguel, one of the Cuban waiters, for a boning knife. I told him I had to cut a piece of leather off my wife's shoe. I wanted to be prepared in case Tommy started anything. He was notorious for always carrying a pair of sharp scissors.

I returned to the table, the knife in my left waistband with my jacket covering it. The floor show was over, and Jiggs and Sophie were leaving. Jiggs and I hadn't had a chance to talk, so we made plans to meet at the track the following day. As I was saying goodbye, Tommy made his way over to the bar. Ten minutes later I heard him calling me over.

"Yeah, Tom, what's up?"

He started kicking me in the shins, screaming, "I'm gonna teach you a fuckin' lesson!"

I couldn't believe what was happening. I never took any bullshit from anyone in my life. Here I show this guy a world of respect, and he's doing this to me in a public place? I reached back and gave him a karate chop in the forehead with the heel of my hand. He went flying on his ass, and his rug slipped halfway off his head.

He got up to charge, reaching into his back pocket, and I grabbed the handle of my knife with my right hand. I lunged my right arm back and forward, like throwing a softball, and as the boning knife was closing in on his groin I was suddenly grabbed by an undercover cop I knew from the area.

"Take it easy, Joe," the cop said to me, and by this time there were people holding Tommy back, too.

Tom left the Diplomat with Lily, but the maitre d' and manager suggested I wait awhile before I headed out. Bobby Anthony had stayed in my corner. But Bobby DeSimone and his wife trailed out behind T.A., DeSimone shooting me a dirty look on his way toward the door. Bobby Anthony caught the look and asked if DeSimone had something he wanted to settle outside. The motormouth declined and scurried through the door.

Bunny was scared as hell, so ten minutes later the maitre d' led us out a secret door through the kitchen. Bobby Anthony came with us and in the parking lot asked me if

I had any weapons at home. "Yes," I answered, and on the drive home Bunny asked if I really thought Tommy would come after me at the house.

"I don't know, honey, but don't worry. I'll take care of it. I guess I should have listened to you a long time ago."

"I'm not going to say I told you so. But I told you so."

We both laughed nervously as I pulled into the driveway.

"Joe, honey, come to bed. It's three in the morning."

I was sitting by the front window with a thirty-thirty rifle, a carbine, and a forty-five pistol. I wasn't taking any chances. I was afraid Tommy A. would retaliate right away. Bruno, our 160-pound brindle-colored Great Dane, haunched next to me.

"You go to sleep, honey," I whispered to Bunny. "I'll be in in a little while. I'm a little worried."

"Joe, he won't hurt the children, will he? I'm so scared. Why don't we call the police?"

"The cops!" I exploded. "Are you crazy? What are they going to do, you fuckin' idiot. They know who I am. They know who I'm connected with. They'll come here and laugh at us. You think they care what happens to us? Besides, I don't call the law. That cocksucker comes near here, I'll kill him myself. Now go to bed. You're pissing me off."

I hated to talk to Bunny that way. But I was really worried and taking my anxiety out on her. I couldn't believe it had come to this between Tommy and me. Twenty-four hours earlier there hadn't been anything I wouldn't do for the man.

"Joey, it's six-thirty. Come to bed and don't yell at me," Bunny called from the bedroom.

I smiled. She was a good person. She deserved better than me. She wasn't materialistic. All she wanted was for me to love her and be faithful to her. I had been, too. Until I became a Mafia tough guy.

"Okay, honey," I told her. "I'll come in on one condition: You see Tommy coming, you kill him. Okay?"

"How about I just wake you up?"

I slept with the forty-five next to my pillow. I dozed off into a coma and dreamed about being bayonetted in Korea. At five that afternoon Bunny shook me awake. Jiggs was on the phone and needed to talk to me.

"Joey, I thought you were supposed to meet me at the track today. What happened? You know I had to talk to you about that thing you asked me about."

Christ, I thought. Here was a capo doing me a favor, and I forgot all about it. I had swiped some diamonds, and I wanted to get rid of them. I didn't want to fence them through T.A., because he'd have glommed them. That's why I'd gone to Jiggs.

"Jiggs, I'm sorry. I just woke up. Did you hear what happened at the Dip last night after you left?"

He hadn't. I explained.

"Joe, did you have to pull that knife on him?" Jiggs asked. "That makes things difficult."

"Jiggs, I did what I had to do. He was going for his pair of scissors. I sat up all night with a bunch of guns waiting for him to come over."

Jiggs laughed at that. "He's not that stupid, Joe. Anyway, I'm going to see him. You stay home, don't go anywhere, and wait for my call."

Three hours later Jiggs called back.

"You know what happened, Joey? When Tommy saw you with that doper Bobby Anthony, he thought you were doing something behind his back. I told him he should put his arm around you and see that no one bothers you because of the money you earn for him. Now here's what I want you to do. Tomorrow morning at eleven o'clock you be at Tommy's apartment. I'll be there. I want the two of you to talk out your differences and settle this dispute. But be there at eleven, because I got to get to the track."

"Jiggs," I said slowly, "nothing is going to happen, is it? I'm going to come dressed, you know what I mean?"

I was telling Jiggs I'd arrive carrying a gun.

"Joey, I told you, I'm going to be there. If you bring anything into my presence I'll make you eat the damn thing. *Capisci?* Don't be late."

10

"Always Watch Your Back"

I LEFT WEST PALM BEACH AT NINE-THIRTY THE NEXT morning. The drive to Hollywood took an hour and fifteen minutes. I parked my car and sat in the underground lot for eight minutes. At three minutes to eleven I knocked on the door of Tommy's eleventh-floor apartment.

I didn't come "dressed."

Tommy opened the door, and as I entered he was walking away from me. No hellos. No embracing. No nothing. I followed him into the dining room, where Jiggs was already sitting. I was scared.

"I want you two to shake hands and discuss whatever problems you have," Jiggs began. "I don't want to hear no arguing, no threats, no involvement physically. If I hear or see any of these things, you will have to deal with me, and I don't think you want that. Now I'll be out on the balcony, so get started. And make it as quick as possible, because I got to get to the track. Talk nice, boys."

I spoke first.

"Tom, I don't know why this happened and I'd love to forget about it and resume our relationship the way it was. You know I care for you like a brother. I've proven what I would do for you whenever you've asked."

"Joey, I don't know what you're doing with that Bobby Anthony, and I don't care. I'm just going to tell you one more time. Be careful of him. He's bad people. Him and his fuckin' idiot partner Rabbit."

"But Tom, I—"

"Just a minute, Joey. I'm not finished. When I finish, I'll listen to you. But right now I have the floor. You know that seventy-five thousand you've got of mine, the

41

money you say is shylocked out on the streets? I want it all back in. You have one month to get it in. And not only that, I want the names of all the customers you got, and where they live."

So this, I thought, is what the motherfucker wants. My mind worked overtime. He was talking like he was doing me a favor by lending me $75,000 at 1½ percent per week. I was handing over more than $1,100 in juice every week. He wanted it in one month. Well, fuck him. I'd get it back to him tomorrow. I had money this asshole had no idea about.

"With all due respect, Tom," I answered, "I'll do the best I can. But as far as my customers go, I won't give you their names or their addresses. They're mine, not yours. Now, I pay you eleven and change every week, so if you're willing to give that up, I'll have your seventy-five grand by tomorrow. You know the good standing I have with the Colombos—there's one of them on the balcony right now—well, I can always go to work for them.

"And as far as the bookmaking out at Gulfstream, that was my idea. You want that, too? Who's gonna run it? That skinny fuck DeSimone you got hanging around you? He doesn't have the brains of a flea.

"And those two paychecks I send once a week from the no-show union jobs out at Century Village? That's about six bills clear every week. Do I find a new *compare* to collect for the absent Mr. Russo and Mr. Demarco, Tom?

"Would you like me to go on?"

Tommy stared at me for a minute and then sprang for me. He hugged me and kissed me on both cheeks. "Joey, I just wanted to see what kind of man you were. And you are a man."

We both laughed and hugged and Jiggs walked in smiling. "All right, that's enough," he said finally. "You look like a couple of *finocchios*." Jiggs hated fags.

We made our goodbyes, and on the way down in the elevator Jiggs turned to me and said, "I'm glad you two are friends again, Joe, but listen to me good. Be careful.

Always watch your back. I won't say any more, and don't ask me no questions.''

Then he changed the subject.

"As far as those stones go, yeah, they're good, and no, I did not mention them to your *compare* upstairs. But the best I can do is five thousand a stone. They're all about a carat apiece and worth three times that amount. But you know how it is. Everyone down the line has to earn a little money.''

"Okay, get rid of them,'' I said, handing Jiggs a bag containing twenty-six diamonds. He promised to have the money for me in a week. We set a date to meet at the track.

Gulfstream had just closed for the 1974 meet, and they were racing at Calder Race Course in Miami. That's where I met Jiggs a week later. He handed me $130,000 cash for the diamonds. I thanked him and gave him $20,000 for his trouble. He tried to give it back, saying he'd merely done me a favor, but I told him if he didn't take it I'd leave it for the waitress.

"You bastard," Jiggs said as he picked up the dough.

Ruby Stein was Jiggs's main tenant. By tenant I mean someone who pays rent. It was said that in any given week Ruby Stein had $2 million on the streets, mostly shylock loans to wiseguys and big businessmen. If that was true, and I had no reason to doubt it, it meant Ruby was pulling in $20,000 a week in juice alone. They said Jiggs took 25 percent of that, or $5,000 a week, which provided him with a nice little nest egg of a quarter million a year. And Jiggs needed every bit of it. He was a degenerate gambler.

"Hey, Joey, I've been watching this horse and he's going off four to one," Jiggs said. "I'm going to bet a G on him.''

"Do that at the window, Jiggs, and he'll go off nine to five. Better to give it to Abbie Roth over there.''

Abbie Roth had been the bookmaker at Calder for as long as anyone could remember. He was the reason our crew didn't have our own bookmaker at Calder. Why start a beef?

"I don't want to meet nobody," Jiggs said softly. "Here, you take it to the Jew. As long as you say he's all right, that's good enough for me."

We both bet $1,000, and the horse went off at seven to two. He went wire to wire and paid $9.20. We won $3,060 apiece. We spent the rest of the day bullshitting about Families. Not families. When Jiggs found out I was close to some of the Colombos like Little Dom Cataldo and had even done some business with Little Vic Orena, he couldn't understand why I was still with Tommy A. and the Gambinos. I just shrugged.

At the end of the day Jiggs had won $5,800 and I'd pocketed $2,000. As we were leaving, he warned me one more time to watch my back.

11

"Uncle Joe, You're Crazy"

THE MENTION OF THE NO-SHOW UNION JOB DURING MY beef with Tommy reminded me that I had to start spending more time on the job site. I'd opened a drywall construction company in January of '74, my legit business on the side, and to this day I think I might have been a success as a "citizen" if I wasn't always in love with the easy buck. As it was, I left most of the construction duties in the hands of my brother Frank, who was also my foreman.

So the day after Jiggs and I cleaned up at the track I decided to run over to Century Village, where my outfit had won a bid to hang the drywall. I got to the construction trailer around one-thirty that afternoon and asked my niece Marsha, who I'd brought down from New York to be my secretary and bookkeeper, what was going on.

"Uncle Joe, most of the men were here at lunchtime," she reported. "They said they wanted their money. They say they want to quit. They say they won't work here as long as Uncle Frank is their foreman, or supervisor, or whatever it is he does.''

Fifteen minutes later there were fifty-two construction workers outside the trailer complaining that my little brother—who carried 220 well-muscled pounds on a six-foot, two-inch frame—was shooting a pistol at them while they worked.

If there was one thing I wouldn't tolerate, it was insubordination from supervisors. So I confronted Frank right in front of the fifty-two men.

"Did you fire a gun at these guys, telling them you were going to shoot them if they didn't get up to work on that building's fourth floor?"

"Hey, Bro," Frank answered. "You think I would do anything like that. You know me better than that. They just don't like me because I'm Italian.''

"Okay, end of story," I announced. "Whoever wants to quit, get the fuck out of here and pick up your pay Friday. Now either go to work or hit the fuckin' road. You got three minutes to decide what to do."

They all went back to work. They all made good money with me, and their checks never bounced. They also knew I could have replaced every one of them in less than three days. My payroll was between $50,000 and $60,000 a week. But the outfit I had the contract with sent their money in like clockwork.

Back inside the trailer, I turned to Frank and asked him what kind of gun he had used. "You fire a thirty-eight?"

"Nah," Frank said. "I used this little twenty-two pistol. No big deal."

"Oh, in that case, that's different." I smiled. "Let's go have a late lunch."

Marsha was aghast. "Uncle Joe, you're crazy. And Uncle Frank, I believed you! The both of you, you're terrible."

Frank and I just laughed and shook our heads.

12
Muscle

"Grrr. Grrr. That fuckin' girl." That was a soliloquy for Gino.

Gino was a big-built lob from Boston. I kept him around the construction site in case I needed some muscle. He had just done ten years inside, and he was good to have at your back. Gino had a lot of balls and would do anything I asked.

"What's wrong, Gino? What are you grumbling about?"

"That girl at the restaurant across the street, she don't want me to fix your coffee anymore. I told her you don't like it the way she fixes it, that she puts too much milk in it and you start yelling. But she says she don't want me touching the coffeepot no more.

"She also said that the manager don't want us in there no more. That we should go someplace else to eat lunch."

The "restaurant" across the street was the Deerfield Beach Country Club. It was built on a beautiful golf course, and catered to a real la-de-da lunch crowd. But it was convenient, right across from the job site, and I'd often take a bunch of supervisors to lunch in the club's dining room. In fact, I left such big tips that the girls were always scrambling to wait on our table. I thought we were liked over there. But one of Century Village's foremen was a good-looking black man named Johnny Coleman. I had a feeling this beef had something to do with Johnny Coleman.

"Gino," I said, "you go back over there and get me my coffee. And if the girl don't fix it right, you take it and show it to the manager."

He was back in five minutes with the container. I lifted the lid. It was almost milk white.

"Gino, did you fix this coffee or did the waitress do this?"

"I didn't touch it, Joe. In fact, the manager told me to wait outside while she fixed the coffee."

"I don't fuckin' believe this. I'm going over there right now."

"Let me come with you," Gino said. I told him no in no uncertain terms.

When I walked through the door of the Deerfield Beach Country Club, the manager was waiting as if he expected me.

"Excuse me, sir," I said to the motherfucker. "I think we have a communications problem here. I've been sending one of my employees here every morning for—"

He interrupted me. "There's no communications problem. I feel that your presence is not desired here, and I will do anything to discourage your motley crew from coming here. As you can see, we cater to a different class of clientele."

I looked at this mook, staring at his jugular vein, wanting to rip it out. But I remembered T.A.'s advice. I stayed cool.

"Well, sir, I'm sorry to hear that," I told the cocksucker. I turned and wheeled out. When I reached the trailer I told Gino to find me Johnny Coleman. Right away.

Within minutes Johnny Coleman was standing at my desk. "Yeah, Joe baby, what's up?"

"John, how many niggers you got working here?" I asked him.

"Joe, man, don't call my men niggers. You know I don't go around calling you wops and all that shit."

"Sorry, John, my mistake," I said. "I just wanted to see if you wanted to make a hundred bucks for yourself and wanted to treat all your, um, blacks to lunch today and tomorrow."

I told him what had happened at the country club. And I explained my scheme. Then I sent Marsha to the bank with a $400 check, and she returned with eighty five-dollar bills. By 11:35 A.M. there were about fifty black guys standing in front of my trailer.

"Listen up, guys," I announced. "I'm going to give you five bucks each, and I want you all to take it across the street to that country club and order lunch. I want you all to go there and sit four to a table and act like gentlemen. But I don't want you to wash up here before you go. Use their washroom. Order your food, leave a tip, but don't take any shit. If anyone tries to throw you out, we'll call the NAACP and close them up. Remember, don't start no trouble. And be back here tomorrow at the same time. Lunch is on me again. But don't rat me out."

You had to see these guys! Two had holes in their pants and their cheeks were hanging out. Most had ripped T-shirts. They were a filthy mess of Zulu construction workers.

I returned from my lunch in town at two-thirty, and Johnny Coleman was waiting for me by the trailer.

"Joe, you should have been there. When we walked in, there was about a dozen regulars in there eating lunch. They got the fuck out of there in about fifteen seconds. Then we all sat down and ordered the same soup, but they ran out. Then we all ordered club sandwiches and the cook quit and ran out. Then, after we ordered, we went to the washroom—ten at a time—and we left that washroom so filthy the rats ran out.

"We acted nice and quiet and they still called the police. And, Joe, get this. Two of the cops that showed were black guys. I went up to them and asked what the problem was. I mean, we work across the street, and this was a public place and all, and with the manager standing right there I told the cops that we were planning on coming in for lunch every day. I asked the cops if they had any objections and they said, 'Fuck no.'

"Then the cops turned to the manager and told him they didn't appreciate the superficial call, and not to do it again."

The two of us rolled on the ground laughing.

I didn't have to wait long for results. Within an hour the big shots from Century Village were in my trailer.

They had been called by the big shots in the country club. They knew I was behind the whole thing. They assured me that it was all a misunderstanding, and that my foremen and supervisors were of course welcome for lunch anytime. As a matter of fact, they said, the manager of the dining room had been fired.

The next morning I summoned Johnny Coleman, threw him $200, and told him to take the black crew from the day before to lunch anywhere but the Deerfield Beach Country Club. Then I rounded up the rest of my foremen and supervisors and we returned to the club. Lunch was on the house. Even the cook had returned. There was only one difference: He had taken club sandwiches off the menu.

13
The Crew

IN A WAY, BEING A MEMBER OF A CREW IS LIKE NEVER leaving high school. The boys are all ganged up and strutting around like roosters, the girls are only food for fucking, and the jokes never get beyond the twelfth-grade level. I remember one Sunday during the spring of '74 when Tommy was still lamming it in his Hollywood apartment. I'd gone to his place to cook for him and the crew. We also had some business to discuss. After we ate.

"Joey," Tommy said, "the maitre d' at the Diplomat gave me these squid. You know what to do with them? My mother used to stuff them. You know how to make that?"

"Yeah, Tom, but you need a grinder to grind the heads up and stuff and we don't have one."

"Won't a blender do the same?" Buzzy asked.

"I don't know," I said. "I'll try it with a sharp knife. I can chop the heads and tentacles up pretty fine."

"Don't forget to remove the eyes, Joey," Bobby DeSimone said. "I think they're poisonous."

"They're not poisonous, you just don't eat them," I said.

"Tommy does," Buzzy said. "He eats eyes all the time. I just heard him tell this guy yesterday that if he didn't show up with the money he would eat the eyes out of his fuckin' head."

It was nice hanging around with the guys. Someone was always joking. And when Tommy was in a good mood (which wasn't often), most of us made him the scapegoat of our jokes.

There were usually five of us, which meant that one guy would have to sit out of the pinochle game, then play the next game with one of the losers. No one wanted me for a partner. Hell, I couldn't remember ten cards, much less forty-eight, like they all did. They always screamed at me, but I didn't care. It was fun. And whoever lost the most had to do the dishes. I went out and bought a pair of rubber gloves. That should tell you something.

Midway through the meal, Tommy announced that the grand jury looking for him had "de-convened."

"My *compare* told me I have to come back in, so I'll be leaving this week," he said. "And just when I met this broad. What a living doll she is. I think she's about twenty-one. I gave her the number here, to the phone in the bedroom. She said she was gonna call today."

Tommy had two phone lines. The living room was for us guys to use. A business phone. The other, in the bedroom, was his "hot-line number." He only gave that number to his special girlfriends. We all had the number, but we never used it.

"Joey, you should see the ass on this baby doll," Tommy went on. "She is just beautiful. I think I'm in love."

I was sitting out of the after-dinner pinochle game and was wondering what kind of mischief I could get into. "Tommy, can I use your phone? I got to call Bunny."

"Go ahead, use the phone. And since when do you have to ask?"

I dialed the phone in the bedroom on the business

phone, and it began to ring. Tommy thinks it's his broad. He got up from the table and walked nonchalantly into the bedroom. As soon as he reached the receiver, I hung up. He came out muttering, "Motherfucker, they hung up. I bet you that was her."

"Don't worry, Tommy, she'll call back," Bobby said. "She probably thought you stepped out, because the phone rang five times before you picked it up."

"Joey, did you call your wife?" Tommy asked.

"The line was busy. I'll call back after we play this next game."

Tommy was my partner and he was aggravated because he hadn't reached the phone. He started nagging me about the card game. "What the fuck you coming in spades for, Joey? Don't you see me pointing to my ring? That means diamonds, you fuckin' idiot."

I'd seen him point but pretended I hadn't. I just wanted to get back on that phone. Whoever was sitting out of the game had the choice of picking his partner from one of the losers, and I was never picked. So I sat out. And dialed again.

Tommy got up a little quicker this time and started walking into the bedroom. "Ooh, ooh, I betcha that's my baby doll," he cooed.

I hung up on the fourth ring.

"Motherfucker, she hung up again."

"Hey, Tommy," I said helpfully, "don't take so fuckin' long to get to the phone."

"Joey, this is a big apartment. I got there as quick as I could. Son of a bitch."

"You know, Tommy, next time it rings, I'll run back there and get it for you," DeSimone said. "I can reach it by the second or third time."

"You don't answer that phone, Bobby. You'll scare her away with that faggot voice of yours. I'll run next time it rings."

I was laughing so hard I had to go into the kitchen. By now, Tommy's talking to himself. "Gee, I hope she calls back. I wanted to take her out tonight."

"Why don't you call her?" I asked him. "Don't you have her number?"

"I don't ever call broads, Joey. I give them my number. If they call, they call. But I never call them."

I lost another hand and Louie Esposito handed me my rubber gloves. "Here you go, Joey, your mittens. Make sure you get everything spotless."

Marrone, but I was tired of washing dishes. But I finished them, went back to the living room, and picked up the phone one more time. The phone in the bedroom began ringing.

Tommy jumped up and bolted for the bedroom. On the second ring he tripped in the foyer. He crab-walked to the phone and got it on the fourth ring. I hung up.

"My fuckin' back," he moaned. "I think I hurt it bad. I think I'll knock the shit out of that broad when I see her."

"It's not her fault, Tommy," Bobby said. "I told you I should have answered the phone and this would never have happened."

"Shut the fuck up," Tommy said. "Joey, you going? I'll see you later. That squid was good. Is there any left?"

"Yeah," I answered. "In the fridge. That maitre d' gave you enough to feed an army."

When I got home I told Bunny what I'd done. We both laughed for an hour. But now, how was I going to let Tommy in on the joke without getting killed? The gag was no good unless he knew about it, and I knew he wouldn't think it was funny. I waited until about eight o'clock that night and called him.

"Hiya, Tip. How you feeling? Your girl call back?" Sometimes I called him Tip, short for Tommy.

"Nah, Joey, the bitch never called. She probably got tired of dialing. Anyway, the back's a little better. But I took some fall. All over a fuckin' broad. You coming to the Diplomat tonight?"

"Maybe, Tom, but listen, first I got to level with you. That girl never called you."

"What do you mean? How do you know? It could have been someone else. But what makes you say it wasn't her?"

"Because, Tom, it was me dialing the bedroom from the living room."

"Joey, you motherfucker," he screamed. "You made me almost break my fuckin' neck! You come down here right now. I'll break your fuckin' head! Get down here, Joey! That's an order!"

"Fuck you," I laughed. "There's no way I'm coming there now. You cool off first, and think about how funny you looked. You really fell head over heels for that girl."

"Joey, I'm gonna rip your fuckin' heart out," he said, but by now even Tommy was laughing a little. Then he hung up.

I told Bunny he'd get over it, and we'd all have a good laugh about it someday. Nevertheless, I stayed home that night.

14
My First Enemy: The *Consigliere*

TOMMY CALLED THE NEXT DAY, LAUGHING. "I CAN'T believe I fell for that shit. I should have known, all those calls to your wife. Anyway, the girl showed up at the Dip last night and I told her about your gag. She laughed like hell. She said all the guys she meets with me act like they're in a gangster movie. Are you coming in tonight? I want to talk to you. I'm leaving tomorrow."

I drove to the Diplomat that night to meet T.A., and he grilled me with all kinds of questions about how I met Jiggs. I told him a mutual friend, a big South Florida bookmaker named Freddie "Freddie Campo" Campagnuolo, another babe in the woods, had introduced us at a Sinatra show the previous New Year's Eve at the Diplomat.

"We had eighteen people at the table," I explained. "Freddie and his broad and Tommy Farese, you know, the Colombo doper. A couple of his lobs. And Jiggs was there with his wife. Jiggs was impressed we had the front center table. Even stars like Jackie Gleason were sitting behind us. I wondered if Sinatra recognized Jiggs, because he sang to our table for over an hour. He even asked me for some ice for his wine. It was red wine. I guess he wanted to cool it off.

"So, after that, I used to see Jiggs at the track and we became friends. I got him front-row tickets for a Liza Minnelli concert in Fort Lauderdale. He asked me because he said Freddie Campo was making too big a deal over it. I even met Ally Boy through Jiggs."

The capo Alphonse "Ally Boy" Persico was brother to Carmine "the Snake" Persico, boss of the Colombo Family. The mention of Persico's name seemed to wake Tommy Agro up.

"Joey, so you know who Jiggs is, right?" Tommy asked.

"Hey, Tom, I'm just friends with the guy. I don't do business with him," I lied. "I heard he was a capo with the Colombos. I told you that already, Tommy."

"Okay, Joey, calm down, it's all right," Tommy said. "I like the guy a lot myself. He's very well respected, and he knows you're with me. He's a man, Joey, not like some of these other cocksuckers. Joey, you're learning. Just try not to make too many mistakes, because I like you very much."

There was always a hint of menace in the heart-to-hearts I had with T.A. I guess otherwise he wouldn't have been T.A. But the beef between Tommy and me was over with. I could see that. I felt comfortable around him again and was glad. Frankly, I enjoyed being around him. And he liked me because I wasn't a freeloader. I earned. That, and I could handle things for him.

"Joey," he asked, "what happened when you met with my *compare?* Remember he called you from Naples?"

Oh *marrone*, I thought. What a fuck-up that had been! Tommy was talking about Joe N. Gallo, the *consigliere* of the Gambino Family. At Tommy's suggestion, he'd called me from Naples, Florida, a few months before, only Tommy hadn't told me who the guy was. We'd gotten on like oil and water. I told him the story.

"He calls me in the morning, Tom, and tells me he wants to meet with me in an hour. I told him I had business to take care of, but I would be glad to meet with him anytime after four o'clock. 'What's this?' he says to me. 'Some kind of joke?' Then he called me a jackass.

"Well, Tom, you know me. I don't take that kind of shit from anyone, and I told him so. I told him the only reason why I was even talking to him was because my *compare* T.A. says you're close to him.

" 'Close to him,' he screams over the phone. 'You be at the fuckin' Diplomat at seven-thirty tonight! And don't be late.'

"I didn't know what to do, Tommy. That's when I called you. I mean, you didn't tell me who he was and all. You know?"

"Yeah, Joey, I know," Tommy said. He was shaking his head. "He called me and told me. I told him you didn't know anything about him. He laughed. A little."

"Yeah, well, anyway, I show up that night at the Dip," I said, picking up the Gallo story, "and he was waiting there at the valet station. 'Joe Dogs?' he says. 'Joe N.?' I say. And we embrace. He apologizes for calling me names. We had dinner and a few drinks, and he asked me to pick him up the next day and drive him around Naples. Said he wanted to build a house.

"So, since you told him I'm in construction, he wants me to build him the house. But, Tommy, the guy wants a quarter-million-dollar house built for nothing. What the fuck?"

"I know, Joey," T.A. said. "All these zips are that way. They think the world owes them. But, Joey, he's number three in the Family. He's the *consigliere*."

"Wow," I answered sarcastically. "Let me say it backward. Wow. How does that sound?"

"Don't fuck around, Joey. He's a good man."

"Hey, Tom, that's just the way I am. I like people. I don't give a fuck if they don't have a dime. But when people start acting like kings, shit on them. I don't like them. We went to the Calder track while he was here. Did he tell you?"

Yes, Joe N. Gallo had told Tommy Agro about our day at the races. It had been a disaster. Earlier in the year my uncle and I had bought a nag, Elfin Water, and the first three times we raced her she finished eleventh in a ten-horse field. Anyway, Little Dom Cataldo had been down from New York a few weeks before Gallo, and he had talked me into experimenting with this new kind of horse dope that was supposed to be untraceable. The first time they were supposed to shoot up Elfin Water, she went off at five to one, and I put $1,000 on her to win. She finished last.

Little Dom had called from New York saying he hadn't been able to get to the stable hand. He promised next time would be a lock. I'd put the matter out of my mind. Coincidentally, the next time my horse ran was the day I took Joe N. Gallo to the track. He didn't want to hang out with me, he didn't want to meet my pals. But before we parted in the grandstand he did ask about my horse. I'd told him I thought she "had a shot." No more, no less. I didn't want Joe N. Gallo throwing his good money after my bad.

For loyalty, I put a twenty-dollar wheel on my horse in the daily double. Five minutes before post time she was listed at seventy to one. I went over to the window and put $200 on her to win. She went off at twenty-five to one. I had $400 invested in her. She won by three lengths and paid $52.80. I won a little over $12,000.

Gallo came running over to me after the race screaming that he hadn't bet her. He was pissed off. I left the track after the second race. Back at home, Little Dom called. He'd bet $2,000 with his New York bookmaker for me, to win. He was holding $50,000 for me. I was up $62,000. Joe N. Gallo was out.

"So that's how it happened, Tom," I said.

"Okay, Joey, but my *compare* thinks you didn't let him in on something that you were sure was coming down. He's still really pissed off."

"Tom, you know I'm not like that," I protested. "In my mind, I really didn't believe that Little Dom could do anything. And besides, I told Gallo we 'had a shot.' What did you want me to do? Split my winnings with him?"

"Joey, all I'm trying to say is that Joe's been pissed at you for a long time now. I tried to explain it, but he didn't buy it."

"And another thing, Tom. In my mind I'm not even sure if Little Dom got to the stable hand and shot up the dope. Because after that race the horse ran second twice and won two more times."

"Yeah, Joey, I know."

Tommy knew? How the hell did he know? I wondered.

"We bet her in New York three of those times," Tommy added. "Didn't you get down?"

"A couple bucks at the track," I said. "Tommy, are you trying to tell me that there was something going on with *my* horse and I didn't know about it?"

"Joey, you don't know Dominick like I do," he said. "He made a fortune off your horse."

"I'm sorry, Tom," I told him. "But in all due respect I have to say that I can't believe that Little Dom did that without letting me in on it."

Tommy Agro bared his teeth. "Joey, you're fuckin' dreamin' if you think Dominick isn't going to do something to your horse without your knowledge. Especially when there's money involved."

"Well, maybe you're right, Tom," I said. "But let me ask you this: If there was something going on, how come *you* didn't tell me?"

Tommy didn't answer me. He just looked at me like he didn't know what to say.

15
Three Points a Week

TOMMY LEFT FOR NEW YORK IN EARLY SUMMER 1974, and things got back to a little more normal. I sold Elfin Water to some guy who wanted to race him at Rhode Island's Narragansett Track, but not before I replaced my trainer with a kid named Howie Ruben. The horse never won under Ruben. I think the best she ran was one second and one third. She was hurting anyway—bowed tendons. In hindsight, I suppose my first trainer knew how to take care of a horse and this guy Ruben didn't.

One day I was sitting in the grandstand at Calder down in Miami when Ruben approached, asking me if I'd like to buy "a real good horse cheap."

"The horse has good bloodlines, Joe," he said. "He's out of Forli, the Italian champ."

What the fuck did I know about horses? I knew how to bet them. I knew how to curse when they lost. I knew how to cheer for them down the backstretch.

"How much can you get the horse for?" I asked. "And who wants to sell it?"

"The owner wants thirty thousand for him," Ruben said. "He's a yearling, and he'll be a good stakes horse. Joe, he's really a bargain at that price. These horses go for at least a hundred thousand at the annual Ocala auction. But you know what? I'll tell the owner we'll give him twenty thousand up front, and then the other ten thousand after the horse wins his first race. We'll run him in a maiden allowance, which is a maiden special weight. This way no one can claim him on you."

Ruben had me all excited now. I was really interested, and I showed it (like a jerk).

"Howie, listen to me," I said. "You don't know me, and you don't know anything about me. Before you do any business with me, I suggest, for your own sake, that you check me out. Do you understand me?"

"Joe, I'll guarantee the horse," he said. "I can't do any better than that."

So I bought the horse. I gave Ruben $20,000 in cash, and two days later he showed me our package.

"Isn't he beautiful?" Ruben asked.

"Yeah, what's his name?"

His name was Glorious Request, although Ruben told me I could change it if I wanted. I didn't bother. I wouldn't know what to call a horse anyway. Just as long as he wins.

"Oh, don't worry about that," Ruben assured me. "We're going to do good with this horse. He might even get to the Derby."

I mean, fuhgedaboudit. I felt like King Tut. I got me a horse that's going to the Derby! Hey, this guy Ruben guaranteed the horse, so I had nothing to lose. What the hell did I know? The horse looked healthy to me. He had legs like a linebacker, thick and strong-looking.

I started getting up early every morning and driving to the barn area. You needed a badge to get in, and since I didn't have one, Ruben would meet me at the gate. Like everything else I owned, the horse was in my wife's name. But I couldn't have gotten an owner's license if I'd wanted one. I had at least a dozen pinches on my rap sheet, everything from B and Es to shylocking, although I was proud of the fact that they were all misdemeanors. I had been arrested a year before for felony assault. But I'd pled down and walked away with a fine. After a few months the guards at the track all recognized me anyway, and I just drove right through.

I'd watch all Glorious Request's workouts. The gallop. The hotwalk. Working out of the gates. The whole bit. In January 1975 the horse turned two years old and I began asking Howie when we were going to race him.

"Joe, he's not quite ready yet," the trainer would answer. "He should be ready for later on in the Winter Gulfstream Meet. Let's get him real sharp."

Meanwhile, Ruben was always bragging about all "the boys" he knew in Detroit, how much they liked him, how they were only a phone call away. He'd mentioned names I didn't recognize—hey, don't forget, I'm the guy who'd never heard of Joe N. Gallo—and, all in all, he was very convincing. I had no reason not to believe him. It really meant nothing to me, other than the fact that my guarantee looked good if things ever came to a head. A sit-down was all it would take.

One morning Howie approached me with a request. "Let me level with you, Joe," he said. "I push a little cocaine here and there, and I need some seed money. Can you front me something?"

"Is there a lot of money in that shit, Howie?" I asked. I knew how much money was in coke. I just didn't want this moron to know that I knew.

"Joe, you have no idea how much," he bragged. "I

can turn twenty thousand into a hundred thousand in one month's time.''

"Are you a user, Howie?" I asked him.

"Once in a while, Joe. I use it to clear my mind. It makes you feel real sharp, Joe. I'll get you some and try it, okay?"

"Nah, nah, Howie. No thanks. But I will loan you twenty thousand at three points a week, and I don't want to know what you're doing with the cash. You just have the money every week. That's six hundred a week juice. *Capisci?*"

"Gee, Joe, that's a little steep isn't it? Can you make it two points?"

"Hey, Howie, you just told me how much you're going to make off of it. So what do you want to do, eat alone? Three points, Howie. And don't—and I emphasize *don't* —be late with the payments. And, Howie, I don't want to try any of that shit. My mind is sharp enough."

"No problem, Joe, three points," he said. "We're friends, right? I just need it for a month or so anyway."

"I don't care how long you keep it," I told him. "That's your business. You know the terms, and you know the complications if you don't meet the terms. I mean, you know all those guys from Detroit, right?"

"Yeah," he answered. "But I don't want to bother them with such a small loan." He was bullshitting.

But Ruben paid his juice on time, no problem. I stopped going to watch the workouts, and he met me every week at a coffee shop in Hallandale, just north of Miami. I'd meet with Jiggs while we waited for the horse trainer to show up. Jiggs, who lived near the diner, would walk his mile, eat half a sandwich, and chew on his cigar. Once in a blue moon he'd light it. "Cigarettes will kill you," he'd tell me every time we met. "I know. I smoked them for forty-five years."

16
The Glass Diamond

BUNNY CALLED ME AT THE CONSTRUCTION TRAILER ONE day not long after I shyed out the money to Ruben in February 1975. She was in a lather. Someone had broken into the house.

"What did they get?" I asked her.

"I think they took your guns."

"Is that all? Did they touch the bowling ball?" Bunny knew what I was talking about. I had about $200,000 in cash stuffed into the bowling bag at the bottom of my closet.

"No, honey," she said. "The bowling ball's still here. Should I call the cops?"

"Yeah, go ahead," I told her. "And don't forget to tell them about how bad you feel over losing your expensive diamond ring and the silverware set. *Capisci?*"

Bunny giggled. "Oh yeah. I loved those things so much." My wife appreciated the way I always thought on my feet, especially if there was a scam involved. She owned an expensive diamond ring but not a silverware set. However, that wouldn't stop me from filing an insurance claim on both. Little did I know that my cleverness would land me in the middle of a shit storm with certain members of the New York Gambino Family.

A few hours later they found the kid who broke into our house. He was a fourteen-year-old from the neighborhood. When they returned with my rifle and my thirty-eight, I asked about the diamond ring and the silverware.

"The kid says he doesn't know anything about those, um, stolen items," the officer told me. The guy was no dummy. He knew exactly what I was doing. "Would you like to press charges?"

"The hell with that," I said. "Somebody must have come in here after the kid left and stolen the expensive stuff. The diamond in my wife's ring was worth ten thousand alone."

"Must have," the cop said dryly and left.

I had insurance with Comine Insurance Company out of Miami. My broker was a guy named Freddy, whose Uncle Nino was a Gambino capo up in New York. So I really didn't foresee any problem collecting on the "stolen" ring. Comine sent me to the Javier jewelry store in Miami, where they "replaced" my wife's stolen ring with what they said was a two-carat $10,000 pear-shaped diamond placed in a beautiful gold setting.

About six months later I needed money and asked Bunny to give me the ring. I'd lost my drywall contract at Century Village because one of my employees had reported me to the IRS, and I'd hired a karate expert to work the guy over. The guy had been hurt real bad, and the head man at Century Village canceled my contract. I guess I was lucky they hadn't known about the no-show jobs and my other tricks or they would have canned me sooner.

"Jiggs, do me a favor," I asked him the next time we met. "See how much you can get for this stone." We were sitting in the Hallandale coffee shop waiting for Howie to come by with his juice.

"How big is it, Joey?"

"It's supposed to be two carats, worth ten grand." I told Jiggs the story behind it.

"I'll see what I can do," Jiggs replied just as Ruben walked through the door.

"Howie, how are you? You're ten minutes late," I kidded him.

He began stuttering, making excuses. He was a nervous fuck. I was beginning to think he was snorting too much of that nose candy. But then that was his business.

"Howie, I'm making a joke," I said. "But be on time next time."

The following week I arrived in Hallandale early to see what Jiggs had come up with on the stone.

"Joey," he said, "this diamond is shit."

I thought he was kidding.

"My guy told me he wouldn't give you five hundred for it," Jiggs went on, and I started to laugh.

"Those cocksuckers in Miami told me it was worth more than ten grand." I had to give those humps in Miami credit. While I thought I was ripping off the insurance company, they were ripping me off. But that didn't leave me any less pissed off.

"Give me their names. I'll take care of it." Jiggs was deadly serious. "Or tell your man Tommy A. about it. He'll straighten it out. Didn't you say Nino's nephew Freddy was in the middle of all this?"

"Yeah, Jiggs," I told him. "But maybe he's not involved. But that's good thinking. I'll call Freddy first and tell him about it. I don't want to bother Tommy with every little thing. I'll take care of this myself."

The next day I called Comine Insurance and got Freddy on the phone. When I explained what had happened, Freddy said that it was impossible, that Javier jewelry was a highly respected outfit. "Are you sure your appraiser is being straight with you?" Freddy asked, and for a moment I felt like scaring him just by mentioning the name Nick "Jiggs" Forlano. But I didn't want Jiggs involved, so I took off on the kid myself.

"What the fuck are you talking about, Freddy? Are you calling me a liar? I'm just telling you what my friend told me."

"Joe, don't talk to me like that," Freddy replied. "I just said maybe your friend made a mistake. I don't appreciate your language."

"Freddy, I don't give a fuck what or what you don't appreciate. Who the hell you think you are? Just get me my ten grand back before I have to take this further than a phone call." I hung up.

About three weeks later Glorious Request was entered in the maiden special allowance race at the '75 Summer Meet at Calder race track. Tommy A. and some of the guys flew down for his debut. I was a big man with Agro now. I owned a horse, and he owned me. He liked to show me off. Tommy was staying at the Diplomat, and a few nights before the race he pulled me aside.

"Joey, Nino come to me in New York. All he says is 'That Joe Dogs down in Florida is starting a lot of trouble.' Joey, I don't know how to answer him. I don't know what to say. What's going on?"

I told Tommy what happened, and he blew his fucking top.

"I wish you would have come to me with this sooner, Joe," he said. "Because I would have told him to go straighten out his fuckin' nephew. But you know what you do now, Joey? Get in touch with this fuckin' Freddy. Tell him to come to the Dip. Tell him I want to see him. And I'll call Nino and tell him I plan to talk to his nephew."

I called Freddy and gave him Tommy's message. Freddy said he'd have to check first with his Uncle Nino. "Do whatever you have to fuckin' do," I told him. "But be at the Dip tomorrow at two P.M. sharp."

Tommy and I were lounging by the pool the next afternoon when Freddy came sauntering in. He hugged Tommy, said hello to me, and added, "My uncle sends his regards." After a little small-talk bullshit, Tommy got to the point.

"Listen, Freddy, my close friend Joe Dogs here tells me he had an insurance policy with you, and that you replaced a ten-thousand-dollar diamond ring that was lost or stolen or whatever. But wherever you sent him to get it replaced, they gave him a bogus piece of glass."

"Well, Tom, in all due respect," Freddy replied, "Joe here could have changed the stone and—"

"Whoa, whoa, wait a minute here, Freddy," Tommy interrupted. "I'm only showing you this respect because of your uncle. Now, if you want to make accusations that Joe here is trying to swindle you out of a few grand, then, my friend, this conversation ends right here. My advice to you is to get out of here, go tell your uncle what you just told me, and I'll straighten it out in New York."

"Tommy, Tommy, I'm sorry," Freddy backtracked. "I'll tell you what I'll do. Me and Joe will take the stone to the Diamond Exchange in Miami, and we'll see what they say."

Tommy just looked at the kid. Tommy wasn't one to be fucked with. He played by the rules. He had listened to Nino's beef about me, had gotten embarrassed because he didn't know what it was all about, and had eaten Nino's shit, so to speak. But now he had the picture, and all he saw was some punk kid trying to throw his weight around because his uncle had a name.

"Listen, my friend," Tommy said to Freddy, "I won't tell Nino the way you talked, because he'll rip your eyes out of your head. Just get this thing with Joey straightened out. If you're right, I'll be the first to apologize. But if you're wrong, then pay him the ten grand, no bullshit. I have no more to say, except that I want this straightened out today."

I told Freddy I had the stone with me, and we went to the Diamond Exchange together. But first Freddy told me he wanted to call Javier's and tell them about the stone. This could go either way, I was thinking. Either the kid is trying to show me he doesn't know anything about the mix-up, or he's telling the jeweler what to do.

We arrived at the Diamond Exchange. There were about fifty jewelers in the place.

"Hey, Joe, let's go to this guy over here," Freddy suggested. "Excuse me, we need an appraisal on this diamond."

The jeweler examined the stone with his jeweler's loupe. Turned it around. Measured it. "Well," he said finally, "this stone can be bought in one store for, say, ten to twelve thousand, or in another for, say, eight or nine thousand. Depends on where you shop. Sometimes you're only paying for the name on the window."

Freddy looked pleased. I wanted to knock the smirk off his face.

"Excuse me, sir," I said to the appraiser. "I was told by a jeweler friend of mine that this stone isn't worth five hundred. To be perfectly honest with you, I hope you're right. Because Freddy here is a witness to what you're saying. And I'm going to get another *unbiased* jeweler to give me an appraisal. In the event this ring is not what you say it is, I will subpoena the both of you, and then sue you."

I was bluffing, of course. Freddy knew it. The jeweler didn't.

"Hold on, I don't want to get involved," the appraiser said. "I received a call from someone at Javier's, and they described the markings on this stone and told me to appraise it for above ten thousand. I'm not going to get myself in trouble or lose my license over this nonsense. The diamond is worthless."

"Gee, Joey, you were right. I'll tell Javier's to replace it." Freddy had balls, I'll give him that.

"Forget about the stone," I told Nino's nephew. "I want the fuckin' money. Call them and tell them I'll be there Friday to pick it up."

My horse was running the next day, and I didn't need this aggravation. I explained what happened to Tommy, and he was overjoyed at being able to go back to New York and put Nino in his place.

"I'll tell that fuckin' Nino how they tried to fuck you, Joey, and I'll tell him in front of people and make him look like shit."

Later, Freddy called Tommy and asked if he could have a little time to straighten this out.

17
A Horse Out of Kelso's Ass

GLORIOUS REQUEST OPENED AT TWENTY TO ONE. HE was running against a field whose owners had paid anywhere from a quarter million to a hundred grand. My horse was the cheapest. Don't worry, I kept reminding myself. He was out of the Italian champ Forli.

It was the winter season, the track was busy, and a lot of money was changing hands. I gave my jockey his instructions. I told him to win. Our workouts had been good, but so had the workouts of just about every other horse in the field.

Glorious Request went off at eight to one. I bet so much money my friends thought I was nuts. I bet with both hands, close to five grand. I think Tommy got down for $1,000, based on my say-so. The rest of the guys were in anywhere from $200 to $500.

They were off. The horse that cost a quarter of a million took the lead. It was a five-furlong race. He reached the quarter pole in twenty-two seconds. Glorious Request was running second, one length behind. The leader hit the half mile in forty-five and three-fifths, which is a pretty fast pace for two-year-olds. Glorious Request was still holding second but losing ground. Seconds later our race was over. My horse ran dead last. He packed it in after half a mile.

I was stunned, in a daze, when my jockey found me after the race.

"This fuckin' horse wasn't ready," the jockey said. "And that asshole trainer knew he wasn't ready. Glorious Request is a long, long way off."

I looked around for Ruben, who was afraid to come near me. I wanted to choke the cocksucker to death.

Tommy grabbed me and said, "Joe, the horse was right there until the stretch, maybe he just needs a little more work. Give the trainer a break."

I snapped out of it. Tommy saved Ruben from catching a beating, and me from being pinched. Everyone offered their condolences. I talked nice with Howie Ruben. And I left the track $10,000 lighter.

I didn't have much time to fool around at the track. I was hustling like never before. Shylocking. Shakedowns. Bookmaking. I started dealing drugs. The whole bit. Losing the construction contract at Century Village had hit me harder than I had expected. That drywall business had been bringing in over $5,000 a week. I used to have money coming out of my ears. Now I was working every angle I could find.

"Hey, Howie, when is this horse going to win?"

Glorious Request had run four times. The best he'd ever finished was sixth in an eight-horse field. We were running him now in $15,000 claiming races. Of course nobody wanted to claim this dog.

"Howie, my friend, I've already lost over twenty grand because you keep telling me he's ready. So be honest. Is he ever going to win, or what?"

It was six o'clock in the morning. I'd gone to watch the horse work five furlongs. Howie and I were standing by the railing at the main workout track.

"All you wops are alike. If your horse don't win, you blame the trainer. Did you ever stop to think that I have feelings, too?"

Smack. I hit him open-handed, like you hit a broad. He landed on his ass, got up, started to say something while covering his face, and I kicked him in the stomach. I was aiming for his balls, but I missed. He doubled up, and I grabbed him by his hair and began smacking him back and forth, open-handed, like he was a broad.

"Listen, you motherfucker," I hissed through clenched teeth. "You know the twenty thousand I paid for that horse that you guaranteed? And you know the twenty thousand you have out as a loan? And you know the twenty thousand that I lost gambling on this fucking horse? You have exactly seventy-two hours to come up with it. Sixty grand, Howie. I suggest you get in touch with your so-called friends from Detroit. Because if you don't have the money by then, you'll be the sorriest motherfucker alive. I'll be back in three days. Have anybody here you want."

Then I punched him, knocked him out, and left.

One thing I must say for Howie Ruben. He may have been fucked up, but he never ran to the law. Maybe he was just too afraid of the consequences. I really didn't expect him to get up the money, and there was no way he owed me my gambling losses. I had merely lost my temper. But just in case, when I drove out to the track three days later I took three of my crew along, in the event that there was a problem. We all had guns.

At the gate the guard stopped me and asked who my friends were. I told him we were thinking of forming a racing syndicate, and they were potential partners. He let us through, no problem. We drove to the area where I had worked Howie over, and there he was, waiting alone.

I got out of the car. He was trembling.

"Easy, Howie. Easy. Nothing's going to happen." I motioned to my crew to go for coffee at the track cafeteria, and Howie visibly relaxed.

"Joe, I couldn't come up with that much money. All I could get was thirty thousand. I had to go to a guy who loans you money on your home. Will you give me more time to come up with the rest?"

"Howie, look," I said. "Number one, I'm sorry I smacked you around, but you shouldn't have talked to me the way you did. Number two, you don't have to pay for my gambling debts, but you did guarantee me the horse, and I'm going to hold you to it.

"So give me twenty thousand for the horse. And if you want to give me the other ten thousand for the loan, then you only owe me ten thousand and your juice payments are three hundred cheaper a week "

Howie said, "Joe, let me give you the twenty thousand, but hold on to the rest. I want to buy some of that stuff, you know what I mean? And I'll keep paying the six hundred a week interest."

"Whatever, Howie. It's up to you. It's your loan."

"And, Joe," he said, "the horse is still yours. You don't even have to pay me to train it. We'll drop him down to a five-grand claiming race and win a big bet, and then the purse will be yours."

"Fine, Howie, fine, whatever you say. But I'm not sure if that horse could win if he was the only one in the race," I said. "And, oh, by the way, I never paid you for training that horse anyway. That was part of our agreement."

"Oh, yeah, Joe, I forgot. And Joe, one more thing. If my wife asks you, will you tell her I gave you all thirty thousand?"

I shook my head in disgust. "Yeah," I said.

I called Little Dom in New York and told him about my horse. I was thinking about what those drugs had done for Elfin Water. He laughed and said, "Joe, there's nothing you can do with that nag."

"But Dominick," I protested, "we're dropping him down to five-grand claimers. And he's out of Forli, the Italian champ! We should win here with a little of that happy juice."

"Joe, I don't care if he's out of Kelso's ass, that horse don't win. Let me explain it to you, Joe. Remember when he finished sixth. You asked me to send in a G on him to win? Remember?"

"Yeah," I said.

"Well, Joe, I didn't want to tell you, but I bet five thousand to win and five thousand to show, because we did that Elfin Water thing on him, you know, and the best that crippled fuck could run was sixth. I wanted to fly down there and get the horse and the trainer and chop both their heads off."

I started to laugh and said, "I already gave the trainer a beatin'. And I let him give me back the money for the horse. He's a coke freak and into me for twenty large. But he's as good as gold with the juice. I wish I had ten guys like him."

"That's good, Joey." Dominick laughed. "But keep him in his place. Listen, I have to go now, but I'll be calling you in about a week. You know that guy at the Bridge Restaurant in Fort Lauderdale? You know who I mean, don't you? I don't want to mention his name on the phone."

He was talking about Tommy Farese, the Colombo doper who had sat with us at Sinatra.

"Yeah, Dom, I know who you're talking about. Why?"

"Are you in good with those guys? Because they're with, uh, my, you know."

Dominick was telling me that he and Farese were with the same Family.

"Dom, you're not telling me anything I don't know. And to answer your question, yeah, they love me. I can get anything I want from them. Why?"

"Good, Joey. I'll let you know next week," he said. "I'll talk to you then."

18
Miami Ice

IT HAD BEEN OVER A MONTH SINCE I'D HEARD FROM Freddy, my top-notch insurance agent. I called him.

"Freddy? Joe Dogs. Howya doing?"

"Fine, Joe, fine. I was just talking to my uncle about you the other day. I was going to call you."

Freddy couldn't say two words without bringing up Uncle Nino. He thought that the name would send shivers down my spine. "Well, do you plan on taking care of your obligation, or do I have to go further?" I asked. "You've had enough fuckin' time."

I didn't care how I talked to this pimp.

"Listen, Joe, why don't you and I go to Javier's tomorrow? I think you'll be satisfied."

"I can't go tomorrow," I told him. "You call that Jew bastard and tell him I'll be there at one-thirty Friday afternoon." I hung up without giving him a chance to come up with an excuse.

Friday came. I picked up my juice from Ruben in Hallandale and mentioned to Jiggs that I had business at Javier's. Jiggs offered to ride along, which I appreciated.

"I know that cocksucker in Javier's," he told me. "If he sees me, he'll shit his pants."

Jiggs and I walked into Javier's Jewelers separately, with Jiggs walking to a corner, pretending to be window-shopping. He was carrying a small fishing gaff under his coat. He told me that if anyone gave me a problem he'd be more than happy to rip their eyes out. I walked up to the counter and signalled to the guy who had originally given me the stone. There was also a woman behind the counter, and I could see a little jeweler working in a room behind the store.

"Here's your piece of glass, you crooked fuck."

"Don't talk to me that way," the guy said. "Who do you think you are? I'm going to give you six thousand for that ring, and that's all."

The woman came and stood next to him. And the worker from the back came out, too.

"Listen, cocksucker, all of you listen. You give me ten grand, and if I have to wait more than five minutes for it, you're going to pay me five points juice, retroactive for the last eight months. And you have one other thing coming."

I reached over, grabbed this fuck by the tie, and backhanded him. He started bleeding from the nose and mouth. Just then Jiggs appeared at my side. "Hi, Joe," he said amiably. "You having a little problem here, or what?"·

"No, Jiggs, I don't think so. My friend here has a nose bleed and I'm trying to tell him what's good for it."

The clerk recognized Jiggs, nodded hello, ran back to his office, and came back with a $10,000 check. "I left the name blank," he said. "I didn't know what name you wanted to use."

I said, "Listen, take this check and get one of your flunkies to cash it right away. I want cash. *Capisci?*"

He went back to the office, returned with the cash, and ordered the salesgirl to bring me a solid gold bracelet. "Keep it, with our compliments," he said.

On the drive back to Hallandale I slipped Jiggs $1,000. He didn't want it, but I insisted. He thanked me. We both went to the track. And won.

I mailed Tommy $2,000 and told him what I had done.

"Did you get me a bracelet, too?" he asked over the phone.

"No," I said, "But you can have this one. I saw some fag wearing one just like it. So it's all yours, buddy."

"Keep talking with your fuckin' mouth that way, Joey, and I'm going to sew it up." He laughed.

PART TWO

The Player

19

"I'll Kill Her Mother and Father!"

I'D BEEN A MEMBER OF T.A.'S GAMBINO CREW FOR FOUR years now. In spite of Tommy's warnings, I was double-banging him behind his back. It just didn't seem right that I could only earn from one *Famiglia*. It was undemocratic. I was forty-five years old and invincible. So when Little Dom Cataldo called me in early 1976 and wanted to know if I could score him some pot, I didn't think twice about doing business with the Colombos. The Gambinos always looked down at the Colombos anyway, like they were junior members of our mob. And it's a fact that they did a lot of Gambino dirty work. Most Colombos were crazy. So I felt like I was working with distant relatives, though I knew Tommy wouldn't have seen it that way.

"I need about five or six hundred pounds, Joey," Dom said. "But don't let them know it's for me."

Tommy Farese would front me as much pot as I wanted. I had a good name with him. Besides, I rented a storage warehouse in Riviera Beach, one town over from West Palm, for his *compare*, John "Johnny Irish" Matera, whenever they brought in a load.

"Fine, Dom, should be no problem," I said. "But who you going to send to pick it up?"

"I'll send Billy Ray down, and he'll drive it to the Auto Train, like that, you know." Billy Ray was part of Little Dom's crew.

The next day I met with Farese and his partner, Harry Roth, and ordered a carload. I had a big trunk and back seat. They loaded the car with 580-odd pounds of Colombian Gold. I told them I'd have their money in two or three weeks.

"Joey, there's about ten extra pounds in there," Farese said. "But you owe us for five eighty at one thirty. Comes to seventy-five four. Make it seventy-five even. Okay?"

"Yeah," I agreed. "I'll get it to you as soon as possible."

"Don't worry, Joey, we trust you."

"Hey, Dom," I said into the receiver. "Call me at this pay phone from outside right away." I gave him the number.

I never had to pay for long-distance calls from pay phones. I had a gadget that made sounds like quarters, dimes, and nickels dropping into the slot. It fit right into a Marlboro cigarette box, and all you had to do was press the buttons on this little machine next to the speaker on the phone. It was a great little gizmo. They still use them to this day.

Dominick called me back. "You got the stuff?"

"Yeah, a little over five eighty. We owe them seventy-five G's. I told them two weeks. Now, Dom, this stuff is Colombian Gold, so don't take no less than three dollars a pound, you know what I mean?"

By three dollars, of course, I meant $300. "It cost me one thirty. *Capisci?*"

"Very reasonable," Little Dom replied. "We're partners, Joey. Okay? And do me a favor. You're down there already, so rent a car and load it up. Cover the stuff with some blankets. I'll have somebody pick it up in Lorton, Virginia. It'll save us a world of time."

"No problem, Dom. I'll call you, then you call me

back outside, and I'll get you the make and the color and the plate numbers and everything.''

I got one of my crew to go to someone he could trust and rent the car. The precautions may sound confusing, but I was just layering myself from the law. We picked up a four-door Buick and I sent one of my guys as a mule to drive it to the Auto Train and meet Dom's guy in Lorton, Virginia. When he hooked up with Billy Ray I had him call me, and I spoke to Billy myself to confirm he'd picked up the load.

Dominick was very pleased. ''This stuff is dynamite,'' he told me over the pay phone. ''I think I can unload the whole shipment in one place, maybe for a little cheaper. What do you think?''

''I don't know, Dom,'' I answered. ''If you're going to price it out piecemeal, get four hundred a pound. If you're going to let it go all in one place, don't let it go for any less than three hundred a pound.''

''All right, Joey, fine. I was just asking.''

''Dominick,'' I said, ''just do what you think is best. I'm not going to question your judgment. Whatever you do is fine with me. Just get me seventy-five thou as soon as possible.''

Little Dom promised he'd fly someone down with the money in a few days. ''You can't mail that kind of cash,'' he added.

Before he hung up, I mentioned to him that Tommy Farese had thrown in an extra ten pounds. ''In case you want to impress some broad, Dom,'' I said.

''Nah, Joey, that don't work,'' he said. ''They want candy—the snow. It gets them crazy.'' He hung up.

I thought it was time I gave my wife and kids a break. We all went on a trip to Disney World. The kids were super happy. Bunny was ecstatic. I had become a lousy husband. I was never home, always out gambling, or bedding down with some broad. And I had added jai alai to my gambling lust. I used to go down to the West Palm Beach jai alai arena, sit in a private room, watch the games on closed-circuit television, and bang the hostess. I also banged two of the waitresses. I mean, I had become a real whoremaster. I was even beginning to disgust myself a little. I'd meet a broad, spoil the shit out of her, take her to bed, and then move on.

Bunny was very suspicious, forever accusing me of fucking this one or that one, and as much as I denied it—"Who do you think I am, King Kong?"—I knew she just knew.

In fact, she turned into something of a detective. Once she even tailed me to a broad's apartment. Knocked on the door, came crashing in, and went after the broad with a knife. *Marrone,* what a fucking scene! I grabbed the blade and cut the hell out of the palm of my hand. Then I carried her out kicking and punching all the way. She was, that is.

I made her feel terrible. It took her two weeks to forgive me after that one. I swore on the Bible I wouldn't do it again. I took her away for a weekend then, too. To Naples, Florida, to a nice hotel. I gave her the salami all weekend, and she seemed to be happy. But she never trusted me after that. She checked up on every little thing.

"Bunny, honey," I'd plead. "I swear I won't do it anymore. So give me a break, will you? I can't take you every fuckin' place I go."

I felt like a prisoner.

Dominick called. "Where the fuck you been? I been trying to reach you."

I told him about Bunny catching me with the broad and the make-good weekend in Naples.

"Joey," he said, "I get caught all the time, and when my wife threatens to leave me, I tell her to go ahead. I tell her if she leaves me I'll kill her mother and father."

"You crazy bastard," I said, laughing. "I can't do that. Bunny's mother and father are already dead."

"Don't worry about it, Joe," Little Dom said. "Where's she gonna go with four kids? Anyway, the reason I called is because of that, uh, you-know-what. I'm at a pay phone. Here's the number. Go out and call me back."

I left and called. "What's up?"

"I let that shit go for two eighty-five," Dom said. "One guy, the whole shipment. It's over with. I got a hundred sixty-five grand. You give those guys their seventy-five thousand and we make forty-five grand apiece. You want some extra for the car rental and the blankets and shit?"

"You calling me petty now, Dom?" I kidded. "Go fuck yourself."

Little Dom told me he'd arranged for one of his crew, a gorilla named Ralphie, to fly down with $120,000, Tommy Farese's money plus my share. "Don't pay him, I already did," Dom added. "Just get him a hotel room and a broad."

"Are you kidding?" I said. "Where am I going to find a broad to sleep with that big ugly fuck? He looks like Godzilla."

"Sorry, Joey," he said. "I already told him you had a nice blonde lined up for him."

Dominick gave me Ralphie's flight number. He was landing in West Palm at eight-fifteen that night. I was at a loss. I knew this animal would go nuts if I didn't get him a broad. Then a light bulb went off over my head. Ruben always had a lot of nice-looking broads working the backstretch. Hotwalkers. Exercise girls. Workout girls. They were a different breed of people. They were also, most of them, young and good-looking. Howie used to fix me up with one every now and then. I called him.

"Howie, I got a friend who just got out of the joint. I need a nice looker. A blonde. I'll pay two hundred."

I went home and told Bunny what was going on. She was incredulous. "You're kidding? With Ralphie? Oh, the poor girl." Two hours later Howie called from the lounge at the Holiday Inn. I met him at six-thirty, two hours before Ralphie was due in. He was sitting with a gorgeous young blonde. She was just beautiful.

"Joe, meet Janice. She's one of my better workout girls. And she just loves Glorious Request."

"Yeah?" I said as I shook her hand. "She can have him."

I ordered a round of drinks, reimbursed Howie for the room he'd taken, and began explaining the facts of life to Janice.

"Look, honey, this guy you're going to meet looks like something of a rugged individual," I told her. "But he's a nice guy, a real pussycat. He's been away for a long time, so do me a justice and be nice to him. He's going to fall in love with you when he sees you. He's a good close friend of mine, and whatever service you perform will be well rewarded."

Janice was insulted. "I'm no prostitute, so don't hand me any money," she said. "I'm just doing this as a favor for you and Howie. What I'd like in return is to work out your horses."

I'd recently bought a couple of cheap claimers to keep Glorious Request company. "Honey," I said, "if anyone else but you ever gets on my horses in the morning, you just give me a call and I'll have a little heart-to-heart with Mr. Ruben here."

Howie left, and Janice and I had another drink. She told me how Beverly, another workout girl, had told her what a nice guy I was. She was making me feel like a heel, and I wondered what Bunny would think if she walked in. Nonetheless, I was hoping Ralphie's plane crashed. I really dug this baby doll.

Soon it came time to pick up the moose. I didn't want Janice to go to the airport with me. I wanted to speak to Ralphie alone. That Dominick, I thought on the drive over, he's doing this just to break my hump.

Ralphie was waiting for me in the lounge. He was wearing a real tourist outfit, right down to the checkered pants. Too bad he didn't wear a mask.

"Ralphie, baby, how you doing?"

He only carried a small bag. He was just staying overnight. Thank God! "Hey, Joe, I thought maybe you forgot about me. Where's the broad?"

"Just hit some traffic, Ralphie, sorry. She's waiting at the Holiday Inn. She's already got a room. And she's dying to meet you."

"Is she nice, Joey? Is she blond?" he asked.

"Ralphie, she's gorgeous and she's blond. Now listen to me, be nice to her. I told her you were a good friend of mine, and I told her you were a real nice guy. So don't be mean to her, and don't hurt her."

"I won't hurt her, Joey," Ralphie said. "No way! I just hope she'll do what I want."

"Yeah, she'll do anything," I said to him. How the hell did I know what he wanted her to do?

When Janice sweetly introduced herself to Ralphie I would have done anything to trade places with that big lob. They made small talk about the weather and about Ralphie's flight down hitting turbulence and about whatever, and I had to get out of there. I couldn't take these two lovebirds anymore. When I told them that my wife and I were going to a late dinner, I thought I saw a shadow of disappointment cross Janice's face.

"My plane leaves at eight-fifteen in the morning," Ralphie said. "Do you want me to take a cab, or what?"

"No, I'll pick you up at six," I told him. "Janice, here's my phone number in the event you have any problems."

Ralphie went to the bar to pay the check and I gave Janice a quick kiss and left.

"How did the girl look?" Bunny wanted to know.

"Eh, she was a little fat. You know, nothing I'd look at. But too good for Ralphie."

"She can only stay with him until midnight. She's got to leave because she's married," I continued lying. "They aren't staying at the Holiday Inn. I took them downtown."

"How is she going to get home?" Bunny didn't miss a trick.

"She'll call Ruben, I guess," I said. "But I gave her our number in case she has any problem with that animal."

Bunny wasn't quite convinced. "I hope you don't have to take her to Miami."

"Hell, no," I said. "That's Ruben's problem."

Bunny bought it. I was glad. I mean, I hadn't done anything wrong anyway. And after a night with Ralphie, there was no way I'd touch that broad now.

"I have to get Ralphie at six-thirty in the morning," I told Bunny. "Take him to the airport, then I'm going to the track to watch the workouts. You want to come?" I knew she didn't.

"No, honey, you know I don't like that Ruben. Does he fool around on his wife?" She smiled. "You know, like you do."

Bunny was a pretty lady, a good mother. She had a lousy husband. Could I help it if I liked girls?

The phone woke me up. It was five-thirty in the morning. A sweet voice said, "Hi! Don't forget to pick your friend up."

Bunny had opened her eyes and was looking at me.

"Sure, Ralphie, no problem, you got plenty of time," I said. "Let me grab a shower, then I'll be right over."

"Oh, gee, Joe, I'm sorry," Janice replied. "I forgot about your wife." She hung up.

"I thought you were supposed to wake *him* up," Bunny said suspiciously.

"I guess he's nervous about making his plane."

I showered as quickly as I could, worrying like hell that Ralphie would call back. He didn't. When I arrived at the hotel room, Ralphie was packed and dressed, checkered pants and all. Janice was splayed out nude, asleep on one of the beds.

"She wants you to come back and take her to Miami," Ralphie said on the drive to the airport.

"Did you enjoy her?" I asked. "Did she do what you wanted?"

"Joe, she was great," he said. "She did everything I asked her to. I left her five hundred. I put it in her purse because she didn't want anything. I'd like to see her again."

"Okay, Ralphie, only let me know a week ahead of time next trip. Tell Dom to give me a call." I dropped him off, parked my car at the airport lot, and took a cab back to the Holiday Inn. I didn't want Mrs. Sherlock Holmes to spot it at the hotel. I had Ralphie's key, and when I walked through the door Janice was sitting on the bed, nude, soaking her hands in a bucket of ice. I didn't ask.

Janice looked at me—a little sad, I thought—and took

her hands out of the bucket. They were red and swollen, especially her right hand.

"What the hell happened?" I asked, and she began laughing hysterically, laughing so hard it was catching. I began laughing too.

"Joe, after you left, Ralphie and I came to the room and undressed," she said. "To be quite frank, he was built pretty good, too. He says to me, 'Joe told me that you'd do anything I wanted.' I was a little apprehensive. I didn't know how to answer. Finally I asked him exactly what it was he wanted. 'I want you to spank my ass real hard while I jerk off,' he says.

"So I told him I'd never done anything like that before, and he'd have to show me what he meant. 'Like this,' he says, putting me over his knees and smacking my ass. It hurt. I didn't like it. But he told me he wanted me to smack his ass real hard."

Janice began laughing again and put her hands back in the cold ice bucket.

"So, he gets on his knees," she continued. "And I start to smack his ass. He's yelling, 'Harder! Harder!' as he's masturbating. I did that for at least forty-five minutes, and then he shot his load all over the sheet and went to sleep."

Janice looked up at me with a smirk. "Different strokes for different folks," she said, breaking up again.

"When Ralphie woke up, he wanted his ass smacked again. He came faster this time. I guess I'm becoming a professional ass beater. At any rate, it made me a little horny, Joe. You interested?"

I looked at her and wanted her. Wanted to make love to her. But something held me back. Something was wrong. I don't know what it was. I just sat down next to her and we fooled around for an hour, kissing and hugging. But I didn't fuck her.

After Janice showered and dressed she found the $500 in her purse. She tried to give it back to me, but I told her she'd earned it and made her keep it.

"Glorious is running today," she said. "I'm going to parlay it on him. Howie told me he's going to win."

I looked at her and said, "Oh yeah? Give me that

money. I'll bet it for you. When you get to the track, go around and tell everyone Glorious Request is going to win today, okay?"

"Sure, Joe, but won't that make him the favorite?"

"Listen, Janice, just do like I say and don't ask me any questions."

I stopped the car on the way to the track to call Little Dom. We had a lot of time. Glorious Request wasn't running until the third race.

"Joe," he reminded me, "that nag of yours is running today. He ain't got no chance, and I got a 'friend' with a horse in that same field. You want down on him?"

"Yeah, Dom, give me five nickels on the front end of the car." My usual bet with Dom was $2,000, or four nickels.

"Fine, Joe," Dom said, adding, "but please don't bet him at the track. The odds, you know. And how come five nickels today?"

"Because I'm in love and one of the nickels is for her."

"Don't let Bunny catch you again," Dom warned with a laugh. "Did Ralphie give you the bazookas?"

"Yeah," I replied. "I had Ralphie taken care of. He's a sick guy, Dom. Did you know that?"

"Yeah, Joe, I knew," he said. "I wanted you to get a laugh. All the guys around here are a bunch of sickos."

We said goodbye.

It was near post time for the third race, and Ruben was dressed in a suit. He thought he was going to get his picture taken in the winner's circle with Glorious Request. Janice had done a good job touting him, and she asked me if I'd bet the $500 for her.

"All on the nose," I said.

Then I went to the window two minutes before post time and wheeled Dominick's "friend's" horse in a twenty-dollar perfecta, as this wouldn't affect the odds. He went off at four to one.

The race was over. Dominick's horse won. A twelve-to-one shot ran second. Glorious Request may still be running. The perfecta came back $168. My twenty-dollar bet paid $1,680. Janice was devastated.

"Janice honey, er, I made a mistake at the window," I

said. "I bet the three horse instead of the five horse. You won by mistake. You won twenty-five hundred. Honest, here's your money. I even won by mistake myself. But let's not tell Howie. Let him think we lost."

"Why?" she wondered.

"Because that's what I want sweetheart. Don't go against me."

"Joe," she said, "I think I could fall in love with you."

"Honey, don't do that. You'll get over it."

I left her at the track and went home.

20
All Fucked Out

I HAD BET $2,500 WITH DOMINICK, SO I HAD $10,000 coming from the book in New York. But my mind was really screwed up now. I felt like I was falling in love. Christ, I thought, this can't be happening. I'd been married for twelve years. I had four kids. It wasn't rational. Plus, and it was a big plus, this was 1976, still back in the Stone Age when the big shots in the Mafia didn't look kindly on a man leaving his wife. Girlfriends were one thing. But second wives were usually young, stupid, and likely to get a gangster in trouble. I had to figure this out in my head. I didn't go near the track for a month, and I didn't answer the phone for anyone except Little Dom and T.A.

But Janice never called. I don't know if that made me glad or unhappy. Ruben called every day, however, wanting to know where I was, wanting to know where he should make his juice payments. Finally, I drove to Hallandale to meet with the horse trainer.

"Where the hell you been?" Jiggs asked. "Ruben's been going nuts. He didn't know who to give the money to, so I took it for you. Here." Jiggs handed me $2,400.

I told Jiggs I'd had a personal problem and I'd been laying low. Then Ruben came in.

"We got a big problem, Howie," I busted his chops. "Jiggs tells me he asked you for the money and you refused to give it to him."

But Howie didn't fall for it. He was smiling. Jiggs said goodbye, and Howie and I talked.

"That girl Janice is crazy about you," he began. "Why don't you give her a break. All she does is pout. She won't even work out your horses. I told her I was going to have to let her go. She even came down here with me the last couple Fridays hoping to see you."

"Let me tell you something, Howie. If you fire that girl, I'll break both your fuckin' legs. And I'm not kidding. And if she comes down here every Friday, how come she's not with you now?"

Howie was still smiling, the dopey fuck, when he said, "She's in the car waiting for you."

I was so happy I threw Howie a hug and went out to get her. Janice was in tears. "What's wrong?" I asked.

"It's just that, Joe, I've been sitting out here so long that I thought maybe you didn't want to see me," she said. "I knew you were here. I saw your car. All the other times I'd never seen your car, and Howie wouldn't allow me to go inside because he said he met with your uncle."

Ruben rose a notch in my estimation with that. I didn't think he was that sharp.

I said, "Come on, Janice, get in my car. We're going away for the weekend."

Howie walked out and she began to protest, saying it was her weekend to work. She needed, she said, Howie's permission.

"What the hell's wrong with you, Janice?" Howie said. "You want me to catch a beating? Take off three weeks, with pay. And if you need three more, take them, too, with pay."

I laughed like hell, and so did Janice. All the way to Key West. We checked into a beach resort but never left the room until checking out Monday morning. Janice wanted me to leave my wife and kids. As I dropped her off at the track Monday morning, I tried to set her straight:

"Look, honey, I care for you, and if we stayed together I could even fall in love with you. *But*. I'm sorry to say this, but I don't think you should bank on a future with me. My wife and children mean everything to me. I'm only being honest with you. There's no sense in leading you on. I'm sorry, honey. Goodbye."

It was too bad. But that's the way these things happen. On the drive back to West Palm I started to laugh, thinking that the one who was going to suffer the most was Ralphie. Who was going to spank his ass now?

When I pulled into our driveway, Bunny came running out of the house. "Joe, what happened? Where were you? Are you all right? You look terrible."

How else would anyone look who had fucked themselves silly for three straight days?

"That's a multiple question," I said sarcastically. "Which one do you want me to answer first?"

"Never mind," Bunny said accusingly. "T.A. wants you to call him. He was worried about you *also*."

Tommy and I had worked out a code, where if I ever had to lie to him over the phone and wanted him to know it, I'd call him "Tipperino." I was hoping he remembered.

"Tipperino," I said into the receiver. "I've been kidnapped since Friday. There were three guys. I think they were with the Colombos."

"You cocksucker," T.A. said with a laugh. "You had us all worried. I hope it was worth it. Is she nice, you bastard?"

"Tom, I got away beautifully, the best thing I ever did in my life. But they left me in bad shape. They were kicking me in the balls all weekend."

"Sure," Tommy said. "You're all fucked out, and you can't take care of the wife. Call me tomorrow. We need to talk." He hung up the phone.

Bunny had been standing right behind me. It was building in her, and she had to let it out.

"So what is she? Blonde? Brunette? Redhead? You bastard!"

"I had one of each," I shouted at her. "I fuck them all. That's what you think anyway, isn't it?"

Then I punched my fist through the bedroom door, unplugged the phone, and went to bed.

21
The Big Fix

"HEY, TOM, WHAT'S UP?" I SAID INTO THE PHONE.

"Listen, Joey, get down to the Gulfstream racetrack. Go to the restaurant in the clubhouse. Ask the maitre d' to point out a guy named Sean O'Leary."

"Why?" I asked.

"Hey, Joey," Tommy Agro growled, "you better stay out of the sun and stop fuckin' around with the broads and start tending to business. I say go see the fuckin' guy. If I tell you over the phone, the whole fuckin' world will know! You idiot!"

He was right. I wasn't thinking. I'd called him at his house from my house. Who knows? Either one of us, if not both, might have been bugged. Anyway, I was sure I already knew why. I'd lay five to one that it had something to do with fixing a race. We were always fixing races. If only the public knew how easy it was to reach jockeys and trainers and hotwalkers. I mean, the track was made for the mob. The '76 Winter Meet at Gulfstream was just about to begin, and I had no doubt Tommy was sending me to set up a scam.

"Yeah, okay, Tip, I'm sorry. I just woke up."

Tom said, "Get down there today. He's waiting for you." So I drove to Gulfstream in Hallandale and the maitre d' took me to Sean O'Leary.

"I'm Joe Dogs," I introduced myself. "I haven't the slightest idea why I'm here. T.A. says you'll explain everything."

Sean O'Leary didn't strike me as a mick. In fact, he didn't strike me as much of anything. He gave new meaning to the term nondescript, the kind of guy who could lose a tail in an elevator.

"Joe, you'll need between forty and fifty thousand, and we can fix a race and cash in on it" were the first words out of his mouth. "That will be the initial investment. Of course, that covers all expenses as well as bets. We can continue to do this throughout the whole meet. I couldn't do it at Calder because I was told by Matty Brown Fortunato that there's already an outfit out of Kansas City that runs things down there."

"Matty Brown" Fortunato was a New York–based capo in the Genovese Family.

"And it can't be done at Hialeah because the stewards are too sharp," Sean O'Leary continued. He pointed to a race on the Gulfstream card. "If you have that kind of money on you, we could fix this here field today."

In fact, I did have that kind of money on me. But I wanted this "fix" explained thoroughly to me. I wanted to know how he intended to do it, the risks involved, exactly who was in on it, the guarantees, and, of course, how much money we could make. Then I would have to talk to T.A.

But I was excited. I loved nothing better than a sure bet.

BETTING. Most people know how to lay two or five or even a hundred dollars on a horse to win, place, or show. It's the so-called exotic betting, the perfectas and trifectas, that confuses their minds.

To bet a perfecta at a horse or a dog track, there must be at least five entrants in the race. In the perfecta, you are betting that you can pick the horses that will finish first and second, in that order. Usually that bet will cost you two dollars.

But say you wanted to "box" four horses in a field of ten, that is, bet that any two of those four horses will finish one-two. That will cost you more. Here is how you figure the cost if the mutuel is a two-dollar bet per perfecta, which it is at most tracks. In this case, the bet would be on four horses. You take the next lowest number, which would be three, and multiply four times three. You have twelve. Then you multiply that number by two. So you'd have to put up twenty-four dollars to "box" four horses. Or say you wanted to bet five horses "boxed." Multiply five times four and get twenty. Then multiply twenty by two. It will cost you forty dollars to "box" five horses, and eighty-four dollars to "box" seven horses. (Figure it out.)

Now a trifecta is a little different, because your entrants must finish first, second, and third, in that order. There must be at least six horses running to bet a trifecta. A straight trifecta bet also usually costs two dollars. I have no cute multiplication table to explain trifecta "boxing," but the track supplies a table showing you how much it costs to "box" any amount of horses in a trifecta. To "box" three horses will cost you twelve dollars, or two dollars down on every conceivable finish those horses could run. A four-horse trifecta "box" costs forty-eight dollars, and so on.

And finally there's the "wheel." When you're "wheeling" a horse or dog, you're essentially betting a perfecta, with the rest of the field covered. In other words, in a twelve-horse field, if you feel certain that, say, the seven horse is going to win, you can bet the rest of the field to finish second for two dollars a horse. Wheeling a trifecta costs a little more. The track usually provides a betting chart on how to wheel a trifecta.

There are also more exotic bets like the "back wheel," where you can bet on one horse finishing second and the rest of the field finishing first, but I think that's enough of a lesson for today, eh?

Sean O'Leary was explaining the scam.

"Joe, the involvement and risks to you guys are minimal. I know the jockeys I can approach. This is done early on the morning of the race. Once I pay a jock to pull and finish no better than third, he's obligated to do so. The only risk involved is an unforeseen act of God. There's nothing I can do about that. However, I will personally guarantee the money otherwise. If there is a double-cross, I pay the money back within thirty days at a reasonable rate of interest. No shylock juice, though.

"So this is how it goes," O'Leary continued, pointing to the program sitting in his lap. "Say there's a nine-horse field, like this race going off next. There are five jockeys I can reach in this race: the one, the two, the five, six, and nine. I've used these jockeys before. This happens to be a high-priced claiming race. I will never approach an apprentice jockey, that's asking for trouble. Anyway, it would cost about twelve grand to fix this race. Look, the favorite is opening at eight to five. It'll take three grand to pay off that jockey.

"This one," he said, pointing, "will cost another three grand. This other horse is five to one. That costs two grand. And the other two I can probably get for fifteen hundred apiece. That leaves four horses—and four jockeys—that are medium prices to longshots. So now, we have to box them in perfectas only. That'll cost us twenty-four dollars per bet.

"So, what we want to do is box them four hundred times. Our total bet would be ninety-six hundred. Then take the change, say four hundred, and throw it on a wheel or two on the slim chance you'll hit it. That makes a total of ten thousand bet, plus eleven thousand for the fix, for a grand total of twenty-one thousand.

"So let's say a twenty-to-one shot wins, and a thirty-to-one shot runs second. Now normally that perfecta would come back paying probably over a thousand to one. But being that we've bet it four hundred times and driven the odds down, let's say it pays, oh, three hundred and twelve dollars.

"We would get back a hundred twenty-four thousand and eight hundred dollars! And if we got lucky and hit the other four hundred on wheels, we could wind up with another ten to twenty grand. Do you follow me so far, Joe?"

I looked at this man. I didn't know much about him. But right now he looked like Santa Claus to me. This wasn't a beat. This was serious stuff.

"Sean," I told him, "let me get back to T.A. with this. Then I'll get back to you."

"Fine, Joe," he said. "But try to be here with the cash on Saturday. That's the biggest handle. And tell Tommy I want an equal share for my part, with no investment."

"Okay, Sean, an equal share with no investment. But you're also holding the guarantee alone," I reminded him.

"That's right," he answered. "But tell Tommy that on some days we're bound to get an eight-horse field, which means we get to five jockeys, box the other three horses, only bet ten to fifteen grand, and maybe wind up with a hundred fifty grand."

"I'll tell him, Sean. I'm interested. I'll probably see you this Saturday."

The more I thought about it, the more I liked Sean's plan. I knew I could come up with the money on my end. And I knew Tommy could on his end. But would he? I rang him in New York and told him to call me back at a prearranged outside number. The pay phone rang and I went over the scam, explaining everything in detail.

"And he said he would stand behind the money?" T.A. asked when I was finished. "And he knows that when he guarantees this thing, that if he don't keep his word, it's like telling God to come and take him?"

I laughed and asked, "What do you want to do? Sean says he needs forty or fifty large. Send me your end, I'll put up my half, and we'll split three ways."

"Send my end," Tommy spit out. "Are you crazy, Joey? This is my thing. You're only in it, my friend, because I'm trusting you to watch out for my back. But better yet, listen. You know that banana-nose Freddie?"

He meant Freddie Campo, the bookmaker. Of course I knew him.

"Go see him and tell him I sent you," Tommy said. "Explain everything to him, and see if he'll put up the bazookas."

"I could do that," I said. "I'll tell him we'll guarantee the money."

"No, no, Joey. Not like that. Tell him me—Tommy A.—guarantees the money. And tell him we split four ways. Tell him how good a deal it is. He'll go for it."

I told Tommy I'd be in touch and hung up. He had a

phone beeper like I had, so it never cost him any money to call long distance. Fuck AT&T.

I had no idea what T.A. had in mind when he told me to see Freddie Campo. Freddie had most of the bookmaking action in Palm Beach County, and he wasn't affiliated with any of the Families. He didn't want to pay rent to anyone. That was nice when you were making it. But on the other hand, if there was ever a problem, Freddie had no one to run to.

When I explained the scam to Freddie, he jumped in with both feet. "If Tommy guarantees the money, I'm in. But I'd like to hear it from him."

This skinny, ugly cocksucker was doubting my word. I was just about to answer him when he said, "On second thought, Joe, your word is good enough for me. I don't even want that fuckin' animal to have my phone number."

I started to laugh. Tommy Agro had some reputation. "Don't worry, Fred, I won't give him your number. So do you have the fifty large? We need it by Saturday."

"*Marrone*, I know I'll have forty grand. Will that be enough?"

"Yeah, that's enough," I said, figuring that if we came up short I'd cover the rest.

I got in touch with Sean and told him it was a go, and that I'd be at Gulfstream on Saturday by noon. He said that if there was a race he could fix, he'd need a minimum $10,000 to $15,000 to pay the jockeys up front, just so there would be no mistakes.

"No problem," I told him. "See you Saturday. Oh, and by the way, Sean. Now it's a four-way split. We got another partner."

That's all I told him. I didn't go into detail with him, because it was none of his business. As far as he knew, he was playing with T.A.'s money, and that was that.

"Joe, I don't want to meet the other guy," Sean said.

"Sean, and he don't want to meet you. In case anything goes wrong. Do you understand me, Sean?" That last was a none-too-subtle reminder to Sean about who he was dealing with.

"Yeah, Joe. See you Saturday at noon."

22
Santa Claus Meets the Mob

SEAN HAD A FIX IN THE SIXTH RACE, A TEN-HORSE field. It was a cheap claiming race for three-year-olds and up, horses which hadn't won more than two races in their careers.

He told me we'd reached five of the ten jockeys, and he broke down the payments, for a total of $9,000. He could have told me it was costing $15,000 to fix the race and I never would have known the difference. So he was being honest, as far as I could see.

"Box the remaining five four hundred times," Sean told me. "This way, we'll take down most of the pool."

"Okay, Sean, that's five horses boxed. That's forty dollars per box, times four hundred. We bet sixteen grand." I thought for a moment.

"Why don't we do it six hundred times," I suggested. "It'll cost us twenty-four thousand. I have that kind of money with me."

Sean liked the idea. Then he gave me a warning.

"Don't approach me at all for the rest of the day. We'll meet at the Diplomat tonight, in the Celebrity Room, and divide the winnings there."

Little did Sean know that nobody was going to be dividing any "winnings" until the end of the sixty-day meet. That was the plan T.A. and I had come up with. We'd pay back Freddie's original investment, of course, but I'd keep everything else until we played out the scam.

I met Freddie in the lower grandstand and pointed out Sean, who was hanging out in a different area of the track. Now Freddie knew what Sean looked like, but Sean didn't know Freddie. That was just in case things didn't happen according to plan. Freddie could take care of Sean. Tommy and I had given this responsibility to Freddie. Whether he did it himself or farmed out the job, we didn't care.

"Here's the numbers, Fred," I explained. "Go to the second floor and wait until the sixth race. Go to the ten-dollar window and get in line about five minutes before post. Try and time it so you hit the window maybe two, three minutes before post time, so no one but the clerk will think anything's up. Hand the guy the numbers on a piece of paper and tell him to box them three hundred times. That's twelve thousand bucks' worth.

"Hand the money up front to the clerk, and he'll punch his heart out. I'll do the same down here. We'll meet back here after the race. I hope this is no fuck-up."

Freddie looked at me and went his way.

The sixth race came and we had the five horses with the shortest odds fixed. None would finish any better than third. Barring an unforeseen calamity—Sean's act of God—we would bang out the perfecta.

I reached the ten-dollar window with just under three minutes until post. The clerk began punching out on that machine and ten-dollar tickets are flying out and the people on line behind me are beginning to shuffle their feet and mumble. With one minute left to post, they began yelling.

"Hurry up, you motherfucker, we're going to get shut out."

Fifty-five seconds to post.

"You should die of cancer, you rotten bastard."

With fifteen seconds to spare I walked from the window with a paper lunch bag brimming with ten-dollar tickets. In those days the tracks weren't equipped with computers, and the highest perfecta ticket you could bet was ten dollars. Today, you can bet $100,000 on one ticket and any moron can punch it in. But before computerization, it took a fast clerk to take care of big bets like ours.

Post time. We'd bet the one, two, five, nine, and ten horses.

The nine horse won at eighteen to one. The two horse, a twelve-to-one shot, ran second. The exacta paid

$382.80. Multiplied by 600, our return was $229,680. Minus the payoffs to the jockeys, and the $24,000 we'd bet, our profit came to $196,680.

"Fred," I said, "go cash your tickets in with the guy you bought them from. Give him a couple hundred for himself. Spread four or five hundred around the rest of the clerks, because then they'll work with you easier."

Back in the 1970s you could bet all you wanted and get paid back in cash. Today a lot of tracks will only give you a check if you win more than $10,000. Not all, but a lot. They say it's for your protection, that they don't want you to get robbed. But I'd rather take my chances in a track's parking lot than with the IRS.

After our windfall, Freddie and I drove to the Diplomat, where we met up with Sean. Freddie could show his face now, because we'd made our seed money back and there was no cause for alarm. I gave Sean the lay of the land.

"Freddie gets his up-front money back, and I hold the rest," I told him. "Tommy says that no one gets any money until we're all through. He told me to let you have fifteen thousand for the next fix, in advance. And he expects it to happen at least once a week. I just got off the phone with him, and he told me to send you his regards and remind you to behave. Do you have any problems with that?"

"Joe, I owe money to shylocks and bookmakers," Sean whined. "I told them I'd pay them today. Could you let me have at least five thousand so I can pay off my juice?"

"Sean, look, I'm only following orders. I'll tell Tommy to call you. In fact, let me call him right now. I'll be right back."

"Tom, Sean needs five grand for some orange juice," I said over the phone in what passed for our half-assed code.

"Give it to him," T.A. replied. "Because I'm the fruit peddler that he's buying the oranges from."

"You fuck," I told him, "you're collecting from all angles."

"Hey, Joey, what did you think? That I was made with

a finger? Give Sean the bazookas, and tell him to see me in a few days. I'll have his oranges for him.''

Actually, I didn't want to say anything in front of Freddie, no sense him knowing Tommy's business. Tommy agreed. I gave Sean the money. Freddie picked up the dinner tab. And we left. On the way out Freddie thanked me for cutting him in, and I rolled him some figures.

"You got your up-front bazookas back, I gave Sean twenty grand, we spread eight hundred around the clerks, so that leaves us with $175,880. That figure coincide with yours, Fred?''

"Yeah, sure, Joe. No problem.''

I got home early for a change and Bunny jumped on my case. "What's wrong?'' she asked. "You got stood up? Or did you finally decide to give me and the kids a break?''

23
Somebody Gets Whacked

BY EARLY '76, THINGS WERE BACK TO NORMAL, AND despite the collapse of my drywall business I was doing good. I had a nice bookmaking operation. I had this thing going at the racetrack. My shylock customers were all paying on time. And I had been doing a little drug dealing with T.A. and Little Dom. Separately, of course. That's where the real money was, in drugs. All in all, I figure I was taking in between $200,000 to $300,000 a year, tax-free, with about 10 percent of that being shipped north to my *compare*, Tommy Agro.

Of course, I could never hold on to a buck. Nobody in the organization could. We all threw our money around. Broads and more broads. Lawyers for pinches, bondsmen for bail. The lawyers got the most, though. We called them whores. They got that name for jumping from one client to another. I had a good lawyer. I got sentenced to a month one time. He got me out in thirty days.

But I loved the life. Of course, not everything about being a gangster was as pleasant as fixing a horse race. Sometimes you had to kill people. I hated that part of it. Well, maybe not hated it, but when it happened I could never eat my dessert after dinner.

"Joe, wake up. It's Dominick on the phone." Bunny's voice brought me out of a nice dream involving Janice.

"Tell him to call back later," I groused. "I'm too sleepy to talk to anyone."

"He says it's important."

"Son of a bitch. . . . Hello, Dom. What's up?"

"Wake up, Joey, I'm flying in tonight," he said. "Pick me up in Fort Lauderdale at nine-fifteen. I'm on Delta. You got to do something for me. I can't come dressed, so have some clothes for me and for you. *Capisci?*"

Dominick Cataldo was telling me he couldn't carry a gun on the plane. He wanted me to secure us a couple. I didn't know what the hell was coming down. Since when, I wondered, did I start taking orders from the Colombos? Even a good friend like Little Dom, who I didn't mind working with when it was on my terms, knew I was loyal to the Gambinos. I'd been a member of T.A.'s crew for nearly four years now. What the hell was the sense of paying rent if every New York mafioso could call up and order me around like a Florida buck private?

"Joey? Joey? You hear me? Are you awake, you fuck?"

"Yeah, yeah, Dom, I hear you. But you better call Tommy and get his okay first. I don't want to get caught in a swindle. You know what I'm talking about?"

"I'm one step ahead of you," Dominick replied. "I already went to him. And he says for you to help me, with his blessings."

"Hey, Dom, that's not what I meant," I lied. "I'd do anything for you, you know that. But if I did something without telling him and he finds out, well, you know what a fuckin' animal he is. What size jacket do you want me to bring?"

"I wear a thirty-eight," Dom said. "And listen, you know those slacks you got for my girl? She has a twenty-two waist. Bring them, too."

"Okay, Dom, I'll see you tonight." I hung up.

What the fuck did Dominick want with a thirty-eight pistol and a twenty-two pistol? I'm sure I'll find out, I thought as I fell back to sleep.

I picked up Dominick and we drove south. He handed me an address in the Keys.

"I got to see a couple of Colombian guys," he said. "You wait in the car. Did you bring the guns?"

I had. Two snub-nosed thirty-eights and a little twenty-two. Dom took one thirty-eight and the twenty-two and stuffed them into his waistband.

"Dom, what the hell is coming down?"

"It's nothing, Joey," he said. "I just want to talk to these guys, is all. I just need the two pieces in case they don't hear so good. I'll only be a couple of minutes. In fact, you don't even have to turn the car off."

I found the place. Small ranch house—cum—fishing shack nestled inside a shadowy cove of bougainvillea.

"Go around the block and park," Dom ordered.

As I backed the car up, Dominick put on a long blond wig. Then he covered his face with a black beard and mustache.

"You go ahead," he said. "Drop me off on the corner, and after I go in, pull up in front of the house with the lights off and the car running. Don't ask no fuckin' questions."

I didn't. I dropped him off and he minced up to the front door like a fag. I watched him enter, and once he got inside I began to pull up the car. I heard about twelve shots. Dominick came walking out and hopped into the passenger seat.

"Let's go," he said. "Take me to Miami Airport and then go home."

On the drive north he told me that a "couple of spics" had beaten him and his *compare,* the Colombo capo Allie LaMonte, out of $80,000 on a dope deal. "I needed the disguise in the event someone else was there," he added.

"It's a good thing, too. There was a broad and two young kids."

"Dominick! You didn't?"

"Naw, Joey, I don't hurt kids or women. But without the disguise, I wouldn't have had no choice. Christ, I'm hungry. Where can we get a quick sandwich?"

He just whacked a couple of guys and now he was hungry. Sometimes I couldn't believe the people I was hanging around with. We stopped for a sandwich at some Cuban joint and then drove to the airport. On the way I drove over a bridge and Dom dumped his two pieces into the Miami River. After I dropped him at his airline gate, I headed straight for the Diplomat. I needed a drink. I went to the Tack Room and caught the last show, met a good-looking chick, and spent the night in a suite. I always got a room dirt cheap. They gave me convention rates.

24
The Big Fix II

I CALLED BUNNY THE MORNING AFTER DOM WHACKED the Colombians, and she relayed a message from Sean. He needed me at the track today, with $30,000. I gave Freddie the word, and we met at twelve-thirty. Sean had already taken care of the jockeys, reaching five in the nine-horse field for the third race. All we had to do was box the other four horses.

"Get them four or five hundred times," Sean said, which annoyed me.

"Hey, Sean, don't tell me how many times to get them," I said. "I know what to do."

On the way to the betting window I ran into two friends, legitimate people, Gerry and his lovely wife, Glenda. I advised them to put a twenty-dollar box on our four horses, without telling them why, and then hooked up with Freddie. I gave him the numbers on our race.

"Let's get them six hundred times," I told Freddie. "It's a twenty-four-buck box, so that'll cost us fourteen four. I got thirty grand on me, so let's wheel and wheel back for another eight hundred each. Here's eight grand. You know what to do. I'll meet you at the Dip after the race. Let's not be seen leaving the track together. I don't want anyone to clock us."

Just as Freddie was leaving, Checko Brown, a Colombo made guy, came rushing over to me.

"Tommy told me what's going on," he panted. "Give me the numbers."

"I don't know what you're talking about," I said.

"C'mon, Joe, give me a break. I just want to get down a ten-buck box."

"Checko, there's nothing happening today, so keep your fuckin' mouth shut. *Zitto! Capisci?*" I turned away and left.

I left the clubhouse and went into the grandstand, where I ran into Gerry and Glenda.

"Joe, these horses look like dogs," Gerry said. "Are you sure?"

"Gerry, don't ask me no questions," I said. "I'm just doing you a favor. Now hit it, and stay the fuck away from me, and don't mention it to no one."

The third race went off, and I had the one, four, five, and eight numbers boxed. I'd wheeled the one horse 300 times just for fun. The eight horse finished first and paid twenty-five to one. The five horse placed and paid three to one. I collected $39,600. Freddie should have had the same, unless he hit a wheel.

I tipped the clerks $600 and left the track with $39,000. At the Diplomat I met Freddie. He'd hit his wheel and picked up an extra $13,000. On two races we'd pocketed over a quarter of a million dollars. I called Tommy and told him and he was content. And I assured him I'd let him know the next time Sean got in the fix. I knew Tommy, he'd get impatient soon and start with the phone calls.

Then I told him about Checko Brown and asked why he couldn't keep his mouth shut.

"That's all we need is to let the Colombos in on this," I said into the pay phone. "He'll tell everybody. You put me on the spot today, Tom. I had to lie to a made guy."

"Well, Joey," he said, "I was testing you. Now I'll tell him not to bother you. But it wouldn't have hurt to get a bet down for him."

"No way, Tom," I answered. "I don't like the fuckin' guy to begin with. And if Sean finds out, he'll fuck us around."

"Okay, Joey, but I think you're making a big thing out of nothing. Checko's a close friend of mine, and I wanted to make him a few bucks. Him being with another *Famiglia* doesn't make him a bad guy."

By now I was remembering that this whole deal was Tommy's. And if T.A. wanted to help Checko out, who was I to stop him.

"Listen, Tip, I'll tell you what I'll do," I said. "The next time Sean calls and we do the thing, I'll put a twenty-dollar box in for Checko, without Freddie or Sean knowing. Then I'll give him his winnings and tell him it's from you. Okay?"

"Good idea, Joey," he said. "But you could tell him the gift is from you."

"Nah," I told T.A. "I don't like the guy anyway. We'll see what kind of mood I'm in."

"Tell him whatever you want, Joey." He laughed. "But take a Midol before you go see him. It usually helps my girlfriend when she has her period."

"Go fuck yourself, Tommy. And thanks a lot for renting me out to Dominick, you bastard. Next time *you* call me and tell me to pick him up at the airport. Not him, or anyone else. You call me! *Capisci?*"

He said goodbye and hung up.

25
A Favor for the Boss

FOUR WEEKS WENT BY, AND SEAN FIXED FIVE MORE races in the '76 Gulfstream Meet. On two of them we must have taken down the entire pool. I was holding over $800,000, and Sean was going nuts. He wanted his end. But Tommy said no.

"If you don't give me my share, I'll quit," Sean threatened one day.

"Tell the fuckin' mope to quit," Tommy told me. "Then he don't get nothing."

When Sean got a little too loud with his threats, Tommy had to fly down and slap him around. There was nothing Sean could do about it. But even Freddie was getting antsy, wanting his cut.

I asked Tom again.

"No. Wait," was all he said.

Tommy was speaking into the receiver. "Joey, you got to come in. I have to talk to you up here. My *compare*—you know who I mean, the number three?—he wants you to do something. I can't get into details over the phone, so fly in tonight. Try and make it LaGuardia. And bring three hundred large with you from our corporation."

He hung up without letting me respond. And I had a date that night with a gorgeous blonde. But I had to go. There was no explaining anything to that lousy bastard, much less his *compare*, the Gambino *consigliere*, Joe N. Gallo. Yet in a way I was proud of myself. In just a little over four years I'd gone from a Florida freelancer to attending midnight meetings with the Gambino Family bosses. I mean, I had management potential.

I arrived at LaGuardia at nine forty-five that night carrying an extra change of socks, shoes, shirt, and suit, as well as a money belt strapped to my waist holding $300,000. I couldn't help but wonder why he wanted the money. We had spoken briefly about the four of us taking $150,000 apiece and leaving the rest in the "corporation." So he was due no more than $150,000. Oh well, I was sure he'd have a good explanation.

"Joey, over here. What the fuck took you so long?"

The plane had vectored for close to an hour, trying to find a hole in the thick New York fog. "I was up in the clouds, Tom, wondering whether or not to come down with all of this money."

T.A. smiled. We embraced. We got in his car.

Driving toward Brooklyn, Tommy asked for the money. I took off the belt and handed it to him. "There's three hundred large there."

"How much you got left over?" he asked.

"A little over five hundred large," I answered.

"Here's what you do," he said. "Give Sean his hundred and fifty grand. You take your one fifty. And what will that leave you with?"

"About two twenty large."

"Okay," he went on, "give Freddie the twenty grand, and don't tell him anything else. I'll tell Sean to say nothing. The rest we'll keep gambling with. I'm making my *compare* a partner, Joe. It will be good for your future. He's still pissed off at you from that last time at the track. Tell Freddie we're all just taking twenty grand apiece."

"Look, Tom, as far as I'm concerned, I'm giving you Freddie's end," I told him. "I don't give a fuck what you do with it. And as far as Joe Gallo goes, I don't care what you tell him. He's got no reason to be pissed off at me. And I don't give a fuck if he is or not."

Tommy pulled the car over to the curb. He turned to me and said nice and calmly, "Joe, do you know what you're saying? Are you that fuckin' naive? You don't think this guy will have you killed in an instant for thinking things like that, much less saying them out loud?"

Tommy was screaming now. "You got to be real stupid, Joe. Now I'm going to tell you for the last time: Don't be disrespectful about him, not even in front of me.

Because I'll hurt you, Joe. And I mean it. The guy is like a father to me. Do you understand me?''

"*Minchia,*" I said. "Take it easy, Tom. I'm only talking to you. I'll show the guy a world of respect. I'm sorry. It won't happen again.

"Forgive me?" I teased.

"All right, Joey, you fuckin' fink." He laughed. "Just remember, I warned you. Now listen, my *compare*'s got a girl, a young girl, down in Naples named Sophia. She's nineteen; maybe twenty, and they fool around a little bit now and then. But this Sophia's got a brother who's giving her trouble. He slaps the shit out of her. My *compare* wants him fucked up. He wants him hurt, Joey, but he doesn't want him dead, *capisci?*

"And it's gotta be done when she's up here with him. He don't want no fuck-ups, and he don't want anyone to know. Joey, we don't even want you to use your own crew. I told Gallo you could take care of it professionally, so don't disappoint me. I repeat, Joey, do not let me down on this."

Neither of us said another word until we got to Brooklyn, where we were supposed to meet Gallo. But he'd left word to meet him instead at the Skyway in Queens. The Skyway was a motel with a nice restaurant and lounge, always a good band playing. Joe N. Gallo didn't go there too often. He preferred the young broads in the hip Manhattan disco Regine's.

We arrived at the Skyway, embraced our "hellos," and kissed on the cheeks in the usual Sicilian ritual. We were not fags by any means. It was just our way of showing respect.

"How have you been, Joe?" Gallo asked me.

"Fine, Mr. Gallo. It's nice to see you. How's your health? You look in great shape."

"Joe, has Tommy told you why I wanted you to come in?"

"He explained," I said. "You need something done, Mr. Gallo, I just want you to know that I'm at your disposal for anything—and let me emphasize the word *anything*. I cannot make it any clearer than that."

"Thank you, Joe," he said. "Now just make sure you do it right. Don't let anything come back to us. *Capisci?*"

I nodded, we embraced again, and Joe Gallo left. Tommy walked him to his car. When he returned, he ordered dinner for two, "the pasta special with the fish, and tell the chef it's for T.A." Then he gave me the particulars regarding Sophia's brother. His home address, where he worked, even a snapshot.

"Get a couple of niggers to grab him and take him to Alligator Alley," he said. "Dump him there. Give the niggers five hundred apiece if you have to. Get them from Miami. Make sure it's a rented car, under a phony name, and do it good. No fuck-ups. If you're caught, you don't know nothing. *Capisci?*"

"No, Tom, if I get caught I'm going to tell them you sent me," I said sarcastically. "Now who's talking like a moron? I mean, you have to say something like that to me?"

"Okay, Joey, I didn't mean anything by it. It's just a habit I have. But don't tell them nothing if you get caught anyway," he said with a smile.

"This pasta is good with the fish," I told him.

"Joey, they treat me like this everywhere I go. In Queens, Brooklyn, Manhattan. I don't give a fuck where it is—I'm always treated this way."

He wasn't lying or bullshitting, either. Wherever I went with Tommy, they would stand on their heads for him if he wanted them to.

I have a vivid memory of Tommy Agro from 1972, back when I first met him. He'd invited Bunny and I to New York for a visit. We stayed in his mansion in Kew Gardens, Queens. The countertops and floors were all marble. His master bedroom was one thousand square feet. He gave the room to Bunny and I the night we stayed.

That same night he said to me, "Joey, would you and Bunny like to see Rich Little tonight? He's at the Waldorf-Astoria."

He called at 8 P.M. to make the reservations. "Hello, Pepi? It's Tommy A. I'm coming in tonight. Hold my table. Yeah, yeah, I'll try to be there. If not, we won't be too late."

We left his house at 8:50 P.M. Drove to Manhattan after he made two stops. We were still in the car when I asked him what time the last show began.

"Ten o'clock, Joey. Why?"

"Because it's ten-fifteen now. We're going to miss most of the show."

"We're almost there," was all Tommy said. "We'll be there in ten or fifteen minutes."

Bunny and Tommy's wife, Marian, were talking in the back seat, having a nice chat and oblivious to time. We pulled into the valet parking area of the Waldorf, and the attendants ran over as if they were expecting the Pope. Before we reached the show room the maitre d' was escorting us through the lobby. He nearly had a heart attack when Tommy stopped to get cigarettes.

"Tommy, please," wailed the little French maitre d'. "It's nearly eleven. I'll get your cigarettes, you take your seats."

We walked into the room through one of the fire-exit doors near the stage, and the place was enormous. It was packed with people, except for one tiny table right in front of the stage. That was Tommy's table. We were rushed to our table with everyone staring at us and making snide remarks. We sat down. And then the show began.

I mean, I couldn't believe it. Rich Little had been held up an hour until Tommy "T.A." Agro arrived. Now, drinking in the Skyway Lounge four years later and having just promised a favor to the third-ranking member of the Gambino *Famiglia,* it all made sense.

"Okay, Tom, I'll leave tomorrow, and whenever you want me to take care of that thing for your *compare,* you call me and consider it done. This pasta's fantastic. I know it's homemade."

"Are you kidding, Joey? If the chef gives me anything but freshly made, he knows he's going to catch a beating. You're going to stay in a good hotel in town tonight, Joey. And don't pay for the room like you did last time. Just sign my name for anything you want."

"*Marrone*," I said. "How many joints you got up here? Fuck, I'm going to move back to New York. All I got in Florida is a bunch of cockroachy motels and old people. They ride around on bicycles, like a convoy, with a flag flying on a long stick. And if you're driving your car behind them, you either got to run them over or poke along behind them until their leader pulls them off the road."

Tommy started to laugh and said, "That's just your speed, Joey, so be happy with it. You can't move back here. You're stationed down there, and don't ask me why. Just do as I'm telling you. Besides, you got it made and you know it. Hey, Joey, let me ask you something, and I want the truth."

"Tom, don't start with that shit about truth and all that bullshit with me. You got something to ask or say, do it. What the fuck do I have to hide? What the fuck do I have to lie about?"

"Yeah, well, okay," he backed off. "It's about our friend, the little guy. Dominick. When you drove him around that time to the Keys, did he tell you what he did?"

I recited the story for Tommy from the start. When I got to the part about Dom prancing into the house like a fag, Tommy laughed. "You get a hard-on?" he asked. But I ignored him and went on.

"So finally I bring him to some Cuban joint. He gets a sandwich and some of their coffee. You know, like espresso only thicker, and he tells me those two spics had it coming. That they fucked him and his *compare* out of eighty large."

"Did you ask him anything?" Tommy wanted to know.

"Naw, I didn't say a fuckin' word," I told him. "You don't have to be a brain surgeon to know what went down. I kept my mouth shut and dropped him off at the airport. Then I went to the Dip and spent the night with some chick."

"You see, Joey, let me explain something to you," Tommy said. "The little guy wasn't supposed to say nothing to you, or let you hear anything. I told him I'd let you go with him, but you weren't supposed to know anything about it."

I started to interrupt, but Tommy cut me off. "Wait a minute. Let me finish. It's got nothing to do with trust. If he gets a quirk in his mind and starts to worry that you know something about him, he'll whack you in a second. Do you understand me now?"

"I see, I see," and I did. "Do you think he's worried about me?" I asked.

"No, no, Joey, don't get paranoid," he said. "I talked to him already. Told him I did him a favor by letting you watch his back. Told him to forget all about it and that you had no idea what went down. Told him you never even mentioned word one of that business to me, which Little Dom is sure to take as a sign that you're close-mouthed."

"Remember what I told you over the phone," I said to Tommy. "Don't farm me out to no one else. Don't have anybody calling me telling me to pick them up, or do this, or bring this, or any of that bullshit, and have them say it's all right because T.A. said so. You call me and tell me yourself. Not them."

"Joey, you're one hundred percent right. What can I say? Except it won't happen again. Could you forgive me, darling?"

"Go fuck yourself, Tom. And take me to a hotel. I want to get an early flight out. And one more thing, Tom. I didn't see you give Gallo that money. Are you sure you're not just going to keep it for yourself?"

He was starting to do a slow burn when I told him I was just breaking balls. "Now how do you like it, your word being doubted?"

Tommy smiled and said, "Joey, slow down. You're learning too fast."

He dropped me off at the hotel and blew the horn. The desk clerk came running out. Tommy said something to him, and the clerk brought me to a room. I entered to meet two beautiful, young girls drinking champagne. They were both naked as jaybirds.

Meanwhile, I was thinking over what Tommy was doing with Freddie's money. I didn't like it, and Freddie

111

knew something hinky was going on when I handed him the $20,000.

"How come we're only taking this much?" he asked. "You're holding a lot of money, Joe. I hope Tommy hasn't got anything on his mind. I was there for you guys when you needed me. And, Joe, I was there for you when you needed me in court."

Freddie was reminding me of the time he'd stood up for me after we'd pistol-whipped some asshole in a restaurant down in Boynton Beach. The guy'd insulted Bunny, and we used his head for a Ping-Pong ball and our thirty-eights for paddles. Coincidentally, by the time assault charges were brought against us, Freddie was already in the middle of a one-year stretch for bookmaking.

He came to court in prison grays and made a deal with the prosecutor to take an extra six months on his sentence for the assault—to run concurrently with the bookmaking time—and I walked out of court with a $500 fine. Freddie was a stand-up guy; not literally Mafia-connected, but stand-up.

And he was right about this payout thing, too. It was hinky. Plus, I didn't like the idea of that asshole Joe Gallo getting Freddie's money. I didn't like it at all what Tommy was doing to Freddie. But I couldn't say or do anything about it.

26
"He Said He Knew a Hitman"

BY 1976 I WAS WELL KNOWN ALL OVER SOUTH FLORIDA as a sort of court of last resort. And my reputation as a slugger was only enhanced by my affiliation with the Gambino Family. So it didn't come as a big surprise when one of my shylock customers named Marty Petro called me and told me a lawyer was trying to find me. People were always calling me out of the blue to solve their problems. I was a good problem solver. In this case, the attorney's name was Roberts, and he was a partner in a firm out of Boca Raton. I made an appointment to see him.

"Joe, I represent an elderly couple, very close friends of mine from New Jersey, and they'd like to meet you," Thomas Roberts began. "I told them all about you, and you can probably earn some big bucks from this. There's one thing I have to say up front, though. Whatever you earn, I want half. I don't care what you have to do, but I want fifty percent of whatever you receive."

I was looking at this Thomas Roberts like he was an idiot. I couldn't believe what I was hearing. Does the Lord really put people like this guy on the earth? I wondered. But I decided that before I broke his fucking head I'd find out a little more about what he was talking about and, most important, how he found out about me.

"Thomas, let me ask you a question first, if you don't mind me being inquisitive," I said. "How did you come to know about me? You don't have to tell me if you don't want. But if you don't want, this conversation is ended."

"Marty Petro told me about you, Joe," Roberts said. "He said he knew a hit man."

I started to laugh. "A hit man? What the hell is a hit man?"

"Well, Marty said that you could take care of anything. That's why I wanted to meet you and introduce you to this couple. They're very close to me."

Right, I thought. They're so close to him that he wants to earn off them! But I kept my mouth shut. And as for Marty Petro, all he knew about me was that if he didn't pay his vigorish on time, he'd get smacked around. Marty Petro had once seen me kick the hell out of a friend of his who'd been late with the juice. But I never had to lay a finger on Marty. Other than that, Marty Petro didn't know me from Adam.

That's how people are, though. You say hello and they feel like they've known you all their lives when they don't even know your last name. But this guy Roberts had me intrigued with his hint of a big score. I decided to meet his clients.

"Joe, my name is Christopher Woods and I'm from Ridgewood, New Jersey." The speaker was an older man, maybe mid-sixties. Nicely dressed but not flashy. A little reserved, looking a touch scared, as a matter of fact. The kind of guy that's got "Good Christian" written all over him and is wondering what the hell he's doing riding in the passenger seat of a car belonging to someone like me. I figured I'd ride with him just a little longer before getting rid of him.

"Here's my problem," Christopher Woods continued. "My daughter Carolyn's husband was killed in an automobile accident back in 1971. She received a substantial amount of money from the insurance policy, and—"

"How much did she get?" I interrupted.

"A quarter of a million dollars," he continued. "And they had about fifty thousand saved when he left this world, God bless him. Well, my daughter was despondent, almost dormant, for two years. My wife and I finally talked her into going on a cruise while we took care of her daughter, our grandchild, who was three years old at the time.

"Carolyn sailed on a two-week cruise. It left from Florida, and when she returned she was ecstatic. She said she'd fallen in love with an entertainer. His name is Joseph DeMarco. We hadn't seen Carolyn this happy since her husband was alive.

"Carolyn was determined to marry this man, even though we protested vehemently. Despite our daughter's happiness, my wife and I both thought this romance was a little too 'whirlwind.' I wish she would have listened to us. We wouldn't have this problem now."

The old man was getting off on the story now. "Yeah, yeah, go on," I said. "I don't have all night." I was an impatient bastard.

"Well, they got married two and a half years ago, and he has made my daughter miserable. He beats her occasionally and is extremely jealous of her. He's spent all the insurance money, as well as her savings. He works as a car salesman for Buick now. And I must get my daughter away from him.''

"So why don't you do that?" I asked.

"Because Joseph threatened to kill us. He said his father was the New Jersey boss of the Mafia, and he could have anyone killed."

I was laughing to myself. Anybody with an Italian last name was in the Mafia these days! That's what people would believe, anyway. The New Jersey boss! Hah! That *Godfather* movie made it tougher on all of us.

"So, okay, Christopher, what do you want me to do?" He was steering me past the house in Deerfield Beach, halfway between Miami and West Palm, where his daughter and son-in-law lived.

"I want you to beat him up bad enough so he won't hurt my daughter anymore."

"Okay," I said. "But you know he's going to retaliate and maybe come to New Jersey and hurt you and your wife. Then he'll take Carolyn back with him, probably beat her, too, and then we'll be right back where we started. Do you want to risk that? I can't be a baby-sitter for your family for the rest of my life."

We began to drive through the neighborhood where his daughter lived, and Christopher started crouching down in his seat. He was nearly under the dashboard.

"Sit up, Christopher," I told him. "Don't be afraid. So he sees us? What's he going to do? I'll run him over with the car."

I was starting to feel sorry for this old guy. We drove by the house a couple of times, trying to get a glimpse of someone. They lived in a nice residential neighborhood. A duplex apartment. No one appeared to be home. I drove Christopher home.

On the ocean side of Deerfield Beach, Christopher owned two—not one, but *two*—condominium apartments right on the beach. One on the fifth floor and one on the top or ninth floor, facing the ocean. The guy had big bucks.

"Well, Christopher, what have you decided?" I asked him after I pulled into a parking space.

"Joe, you're absolutely right," he said. "I can't risk

having Joseph retaliate against my family. The only thing to do is rid him of his life once and for all. But won't there be an investigation?"

"Not if there isn't any body," I answered. "Who would know? But that's expensive Christopher. Do you have any idea what something like this is going to cost you?"

He muttered and moaned for a while, finally asking, "Would it cost about a thousand dollars?"

I looked at him, smiled, reached into my back pocket, and pulled out a wad of hundred-dollar bills. "Christopher, there's about eight grand here. That's my walking-around money. I wouldn't even beat him up for that parsley sum."

"Well, how much would it cost." He didn't say it like a question. He said it like a statement.

Truthfully, I wanted to get rid of this guy and his whole problem. So I said, "Sixty thousand dollars." He didn't blink an eye.

"Wait right here," he said after a minute. "Walk to the end of our hallway. There's a balcony there. I have to consult my wife." We were on the ninth floor.

"Christopher, I don't want to meet your wife," I told him. "And I don't want to discuss it in front of her."

I lit a cigarette and waited on the balcony. Five minutes later a little old lady appeared, like a ghost. She couldn't have been more than four feet eight inches tall.

"Are you Joe?"

"Uh-huh."

"Do it. We're flying back to New Jersey tomorrow. Give us a day to raise half the amount to pay you upfront. The balance we'll pay after the job's done. All I want is your word that you won't rip us off for the thirty G's."

I stared until my cigarette burned my fingers. At one time, I thought, this broad had to be a street person. She certainly talked like one.

"There's no beat here," I said. "Let's not discuss any more. Send your husband back out here now, please. Alone." I only wanted to talk to these people one at a time. If I spoke to both of them, it could place me in the middle of a conspiracy, and these two could one day corroborate each other's story in court about any crime committed.

"I understand," she said and walked off.

"Christopher, are you sure you know what you're getting into?" I asked when her husband returned. "Once you start, you can't back off. I mean, a handshake is like a contract."

Christopher understood. He gave me his home number in Jersey and told me to call him. He'd have, he said, the $30,000. I could pick it up at my leisure. Then I left.

On the way home I stopped and called Little Dom. "Call me from the outside right away." I waited ten minutes and the pay phone rang. I gave Dominick all the details, and there was a brief silence on the other end of the line.

"Jesus, Joey, sixty large!" he finally said. "How did you come up with that figure?"

I explained to Dom how I was just trying to get rid of the guy, but he hadn't batted an eye.

"You should have said a hundred, then." Dom laughed. "He probably would have went for that, too. The only problem, Joey, is that if we do it, what about the people? You want to whack them, too? It doesn't sound like you want to do that, too. But you're definitely going to have to whack that guy Thomas Roberts, because he wants half the money.

"I don't believe these fuckin' people down there," Dom continued. "They must bake their heads in the sun. Anyway, look, pick up the thirty large tomorrow, then take a cab to Queens. I'll meet you at the Palmer Avenue joint. You know the hotel. I'll be in the lounge, say eight-thirty, nine."

I met with Mr. and Mrs. Woods at Newark Airport the next day. We drove to a restaurant, sat at a table, ordered a drink. The place was crowded. It was happy hour. Christopher handed me a paper bag.

"Do you want to count it?" he asked. "I can assure you, there's thirty thousand there."

I declined and gave him a slip of paper. "This is my phone number, Christopher. Call me only if an emergency arises—and don't say anything on the phone. I'll call you back from a pay phone immediately. Don't call me just to say hello, or to see how I'm doing, or to ask when I'm going to do this thing. I'll do it as soon as I can.

"And I want to warn the both of you: Forget all about this. Mum is the word. Don't talk to no one. Understand? Now I have to bring the money to the office, because they're the ones who'll take care of this. One more thing I forgot to tell you. You'll have to pay for expenses involved, not to exceed six thousand."

I was taking a shot. I don't know where I got these figures. But anyway it worked.

"No problem," Mrs. Woods said.

I grabbed a cab back to Newark Airport, then grabbed a different cab to Queens. I always covered myself in case I was wearing a tail.

I gave Little Dom $15,000, and we discussed the matter briefly.

"Joey, do the legwork and then I'll send Billy Ray down to do the job." Billy was part of Dominick's crew. "Put the guy in your Lincoln, they got big trunks. Drive to the 'Glades. Billy'll dig the hole, because I know you don't want to get blisters. Just have everything ready, like the lime and everything, you know?"

I knew. We picked up a couple of hookers, had a few drinks, banged them. It cost $200 apiece. I flew back the next morning. My lovely wife greeted me at the airport.

"Honey, some guy called you last night and sounded annoyed that you weren't home." Bunny said. "Said he was Tommy's friend. Said Joe G."

Joe N. Gallo, the *consigliere*.

"I told him you'd be back today, Joe, and he said he'd call at three o'clock sharp and for you to be there. What's up?"

"Oh, that's Tommy's *compare*," I said. "I have to do him a favor. Will it ever stop?" I added, looking up to the sky and making a gesture like I was talking to God.

27
Break a Leg

GALLO CALLED AT EXACTLY THREE O'CLOCK AND ASKED me if I remembered my conversation with Tommy several months before. Of course I remembered, the moron!

"Yes, sir," I answered. "I can have that room ready for you no later than tomorrow night. When is your niece going to return?"

"My niece will be returning Friday," he answered. This was a Wednesday, so I had to hurry. I really appreciated all the time he was giving me, the bastard. Luckily, I'd already done a little legwork, found Gallo's broad Sophia's brother's house in Naples, Florida, cased it, and spent a few days in the neighborhood. It had been a while since Tommy had told me in New York that Gallo wanted his girlfriend's brother messed up, and I thought he'd forgotten about it or changed his mind.

"Okay, Joe," I signed off. "Consider the job done."

I did like Tommy said. Drove to Miami that day. Got two spades. Told them what to do. Then I rented a car with a phony credit card and drove to the guy's house. I knocked on the door, and when Sophia's brother answered I made up a line about my rented car overheating. I knew he was a zip—that's what we call Italians from the other side—as he communicated in a fractured mixture of Italian and broken English.

"Whatsa matta? You car—shesa no good?"

My Italian was limited, but I could get by. The zip looked to be in the late twenties, about five feet eight inches tall, and built real hard. The spades had their work cut out for them.

"Cumma in. The telephone, shesa inna kitchen."

After going through the charade of calling the car rental

company, Sophia's brother offered me a glass of red wine, and we sat and talked. He began telling me about his "beautiful" sister, how she was in love with some old man who was a big shot in the Mafia, how much he disliked the bastard. "If I see him, I breaka his fuckin' head," he said.

His name was Alberto. Alberto poured me another glass of wine and we continued to talk. Broken English and broken Italian. He showed me a picture of Sophia. I had never seen such a beautiful Italian girl in my life. Jet black hair and black eyes. What the fuck was she doing with that old cocksucker Gallo? I wondered.

"Giovanni, another glassa wine?"

"Just one more, Alberto. The car people should be here soon."

I knew I was showing my face, a cardinal no-no in the leg-breaking business. But there was no way Alberto could connect me with the coming events. I lived too far away and never came to Naples anyway. Almost never.

Finally there came a knock at the door. Alberto rose to answer it, and it was the two spades. They asked him to use the phone, to call Hertz and let the office know they found me.

As Alberto was following one guy into the kitchen, the other dropped a canvas sack over his head and the upper part of his body. He was struggling and yelling in Italian for me to help. The other spade hit him on the head with a lead pipe and knocked him out. We tied his hands behind his back, lashed his ankles together, and threw him in my trunk.

I shot over to Alligator Alley and began the long drive to Fort Lauderdale on that dark, desolate road. I figured I'd drive about sixty miles before dumping him. I wanted to get off the Alley before he came to or was discovered.

When I found a nice dark pull-off, I stopped the car. Alberto was still unconscious. I told the spades to break one leg, smash the knuckles on his right hand, and blacken both eyes. It took them two minutes.

We left Alberto on the side of the road. I took the guys to Miami, gave them a grand, and returned the car. Then

I went to the Diplomat for a drink. I was in the Tack Room when Tommy called.

"Your wife told me you'd probably be there," he said. "My *compare* called and told me that you told him you'd take care of that thing by tomorrow night."

"What thing?" I asked, acting stupid.

"You know what thing!" I could hear his aggravation building.

"Hey, Tommy, are you home or at a pay phone? If you're home, call it a 'thing.' But if you're at a pay phone, talk straight. Because I don't know what the fuck you're talking about. Tomorrow night, you say? I'm supposed to do something for your *compare?*"

I was really breaking his balls now. I could picture the flecks of foam spraying out of his mouth.

"Hey, Joey, remember when you came up to New York and you met— What the fuck are you laughing at?"

"Tell your *compare* it's done," I said. "I did it tonight. Would I be here if I didn't do it tonight?"

"*Marrone,* Joey, that was fast. Did you do it like I told you? You know, rent the thing and get the two eggplants and all?" He meant the black guys.

"No, T.A., I got two egg rolls instead," I answered. "It cost me over a G. I hope the old fuck appreciates it."

"Don't worry, Joey, he will. Let me call him now and tell him. He'll cum in his pants. Call me tomorrow." And he hung up.

I went home that night and called Dominick at the Casbah Lounge in Queens. I warned him not to tell Tommy about that deal we had going with the sixty large from the old Jersey couple.

28
The Double-Bang

A WEEK AFTER I TOOK CARE OF THAT JOB FOR THE *consigliere*, Sean O'Leary called.

"Joe, it's the last week at Gulfstream, so let's get together this Saturday and do a good one."

I made arrangements to meet Sean at the track and decided to get to work on that Christopher Woods package. I found out where Joseph DeMarco worked, and I even stopped by the dealership pretending I wanted to buy a Buick. He was in the used-car department. I became a little friendly with him and we went out after my test drive for drinks.

He wanted me to stop by his place for a drink, as well as to meet his wife. I declined. I didn't want to meet her, as she could finger me as a new acquaintance of his in the event anything went wrong. I told him I'd let him know about the car.

He asked for my phone number, but I stalled him with a story about being in the process of moving. I told Joseph I'd call him when they connected my phone. He thought I was a vacuum cleaner salesman by the name of Joe Russo. That was the phony ID I was carrying at the time.

"Joey, that guy who says that his father is the New Jersey boss . . ."

"Yeah?"

"Well, his father is a guard at a New Jersey state prison. A working stiff. He's nothing. Not connected at all." It was Little Dom calling from New York.

"Okay," I told Dominick. "I never thought he was

anybody. I'm almost set down here. I just have to pick up the lime. When are you sending Billy Ray down?"

"Whenever you want. He's ready. He can come this weekend if you want."

"Nah, wait until next week, after Gulfstream closes," I said. "I'm doing something for Tommy over there."

Dominick was interested. "What you got going, Joey? Can I get down?"

"Sorry, Dom. No sense getting in now. It'll be over in a few days and I can't go into details."

"Yeah, okay, Joey. Let me know when you want me to send Billy down." He hung up.

"Jesus Christ, Sean, couldn't you get a couple more jockeys? Boxing seven horses is going to cost us eighty-four bucks a ticket!"

It was a twelve-horse field and Sean had reached only five of the jocks. True, they were the five favorites, and Sean was sure we'd do real well boxing the longshots, but still. Seven horses?

"We can do real good here, Joey," Sean assured me. "How much money did you bring?"

"I'm carrying a hundred large," I told him.

"Good. Bet it all. You should have brought more. Now start betting early, it takes a long time to box seven horses. The three horse and the eight horse got speed. Gamble a little and wheel them a couple a hundred times on top of the box."

What could I do? There was something about the whole thing I didn't like, including the fact that Sean had "fixed" a new jockey. But he assured me this jockey had pulled for him before in California and told me to quit worrying and start betting. When I met with Freddie he almost had a heart attack when I told him what we were doing.

"Seven horses!" Freddie blurted. "What, is he crazy? What the fuck are we gonna make?"

"Well, he claims we'll do good because they're all longshots and because of the big handle the last Saturday of the meet brings in."

"And who the fuck is this new jockey?" asked Freddie, not mollified in the least. "He was never in our fix before. I don't like it, Joe. I think somebody got to Sean. I'd like to pass on it."

"Yeah, me, too," I told Freddie. "But what if we pass and it comes back big? What do we tell Al Capone up in New York? You know he's not going to believe us."

"Yeah, I guess we better go after it," Freddie said.

"Here's your half," I said, handing him fifty large. "Use the balance on the box but save some for wheels on the three horse and eight horse. Sean said they both got speed. And start betting early. Seven horses take a while to box."

Post time. The race was a six-furlong event. That's three quarters of a mile. The rider we were suspicious about was aboard a four-to-one shot, the third choice on the board. He won by eight lengths. We lost $100,000.

I met up with Freddie, and we both wanted to puke. We couldn't go after the jockey, so we went looking for Sean.

We found him behind the barns, and I backhanded him to the face. He reeled backward about ten feet, fell to the ground, and when he got up I hit him again.

"Be at the Diplomat Wednesday," I told him quietly. That's when T.A. would be down. I was about to smack Sean again when Matty Brown Fortunato, the Genovese capo, appeared out of the blue. Matty Brown's turf was Calder, not Gulfstream. Freddie and I just looked at each other knowingly.

"Fuck it, we got double-banged," I told him on the way out. "Let Tommy take care of it."

Murphy's law. Everything was going down the tubes. Not only did we lose a hundred grand but I got a speeding ticket driving home from the track. I called the cop a cocksucker, and he pinched me. Bunny had to bail me out for a G-note. To make matters worse, the next afternoon I got a call from Christopher Woods in New Jersey.

"Joe, please call me" was all he said.

When I reached him from a pay phone he told me his daughter was going away with her husband. Joseph and Carolyn were taking a two-month European vacation.

"Christopher, call up your Joseph and Carolyn, get them on two different extensions, and tell them this: Tell them that your wife has been sick and that she plans to leave Carolyn half a million in her will. Tell them that in the event Carolyn isn't around to collect, the money goes to your grandchild on her thirty-fifth birthday. I guarantee you, Christopher, that gold digger will treat Carolyn like a queen on their European trip. In fact, I'm surprised the dirtbag hasn't shaken down your wife already."

"Oh, he has," Christopher said. "He made us buy a new car, paid for in Carolyn's name. He drives around in it now. He said if we didn't, we could never visit our grandchild again. We feel like we got away cheap. But we expect him to come back for more."

I couldn't help wondering exactly how much money these people were worth. But this was beyond bazookas now. After listening to Christopher's story, I couldn't wait to whack that cocksucker DeMarco myself.

"Okay, Christopher, we have to wait, that's all. Our deal still stands. In the meantime, don't mention anything about me to Carolyn. And don't worry about her returning from her trip. With half a million dollars awaiting her return, Joseph will be carrying her down the gangplank like they were newlyweds."

29
"Straighten Joe Dogs Out!"

"LOOK, TOM, WE WERE FUCKED BY SEAN AND THAT'S all there is to it," I said into the pay phone. "It's no coincidence that the Calder outfit from Kansas City suddenly shows up at Gulfstream and we lose a hundred large. And Freddie is pissed off. He wants his end. Now."

"Fuck Freddie," Tommy growled. "How much we got left?"

"About a hundred grand."

"Yeah? Well, bring that with you Wednesday to the Dip, Joey. Is Sean going to be there?"

"Six o'clock sharp. I told him the Tack Room."

"Okay," Tommy said. "We'll straighten this out then. And, oh, by the way, I have a message for you from my *compare*," he added. And then he hung up.

I called Little Dom and told him to hold off on sending Billy Ray south.

"Gee, Joey," he complained, "I was counting on that extra bread. I took a bath at the track. But maybe that's how these things happen. Who knows? Maybe it's for the best. Maybe they'll change their minds. Maybe they'll forget about the whole thing."

"Yeah, maybe," I said.

I was sitting with Tommy in the Tack Room of the Diplomat that Wednesday when Sean O'Leary walked in with Matty Brown Fortunato. We all discussed what happened, Sean's story being that the jockey double-banged us. Then Sean complained about me smacking him around.

Matty Brown took Sean's side on the beating—if you could call it a beating—and wanted Tommy to do something about it, or else he would take it further himself.

"Tommy, I'm only showing you this respect and consideration because I've known you for a long time and you're close to Joe G.," Matty Brown said. "So show me the respect and straighten Joe Dogs out."

Tommy replied, "First of all, Matty, in all due respect, this Irish cocksucker fucked us out of one hundred large. You're the one who's intervening on this thing and, I might add, going against your own people. As far as taking this any further, you can do what you want. But it's on record that Sean is with me.

"And I'm telling you up front, Matty, that I will take this right to the top. And let me go even further. It was me who told Joe Dogs to kick the shit out of Sean if this ever happened. Sean got away easy, because I was going to rip his fuckin' eyes out. I'll show you the respect and not touch him. But I do expect you to straighten him out.''

Matty looked at Sean and smacked him and said that he hadn't known what this whole thing was about. He wasn't aware, he said, that we'd lost so much money. Then he asked Tommy to promise not to harm Sean.

Tommy declined, saying, "I can't promise you that. I have to see first what my *compare* has to say.''

Matty Brown and Tommy A. shook hands, and Matty and Sean walked out the door.

"Tommy, they just gave us the nicest hand job that I ever had,'' I said.

"Yeah, Joey, I know. I came in my pants, too. But there's nothing I can do about it. Matty Brown's a capo. Let my *compare* handle it. It's a good thing I cut him in.''

"Well, Tom, I'm glad you did, too. So what do you say, how about I give Freddie the hundred grand we got left?''

"Joey, you give me the money, and tell Freddie to come see me. I'll give him something. You listening to what I'm saying?''

"Yeah, Tom, I hear you. I'll tell him. Do whatever you want. I'll bring you the money tomorrow—unless somebody robs it.'' I smiled.

"Hey, Joey, they steal the money, they better steal you with it.''

The next day I delivered Tommy's one hundred large, and told him I'd pass on his message to Freddie.

"Wait until next week, Joey. I'll be back in New York. You tell him what to do. But don't tell him how. Let's see if Freddie knows how to reach out.''

Tommy A. was testing Freddie. He wanted to see just how much pull he had outside of Florida. Ten days later I delivered Tommy's message.

"But what about what Sean did?'' Freddie wanted to know. "Isn't Tommy going to make good on that money we lost?''

"Freddie, I don't know what he's doing. You ask him. It's out of my hands. I was told to mind my own business, and that's what I'm doing. I'm just delivering a message from Tommy. He has your money."

30
"God Will Punish All of Us"

I WAS DELIVERING A LOT OF MESSAGES FOR TOMMY around then. Gradually, over four years, I'd leapfrogged Skinny Bobby DeSimone and become T.A.'s top guy in Florida. I think it was because of a combination of Tommy's lessons in Mafia attitude and my own ability to think quick on my feet. I never thought about if what I was doing was *right*, or *wrong*. My only concern was whether it was good for us. That's why I was able to take a case like Christopher Woods's.

Nearly three months went by before I heard from Woods, the good Christian from New Jersey who wanted his son-in-law whacked. He called in the summer of '76. Sean O'Leary's double-bang was fading to a bad memory.

"Joe, they're back," Christopher Woods breathed into the phone. "Your plan worked beautifully. Carolyn said Joseph treated her like a queen. And all he could talk about was what they were going to do with the money when my wife passed away. Can you believe the audacity of this guy? Carolyn said he made her sick, and she couldn't wait to get home, because now she has enough courage to leave him. They're back home in Florida, have been for ten days."

"Christopher, don't call me, I'll call you—unless it's an emergency, of course."

I rented a car and did some surveillance. The thought occurred to me, not for the first time, that I should have been a cop. I wore this goofy fishing hat, and sunglasses, and I followed Joseph and Carolyn and their daughter on a Sunday when they went to the park. Carolyn was about five feet six, lovely figure, and extremely beautiful. She had soft, reddish-blond hair, the same as her daughter.

What a jerk this dumb wop was! Here he had a million-dollar family, in both senses of the phrase, and he was fucking it all up because of his greed.

And to tell you the truth, they did look like the perfect family. Carolyn walked with a slight limp, nearly imperceptible, but Joseph took her arm and helped her in and out of their car. He looked like the perfect husband, and I began to wonder if Christopher Woods was lying. I didn't know anything about these people except what Christopher told me.

Hey, Joe, I told myself, don't start making judgments. Just do what you're supposed to do, and collect the rest of the money. That's where my Mafia training came in handy.

Nonetheless, when I called Dominick and told him to send down Billy Ray, I mentioned my second thoughts.

"Joey, maybe the guy's being nice to her because of that half-million," Dominick said. "This is some story you're concocting. You should have been a screenplay writer. I'll send Billy down, and don't take a year doing this thing."

Two weeks later Billy Ray flew into town, and I booked him a room at the Holiday Inn in West Palm. We made plans to case Joseph's dealership the following day, and I told him to stay out of trouble.

"No problem, Joe, whatever you say. You have everything?" he asked. "Like a piece and all?"

"Yeah, yeah, Billy, I got everything. Including a pick and shovel."

The next morning Bunny was in my ear. "Joe, wake up! Some guy named Christopher wants you on the phone. He says it's an emergency."

I left the house and called Christopher Woods from a pay phone.

"Joe, you didn't do it yet, did you?"

"Hey, Christopher, I told you not to break my balls about this thing." I felt like calling the whole deal off. "What the fuck are you calling me for? It's in the process right now."

"That's why I'm calling, Joe. Please, please stop it. We beg of you. My wife and I will never be able to live with it. We'll take our daughter away from Joseph, and we'll have the law take care of him. Keep the money we gave you, only don't harm him."

I didn't believe what I was hearing. Sure, I could stop it. But after all the rigmarole with the setup, what with Billy Ray traveling down and all, I wanted to go through with it if for nothing else than the laid-out expenses.

I gathered my thoughts. And lied. "First of all, Christopher, I don't even know if I *can* stop it now. Number two, the office is expecting the balance of the money by tomorrow, plus expenses. Number three, I'll have to go crazy hunting down the guy the office sent to actually do the job. And number four, I have to call the office to get their permission to stop it."

"Joe, please," Christopher begged. "I'll give you the balance of the money tomorrow, or even today. If you do this to Joseph, God will punish all of us. Call your office and tell your people we'll come up with the balance, plus all expenses. Please call them, Joe, and call me right back."

"Hey, Billy, wake up, you punchy fuck," I said into the pay phone. "It's cancelled. But I want you to stay a few days. I'll clear it with Dominick. I'll pick you up in an hour."

I went to have coffee, and then called Little Dom, explaining Christopher Woods's sudden change of heart.

"We might be better off this way, as long as we're still getting the money," Dominick said. "I didn't like the idea of so many people knowing who you were, anyway. I'm surprised, though, that they're still paying off the balance. Here's what you do, Joey. Let Billy keep five G's, take it out of my end, and keep him there, if you want, for another week."

I called Christopher and told him that I'd managed to

call it off in time, that the office understood, but unfortunately he'd still have to come up with the $30,000.

"God bless you, Joe, God bless you. Fly in tomorrow, we'll pick you up at the airport and have the money. Or if you want, my wife and I will fly down to you, so it won't be an inconvenience."

My God, what nice people this family was. I couldn't just let it go at that. So naturally I came up with a plan.

"Christopher," I said, "you fly in Monday, and check into that Howard Johnson's near your daughter's. What time does your grandchild get out of school?"

"Three o'clock. Why?" he asked.

"Never mind why, just call me at noon Monday, from the Howard Johnson's at Deerfield Beach. Don't bring any money with you. Maybe we can cut through all this nonsense without anyone getting hurt."

"We'll fly in Sunday," he said. "And I'll call you on Monday."

"Okay, Christopher," I said. "And don't let Carolyn know you're coming down."

Over the weekend, I told Billy what I had in mind. "I don't think you should show your face to them," I said. "You never know what could happen down the line."

Billy agreed.

At 1:30 P.M. on Monday, I met with Christopher and his wife at the Howard Johnson's. There were just a few things I had to get straight in my mind.

"Christopher, do you actually know that your daughter wants to leave her husband?" I asked. "She's willing to take her kid and come back to New Jersey with you?"

"Joe, to be perfectly honest with you, I don't actually know," he answered. "She's mentioned leaving him. She's told us how unhappy she is. Carolyn said she was sad and sorry six months after their marriage. She's told us he beats her, but we've never seen the bruises. But then again, we do live over one thousand miles away. I can't imagine, however, that Carolyn has been lying to us. We are, or were, a very close family. But I don't even know how Carolyn would feel if we went there right now unannounced."

"Okay, listen, Christopher. Here's what I have in

mind," I said. "At three o'clock this afternoon the three of us will go to your daughter's apartment. You will call her first, tell her you're here, and explain that you'll be right over. I'll drive you there, and in front of me, we will ask Carolyn if she wants to leave Joseph.

"I have two men parked in a moving van on her block right now. If she says yes, the men will load all her furniture and take it anywhere you want, even to New Jersey. Now don't worry about Joseph. No one will get hurt unless they ask for it. And I don't want any money for this. It's a gift."

"God bless you, Joe," Mr. and Mrs. Woods said in unison.

At three o'clock, Christopher dialed his daughter. "Hello, Carrot Top, Mumsie and I are at the Howard Johnson's. . . . That's right, around the corner. . . . Honest. . . . Yes, we're coming over."

I'm looking at Christopher, and I gave him a gesture to hurry it up and make it short while I'm ushering his wife out the door. They jumped in my car, and as we were leaving I saw Billy Ray pulling into the Howard Johnson's parking lot, just as we planned.

Within thirty seconds we were in front of the duplex, and Carolyn was already waiting at the curb. She had a black eye. As I got out, the two big lobs from my crew left the moving van and began walking up the street to meet me.

"Who are you?" Carolyn asked me, shooting her parents a concerned look.

"I'm a friend of your mother and father," I answered. "And we don't have much time. Do you want to leave your husband?"

Carolyn was obviously confused. She looked from me to her parents, who were both nodding as if to say, Yes, it's true, and then she burst into tears and ran into her parents' arms.

"Oh, Mama," she sobbed like a little girl, "I've been waiting so long for you and Daddy to come and get me and take me and the baby away from this nightmare. Thank God it's finally over."

I broke up the happy reunion and told my boys to get started, with Carolyn eventually pointing out what she wanted them to load. She left most of the furniture and packed only clothes. And on the short drive back to the Howard Johnson's I assured her that she would be safe from Joseph.

"What happened to your eye?" Christopher Woods asked his daughter, but Carolyn looked too embarrassed to say anything in front of me or her daughter, whom she was now cradling in her arms.

I didn't have time for explanations, at any rate, as I saw Billy Ray sitting in his rental car and pointing to his watch. It was now three-thirty.

"Look, Christopher," I said. "I have a lot to do. This thing isn't completely solved yet. Take a cab to the airport at West Palm Beach and get back to New Jersey. I'll call you late tonight, around midnight, maybe later. I have to go now."

I reached our rendezvous before Billy and quickly changed the license plates on my car. I lit a cigarette and waited. Fifteen minutes later Billy and Joseph pulled up in a powder blue Oldsmobile.

As I approached their car, I noticed that Billy had pulled a gun and was pressing it into Joseph DeMarco's ear. I walked up, opened the passenger-side door, and ordered Joseph into the back seat. Billy climbed in next to him. He was limp, begging for his life. He had no idea what was happening. He did, however, recognize me as Joe Russo.

"What's wrong?" he stuttered. "Joe, what did I do? Why are you doing this to me?"

"Billy," I barked, "shove the gun in his mouth and let him suck on the muzzle. I don't want to be disturbed while I talk to this cocksucker."

I drove to a secluded parking lot and pulled into the back next to a fence. I clicked off the ignition and turned in my seat. "Joseph, I'm going to tell you this one time, and I want you to pay attention. I don't want to hear one word from you. Billy, take the piece out of his mouth. If he says one fuckin' word while I'm talking, hit him in the eye with the gun. Is that what you used on Carolyn, you motherfucker?''

I wanted to kill the guy. I wanted to cut his balls off. But I had to be a professional now.

"Joseph, your wife left you," I said. "I'm even going to tell you where she is. Because I'm sure by the time we're through here, you're going to do as I say. She went to her mother's house in Ridgewood, New Jersey—Carolyn and her child, who I am going to adopt after Carolyn divorces you and we get married. Joseph, I'm not going to kill you here today. But I—"

"You don't know who the fuck you're talking to," he blurted out. I gave Billy a nod. "My father—"

Billy smacked him in the eye and over the bridge of his nose with his forty-five. He opened a gash from Joseph's eyebrow to his nose. I threw him a towel.

"Open your fuckin' mouth again while I'm talking and the other eye gets it," I said. "Now, you were mentioning your father. Joseph, listen to me. This is where your father works."

I told him the prison, and Joseph's good eye went wide. Then I handed him a slip of paper with an address. "And this is where your father lives with your mother."

All the color drained from Joseph's face. He slumped back in the seat.

"Now, Joseph, if you don't do what I tell you, I'll kill your father. I won't kill you, but I'll maim you. And you will have to live with the fact that you got your father killed. We will even let your mother live, but let her know the reason her husband got killed.

"Now, you wouldn't want that to happen, would you? Don't answer. Just nod yes or no."

He shook his head back and forth.

"Now, Joseph, you know we could kill you now. But I'm going to give you a chance. One month from today, you will call Carolyn and see if she still feels the same way about having left you. Other than that one call, you will have no contact with her. She'll be with me most of the time, and she knows how to reach me. In the event that something happens to her, her daughter, or her parents, your father will be killed within the hour.

"If you want to know how well I know Carolyn, she has a birthmark on the right cheek of her ass and a scar on the inside of her thigh just below her pussy."

I'd gotten this information from Christopher and his wife.

"Carolyn and I see each other while you're working, you jackoff. Every time I fly in from New York, we get together. This has been going on for six months. She doesn't love you at all, you fuckin' moron. She just doesn't want you killed, and I'm only letting you live because I made her a promise. But, Joseph, I could break that promise. Do you understand?"

Joseph DeMarco nodded his head vigorously as I started Billy's car.

I drove back to our rendezvous and told Billy to open the trunk of the Olds. Joseph went white again, and his body went stiff. But I was only looking to see if the car had a spare tire and jack. It did. I took the gun from Billy and shot out a front tire.

"Okay, Joseph," I said. "Change the tire. And when you get back, tell your boss the jack slipped and hit you in the eye. Billy, let's go."

Billy was a chatterbox on the drive back to West Palm. "Joe, that was so sweet and beautiful, I can't wait to tell Dominick. I know you really wanted to whack that guy. His wife is a baby doll, even with the shiner."

"They're a nice family, Billy, well educated and all," I said. "She just got tied up with a moron who didn't know how to handle a wife and family. He could have milked them for the rest of his life if he had any brains."

"Here, Joe," Billy said, "here's your five large. All you have to do is pick up my hotel bill. Dominick paid for the plane tickets."

"No, Billy, that's yours," I said. "Dominick knew what was coming down, and he said to let you keep it. He'll straighten it out with me later. And here's another three grand from me. I know you didn't have to do anything, but you were here if I needed you. Let's stop at my house and have a drink before we go out."

31
He Loved Her So Much He Killed Her

BILLY RAY WAS PRETTY TYPICAL OF THE KIND OF FELlows who became mobsters, the type of person I was now calling "colleagues." He might not have been the toughest guy who ever came down the block, or the smartest, or the shrewdest. But, Jesus Christ, he was one of the craziest. I mean, not ha-ha crazy, but kill-your-wife insane. Even for my taste, and I was pretty nuts. I remember him telling me a story, right after the Joseph DeMarco bang-up, that still has my head shaking. It was about how he'd been "forced" into the unpleasant position of having to murder his lovely wife.

The two of us had barely walked through my front door after scaring the shit out of DeMarco before Bunny was on me like a fuckin' Ban-Lon shirt. "Joe, a Tony Esposito has been trying to reach you. He said he's been waiting in Deerfield Beach for three hours. He wanted to know what to do with the load of clothes you ordered moved. So I told him to drive to West Palm and check into the Holiday Inn. Here's his room number. Joe, what's he talking about?"

"Tony? Tony? Oh fuck!" I said, remembering the moving van with Carolyn's wardrobe. "I'd completely forgotten about him. You did the right thing, Bunny, telling him to come here. Thanks."

"And you got another call," she continued. "Guy named Christopher called and said for you to deliver Carolyn's stuff to the house in New Jersey.

"Who's Christopher?" Bunny asked. "And, more important, who's Carolyn?"

I had to hand it to Bunny, she didn't miss a trick. I really loved her. I explained that I'd done a piece of work for a guy named Christopher and his daughter, and that Tony—who was Louie Esposito's son, by the way—was delivering a truckload of stuff to New Jersey.

I met Tony, bought him breakfast, threw him a G, gave him the Woods's address in Ridgewood, New Jersey, and sent him on his way. Then I told Billy that before I put him on a plane I needed him for one more job. "We have to see a lawyer named Thomas Roberts."

During the ride to Roberts's place in Boca Raton, Billy started musing on the crazy relationships between men and women. He told me he understood how much I loved Bunny, but he also sensed how much I wanted to bang that baby doll Carolyn. Billy was on intimate terms with such matters of the heart, he explained. He'd been in love once, too.

A few years back, he said, he'd married his childhood sweetheart. Their honeymoon was interrupted when Billy had to go in for an eighteen-month stretch for assault.

"When I came home, I found out she was fucking one of my so-called friends. From the first day I went into the can! I couldn't believe it. I wouldn't believe it. I told her I had to go to California on a piece of work. I told her I'd be gone for a week, maybe ten days, but that I'd call her every night. When I called her that night from Los Angeles and told her I loved her, she said to me, 'Ditto.' Ditto, Joe, can you fucking believe it? I knew he was there in the bed," Billy said, beating his fists into his thighs for emphasis.

So Billy picked up a hooker and banged her for $200. The next day he made arrangements with the hooker to stay in his hotel room and for $500 to play a role in what he told her was a practical joke. Billy gave the hooker his home telephone number and asked her to call his house —collect from Billy—at midnight eastern time. Then he hopped a flight back to New York under an assumed name and picked up a forty-five with a silencer.

"I got to my house at about eleven-twenty P.M., parked a block away, and opened the front door with my key," Billy explained. "I heard a bunch of rumbling around in the bedroom. I walked in, flipped the light switch, and there they were, trying to get dressed. I shot him twice in the head and once in the heart.

"She was so scared she couldn't speak. Believe me, Joe, I didn't want to kill her. I loved her so much. If she would have fucked around with some stranger, I'd probably still be with her. But my close friend! I let her have the other three bullets in the head. Then I turned off all the lights and poured myself a drink. At midnight the phone rang. The operator said, 'Collect call to anyone from Billy,' and I accepted.

"I disguised my voice like a broad's for a few minutes, hung up, turned on the lights, put the television on loud, and flew back to California that night.

"Joe, I had the perfect alibi. They checked it out with the airlines, the hotel, the phone company. Everyone that knows me knows that I did it. Even the law knows. But go ahead, prove it. They can't. Joe, if it happened to you, I know you'd do the same. I had to do it to save face."

"I don't think so, Billy," I answered. "I'm no analyst, but I don't think I could ever kill Bunny if I caught her with anyone. To you, face-saving meant more than your love for your wife. That's not the way I am."

I stopped to call Thomas Roberts, and told him I had good news. He was so excited when I said I had something to give him that he invited me to his home. I warned Billy to keep an eye on Roberts's wife, Sarah. I had asked around and found that she was known for carrying a little twenty-five caliber in her purse. They said she wasn't shy about using it.

When I introduced Billy to the Robertses at their front door, Sarah was carrying her purse. Billy noticed.

"Let's all go into the living room for a drink," the lawyer suggested. Sarah sat on a love seat and I sat on a large sofa. Billy sat down next to Sarah. Thomas brought over a round of drinks and I offered a toast. Then I told the lawyer, "Thomas, I made a mistake over the phone when I said I had something to give you. You won't get anything from me."

"I don't understand," Sarah Roberts interrupted. "Why won't you give it to him? You must have earned a lot of money from our Woods family connection. At least we deserve some."

"Well, it wasn't money that I was going to give to your husband," I told Sarah. "I was going to give him a few smacks in the mouth. And if you want one of them, I'll be happy to oblige. Since you're talking like such a tough fucking guy, I'll be happy to treat you like one."

Sarah reached to unzip her purse, but Billy Ray backhanded her, nearly knocking her head off. He grabbed her pistol and began walking toward Thomas.

"Nah, Billy," I said, stepping between them. "Let him go, he's a cunt. He squats to piss. You've already smacked the man of this house."

I turned to Sarah. "Before I leave, lady, remember this: If you decide to call the law, don't forget to tell them that you hired me as a hit man to commit murder and that you were going to profit from it."

We left their house feeling good. "Hey, Billy," I asked on the way to the airport, "do you always smack broads like that?"

Two days later I wound up my business with Christopher Woods and family. He and his wife picked me up at Newark Airport. I was a little disappointed that Carolyn wasn't with them, but fairy tales don't come true. Once in their car, Christopher passed back a bag containing $30,000. They had offered me the front passenger side but I don't sit there with strangers, as that is the seat where a lot of people get whacked.

The Woodses even offered me expense money, but in all good conscience I had to decline. "The only other thing you owe me is a Dewar's Scotch on the rocks," I told them as we headed for a restaurant near the airport.

Carolyn was waiting for us when we got there, and I proceeded to relate to all three the tale of Joseph DeMarco's scary little test drive. I left out the part about Billy cracking Joseph with the gun, although I did mention that I had given her former husband a payback black eye. Carolyn hugged me and kissed me—I had warned her parents not to mention that I'd been paid for this job

139

—and I felt great, if a little out of place drinking with ordinary "citizens." After dinner I called Dominick from the restaurant and told him to meet me at Newark Airport for his share.

"In the event Joseph calls before the month is up, get in touch with me right away," I told Carolyn before we parted. "In fact, Carolyn, you can call anytime."

I meet Little Dom at midnight, one hour before boarding, and flew back first class drinking double Dewar's all the way. Sometimes you run into situations where the law just can't cut it. This had been one. The Woodses had no choice but to seek help for their problem from someone like me. So it cost them sixty grand? So what? They did it to save their daughter. They would have paid double that price if necessary.

Bunny was surprised to see me come home. She was punchy from sleep—it was early in the morning—but not sleepy enough to hold back a crack. "What's wrong, honey?" she asked. "Don't you like to fuck in New Jersey?"

"Go back to sleep, Bunny. I had a rough day and I don't want no bullshit. I just left some nice people, not like you and I. Nice people, and a lady. Now shut the fuck up."

32
Shakedown

SOUTH FLORIDA IN THE MID-1970s REMINDED ME OF the Wild West. Everything was there for the taking. The state was growing like a weed, and northerners were pouring in. That meant restaurants and construction sites to be shaken down, money to be shylocked to new entrepreneurs, racetracks to be divvied up, drugs to be dealt, and lots of easy money to be stolen. Whoever had the most muscle took. Between my slugging and Tommy A.'s reputation, we grabbed with both hands.

Crime was just another business, and to get into any other line of work, we figured, was just plain stupid. We never gave a second thought to punching a clock or pension funds or safety nets. We wanted all the money now, and we wanted to spend it all now.

And, believe me, we literally had people begging us to take it from them. One night in 1975, for instance, Bunny and I were sitting in one of our favorite local places, Lord's Restaurant and Lounge in downtown West Palm, when Benny Lord, one of the owners, came over and asked to speak to me for a moment. "I have something of great importance to ask you," he whispered.

"Yeah, Benny, sure. What is it?"

"I'm having a problem with Stanley Gerstenfeld," the restaurateur began. "He comes in here, pushes everyone around, and won't pay his bills. I'd like to talk to you about helping me."

I knew Stanley. He was a local bookmaker and hustler. He was also a doper and a lush. He'd pop Quaaludes all day long and chase them with vodka. Frankly, I don't know how he did it. If his customers won big, they rarely got paid. If they lost, he'd hound them to death. I'd bet the Preakness once with Stanley, won a big price, and he'd had to run to Freddie Campo to get the money to pay me. So I had no personal beef with him despite his reputation.

"Listen, Benny," I said, "I don't discuss business when I'm out with my wife. Tomorrow I have a big day, so I can't see you then. The problem can keep. Don't misunderstand me now. I'm not passing on it. It's just that the wife and I are celebrating our anniversary, and I really don't have time to take care of you tonight."

"Of course, Joe, I understand. But please don't forget me. Come and talk to me," Lord said as he motioned a waitress for drinks on the house.

"Happy anniversary, Bunny, and you, too, Joe. Many happy returns."

Bunny was crimson as the guy walked away. Our anniversary wasn't for another six months. What, she wanted to know, was that all about?

"I just didn't want to talk to that Jew bastard," I said. "What do I care if Stanley's shaking him down? I'm not a priest for all these people. I'm tired of doing favors for all these fucks and getting nothing in return. Let him go to the cops."

"You're right, honey," Bunny said. "I hope you don't get involved, because I like coming here. This is my favorite spot."

But it wouldn't go away. A few months later I got a call from Benny Lord. "Joe, can you stop over this afternoon? I'd like to talk to you." I told him I'd meet him at his joint at four that afternoon.

"Joe, this Stanley is driving me up a wall," he began. "He won't pay for anything he orders, and everyone here is afraid of him. All the help is threatening to quit because not only is he robbing us, he and his gang never even leave a tip. He sends rounds of drinks to every other customer in the place, and I don't know what to do. Can you help me?"

"Benny, why don't you go to the police?" I couldn't believe I was telling somebody to run to the law. "If I help you, it's like I become your protector. Otherwise it's really none of my business what Stanley does here. Why should I stick my nose in his business? I wouldn't like it if someone did that to me. Besides, what could I gain if I did it for you? I can't do it as a favor, because I don't do those kinds of favors."

"I threatened to go to the police," Benny Lord said. "Stanley said he'd kill me, and my brothers. It was my decision, with my brothers, to ask your help. And we don't expect you to do this for nothing. We'd certainly want to give you something for your efforts and trouble."

I asked Benny exactly how much he thought my "efforts and trouble" were worth. And I reminded him that I'd have to take any offer to "my people." That made Benny jump. He was always nervous around me, he admitted it himself. Now this protection thing was driving him out of his skin.

"Relax, Benny, I'm not here to shake you down. You

called me, remember," I reminded him. "Now make your offer. And while you toss it around in your head, remember we are not going to do this for a ham sandwich."

"How about this, Joe?" he proposed. "For the six-month in-season I give you eight hundred a month. Off-season, four hundred a month. And anytime you or anyone in your, er, company comes in, I pick up the tab. If I'm not here, you just sign it. I don't even want to mention about gratuities, as I know you're a man of integrity. Every time you come in the entire staff fights to wait on your table."

"Benny, are you sure you're not patronizing me?" I smiled. "I'll let you know about this by the weekend. In the meantime, play it cool with Stanley." I left.

I drove south to Hallandale that night and told Tommy A. and the crew about the offer. Tommy was down making one of his periodic visits to check up on his territory. He said he had to check Stanley out in New York, because Stanley had been shooting his mouth off about being connected with Henry "Chubby" Buono, who was a made guy with the Genovese Family. It was a Mafia no-no to move in on another *Famiglia*'s joint.

After we got through playing cards we headed over to the Diplomat to catch the show in the Tack Room. There was a good-looking broad singing there, and Tommy was trying to get her in the sack. He sent her two dozen roses, which sat on top of her piano.

"Do you like the roses, sweetheart?" Tommy asked her during a break. "I sent them from my heart, darling."

"Tommy, I'll sing all night just for you," she said on the way back to the stage.

"I hope she plays the flute for me later. Those fuckin' roses cost ninety-five bucks, and then I had to give the cutie-pie salesgirl a ten-dollar tip for making them special. A buck, five, *minchia*, what is that? Zinc, Joey? She better not have a toothache tonight." Tommy was rocking back and forth in his chair. That thin line of sweat had appeared on his forehead.

Then I remembered something. "Tommy, I forgot to tell you. This guy Stanley is close to Freddie Campo."

Freddie had never collected his end of the Gulfstream fixes from Tommy. As Tommy had suspected, Freddie, the babe-in-the woods bookmaker, unaffiliated with any *Famiglia,* had no pull in New York. And when Freddie had failed when Tommy had practically dared him to come get his money, Tommy, like a shark, lost all respect for Freddie. Not that he had that much to begin with.

"Joey, I don't give a fuck about Freddie," T.A. exploded. "He's shit. In fact, let me go check if I can track down that Chubby Buono now."

When Tommy went to the phone I was left drinking with his crew, Louie Esposito, Buzzy, and the kowtowing Bobby DeSimone.

"Joey, Joey," DeSimone said in his faggy voice. "If we have to, we'll come up to West Palm this weekend and straighten this guy Stanley out. We'll sit him down and let Tommy talk to him. Tommy always makes everybody understand. This restaurant thing looks like a nice earn for us. And if we never have to pay for anything, Christ, I'll drive up with Betty once a week to have dinner."

DeSimone was the freeloader in the crew. He always wore pants with no pockets. A real cheap bastard, he sent his wife Betty out to work while he stayed home. A real two-time loser who talked way too much. As we were sitting there I couldn't help but wonder just what it was that made Tommy Agro feel so "obligated" to Bobby DeSimone.

The music had stopped, and the torch singer headed straight for our table. "Where's Tommy?" she asked. "Did he leave? I wanted to kiss him for the roses."

"No, honey, he didn't leave," I said. "He said he liked you so much that he wanted to get something else for you. He went to the phone to order it, I think. I know he wants to see you after the show." It was a weekday, so there was only one show.

"In fact, here he comes now. Pretend like I didn't tell you anything about the gift. Okay, honey? Please?"

"Okay, Joey, I won't say a word," she said.

"Hi, darling," Tommy said to the broad. "Is Joey behaving or should I break his legs?"

"Oh, no, Tommy, we're just talking. And Joey told me how much you like me. I have some things to do. Can you wait another hour or so for me?"

After Tommy told her he'd wait all night, she left and he turned to me. "*Minchia,* Joey, what did you tell her? She looks like she wants to rape me. But wait, before I forget, let me tell you what Chubby says. I mentioned that guy Stanley's name—I couldn't even remember his last name—but Chubby knew it. And when I told him that Stanley's been bragging that he's close to him, Chubby laughed like hell.

"Chubby says Stanley's a broken suitcase, a beat, and to do anything we want to him. But listen, tell that other Jew, Lord, we want to make it twelve hundred in-season and six hundred off-season, and we still never pay for nothing when we walk in. *Capisci?* Now tell me what you told my baby doll at the piano."

"I told her that you went to buy her a flower so rare that you had to order it over the phone," I said.

"Where the fuck am I going to get a rare flower at this time of night?" T.A. screamed. "You put me in the shitpot, Joey. Now I'll never get her over to my apartment."

"Nah, listen to me Tommy, here's what you do," I said, trying not to bust a gut. "Tell her the flower's at your apartment, and if she wants to know what it is, whisper 'cunnilingus' in her ear."

"Cunna what? What, Joey? What?"

"Cunnilingus, Tommy. Let me write it down for you in case you forget the word. Now listen to me. Don't blast it out and let everybody hear it, like you're showing off. It's a personal love flower, and she won't appreciate it if you shout it out for everyone to hear.

"So, if she wants to know what you ordered for her, whisper it in her ear, and then kiss her ear. Tell her you've thought of nothing but that since you met her. *Capisci?*"

"Yeah, Joey? She'll like that? If I do it that way?"

"Hey, Tip, would I lie to you?"

I figured it was time to get out of there, and I suggested that the crew leave with me, "so Tommy and his broad can be alone." When I got home and told Bunny the story, she burst out in hysterics and advised me that Tommy was going to kill me.

"I can just see his face when he finds out she wants the blowjob he promised her," I said to Bunny. "Fuck him, I'm not going near him until next week. He's going to need some time to cool down."

I didn't hear from Tommy the following day, and I sure didn't call him. It was Friday, so I took Bunny out to dinner in Palm Beach, and we then went to Lord's for some drinking and dancing. The place was busy, but we got a table with no problem. I had the waitress summon Benny Lord and told Bunny to hit the ladies' room for five minutes.

"That problem you have, Benny? I'll take care of it," I said. "But . . ." and then I gave him Tommy's figures. To make them easier to swallow, I mentioned to him that this meant he was not only protected from Stanley Gerstenfeld but from anyone else who might try to strong-arm him.

"I'll bring the crew around tomorrow or Sunday," I finished. "We'll sit Stanley down, and we'll explain to him about the birds and the bees."

He took the offer on the spot, peeling twelve hundred-dollar bills off a roll and shoving them into my fist. Then I noticed him calling our waitress aside. In a moment she came over and announced, "Mr. Lord says that you're not to pay for anything, Joe. He would like you to sign the check, though, for his own records."

"Fine, honey," I answered. "And just tell Mr. Lord to give me a duplicate copy saying with his compliments."

I didn't trust that Jew. Down the line he could say that I was shaking him down.

Bunny and I were dancing when Stanley came in. He had a slugger with him, a local karate instructor. I'd once used this guy to beat up a client late with his juice payment. Paid him well, too.

The place was packed and everyone was having a good time when suddenly I heard Stanley's voice above the din, yelling something at the bartender about his drink.

Then Stanley leaned over and smacked the guy in the mouth. The bartender looked to Lord. Lord looked to me. I couldn't let Stanley get away with this, not in front of all these people. I left the dance floor and walked to the bar.

"Stanley!"

He ignored me.

"Yo! Stanley! Stop hollering like you own the fuckin' joint."

He turned, put his nose up against mine, and shoved me backward. "Who the fuck do you think you are, Joe Dogs?" he asked. "I do own this fuckin' joint."

The place was so quiet now you could hear a pin drop. I had to take a stand. There would be no waiting for T.A. and the crew.

I may have had Stanley by a couple of inches, but he had me by at least twenty pounds. I could feel the entire room staring at the back of my head. I walked up to Stanley and grabbed him by his hair. I smacked his head back and forth, like a broad's, opening a cut in his mouth. Then I gave him the knee in the balls, and when he doubled over I straightened him back out with a left-handed uppercut. I grabbed him by the shirt and dragged him into Benny's office.

As we entered, I noticed the karate instructor trailing behind. "You want to get involved with this?" I asked him. "Then you just come right on in with your friend."

"Fuck, no, Joe, are you crazy?" He smiled. "I don't want my ass washin' up in the 'Glades."

From Benny Lord's office I dialed T.A.'s apartment. Luckily I caught him at home.

"Tip, you know that thing about Stanley? I had to take care of it tonight. It couldn't wait. He got out of hand and I had to smack him around. I wanted you to tell him personally to stay the fuck out of our fucking joint."

I handed the receiver to Stanley.

"Hello, Tom," Stanley said ruefully. Then he listened for three or four minutes. "Okay, Tommy, I promise. I'll never set foot in here again. And, yes, I'll tell Freddie what you said."

"He wants to talk to you," Stanley said, handing me

the receiver and starting to leave. I grabbed his arm and motioned for him to wait.

"Yeah, Tom, what's up?" I asked.

"Joey, be careful. And call me tonight when you get home. But don't make it too late." He hung up.

"Stanley," I said, "I'm sorry this had to happen this way. Tommy was going to talk to you tomorrow night, but you forced my hand. Now, be a good boy and stay away from here, because if you don't . . . well, I don't have to tell you."

"Yeah, okay, Joe." We shook hands and left.

Back at the bar I was the hero. Every waitress in the place came up and kissed me when I told Benny Lord that Stanley would never be within a half-mile of his place again.

"See?" I asked Bunny. "See what a nice guy I am?"

She looked at me and made a gesture like she was going to puke.

"Yeah, Tom, I'm home. Stanley left quietly after you talked to him. What did you tell him?" It was later that night.

"I told him I was going to give him some cunnilingus, you dopey fuck," T.A. said. "When I whispered that in her ear, she started to laugh like hell. She says to me, 'Tommy, who told you to say that? Do you know what it means?' So I thought I was going to be a smart guy and impress her, so I told her it's a rare flower.

"She laughed even harder. That's when I knew that fuckin' Joey had got me again. But when she told me what it was, I had to laugh myself. We had a good time, you punchy fuck, but I'll never trust you again."

For a minute I laughed too hard to speak. Finally I said, "I'm glad you had a nice time, Tommy. She seemed like a nice person. And very promiscuous-looking."

"And what does that one mean?" he asked. "Go ahead and tell me another fuckin' lie."

"No, Tom, honest. It means very pretty. You can tell her when you see her that she looks very promiscuous."

In the background Bunny yelled, "Don't believe him, Tommy." So I handed my stool pigeon the phone, and

Bunny told Tommy what the word meant. "And if you tell her that, it's like telling her that she looks like a whore." Bunny handed the phone back.

"I was only kidding, Tom. Don't be mad."

"I'm not mad, Joey. She does look like a whore. Maybe I'll tell her that tonight. What's that word— permis-what?"

"Forget it," I said. "Just have some fun with her. Because you'll be tired of her by the end of next week."

"Yeah, you're right, Joe. All those broads fall in love with us because we throw our money away on them. But, hey, Joey, it's a nice life, eh? Now go out and make a score, will you. I have to go in soon."

"Yeah? For how long?"

"For a year. Though I'll probably only do ten months. I want you to run things down here for me while I'm gone."

"But what about Bobby?" I asked. "I thought he was going to do it. I know he expects you to ask him."

"Are you crazy, Joey? I told you I only keep him around as a go-fer. I feel sorry for him, because—Oh, I'll tell you in person sometime."

"Okay, Tip. I'm going to stay home for a couple of days. Call me if you need something." I hung up.

Bunny was glad to hear that. "Wow," she said. "I have you all to myself for the weekend!"

33
The Cocaine Cowboys

In June of '76 Tommy went in again. He got ten months in the state pen for that extortion bit he'd been running from for years. He left me in charge of his Florida operations. I'd come a long way in four years.

Benny Lord paid his rent. Twelve hundred a month

like clockwork. We started collecting in February of 1976 and dropped him down to $600 in May. He sold the place that summer, while Tommy was in prison. With T.A. in the can, I sent his share, as well as whatever else he had coming, to his mother.

Stanley Gerstenfeld never once set foot in Lord's Restaurant and Lounge. In fact, he got married. He married a pretty little redhead, and I went to the reception. I gave the bride a sympathy card with cash in it. It got a laugh from everybody but her. I never did find out the "message" Tommy gave Stanley to send to Freddie. I didn't care to find out, either.

Toward the end of July—just as T.A. was settling into jail time—Little Dom called from New York with big personal news, as well as a piece of work. Florida was filling up with drugs, and this was typical of the kind of schemes Dom always came up with. All he needed was a partner on site with muscle and balls. I was secretly proud that at the age of forty-four, people knew I still had both.

"Joey, I have a friend down there with the Geno. A made guy, Joey. He's like me, only with a different you-know. *Capisci?*"

Congratulations were in order! Dominick, in comparing himself to his friend who was a made member of the Genovese Crime Family was telling me that they'd opened the books up north and Dom had gotten his button. He was a wiseguy.

When they open the books, they open them for every *Famiglia*. Dom was with the Colombos. But that didn't mean the Gambinos weren't swearing in new soldiers.

"Yo, way to go, Dominick. Did Tommy get his?" I asked.

"Joey, I haven't heard. Maybe when he gets out of the joint, eh? But that's not why I called you. I don't give a fuck about that thing. Tommy does, but not me. Anyway, my friend's name is Pete Conte. He's new down there, just moved in, from up here. Go to the Tender Trap in Hollywood, a steak joint. He'll be waiting for you there. See what he wants. And get twenty large up front, because Saratoga's opening up next week and I need some money."

"Hey, Dom, you just told me this guy's a wiseguy, and you want me to ask him for twenty large up front? What are you, wacky?"

"Joey, don't let him know that you know he's a wiseguy. You're not supposed to know. He's got a big problem, and we'll make a lot more than twenty large. Go see him and treat him like a doper. Then get back to me." He hung up.

The Tender Trap was a bleeding-meat joint on U.S. Highway 1. A lot of Colombos, Gambinos, and Genoveses hung out there. Vincente "the Chin" Gigante spent a great deal of time at the place. Gigante would one day succeed Anthony "Fat Tony" Salerno as boss of the Genovese *Famiglia* in New York.

Pete Conte was waiting for me in the lounge. His story was all sob. A local cocaine dealer named Bobbie Kelly had ripped off Pete for $300,000, the down payment on a 200-kilo load of powder. "For six months all I've been getting from him is a hand job," Pete said. He wanted me to either retrieve the money or collect the dope.

"Okay, I want a hundred large as a finder's fee," I said. Pete stiffened. "And if I get you your dope, I want five keys, too. I want thirty large up front right now. And I'll start tomorrow."

Pete haggled. But he gave me $30,000 that night.

"Bingo jackpot!" I was on the pay phone talking to Dominick, who was ecstatic over the deal. I told him to send his boys down, because there might be some "hard work" involved.

"I'll get you three or four guys," Dominick said. "You just guide them, and they'll take care of everything. But see if the deal can be done without you-know."

He was trying to tell me that he'd prefer if this went down without anyone being killed.

"Hey, Dom, I'll do the best I can. What do you want me to do with this money?"

"Joey, hold it for a week, and then maybe you and Bunny would like to go to Saratoga for a week with me and my wife. I'll whack the money up with you. Did you get that guy Pete's phone number?''

"Yeah, and he wants this done right away," I said. "You better send those guys down."

"Don't worry, Joey," Dominick said. "I'll get you Billy Ray. And Ralphie. You've worked with both of them. And I'll find somebody else. Since I got made I got a million fuckin' worshippers hanging around. I'll call you later." He hung up.

Since Tommy'd gone inside, I was home more. That made Bunny happy. "It seems like old times," she said to me that night. "I hope they keep Tommy in prison forever."

34
Just Kill Peter, Then Rob Paul

THE DOPER BOBBIE KELLY'S HOLLYWOOD HOME WAS set off the street, secluded behind a thick stand of palms, and surrounded by a ten-foot wrought-iron fence. A telephone was attached to the empty guardhouse at the front gate. Billy Ray noticed video cameras nestled into crooks of the trees and atop the fence.

"*Marrone*, this guy is sitting pretty good here." He whistled. Billy Ray and Ralphie had flown in with two other lobs from Dom's crew. I parked the car about a block away from Kelly's front gate. My plan was to just go up and knock on the door. I was going to pretend I was a lawyer. I wanted to get a look at the inside. "Wait here," I told Billy. "Don't try and come in."

"What do you want," a male voice said into the phone receiver. It wasn't really a question, more like a warning.

"I'm a friend, a lawyer for Pete Conte," I said. "I'm alone, and I'd like to discuss a matter with a Mr. Bobbie Kelly." I tried to sound professional.

"Where's your car?" the voice asked.

"I parked it down the street. Do you want me to get it?"

The gate clicked open. I hiked the length of one football field along a hedged-in driveway. It looked like a fisherman's house, with all kinds of nets and fishing poles, buckets, lures—that nautical shit. On the canal side, where I approached, there was a screened-in porch. Three broads in bikinis squatted over a huge oval mirror striped with lines of coke. Behind them, two guys dressed in blue jeans looking stoned.

"I'm looking for Bobbie Kelly," I said through the screen. One of the girls yelled for Bobbie, saying there was a salesman at the door. A third guy then entered the porch carrying a shotgun. When he reached the screen door the other two guys stepped to either side of me. They pulled pistols. The guy with the shotgun opened the door, grabbed my arm, and yanked me inside. *Minchia*, I'm thinking, what the fuck did I walk into here?

"I'm Bobbie Kelly," the thin guy with the scatter gun said. "What can I do for you?" He motioned for the girls to leave. One tried to grab the mirror and take it with her, but Kelly barked, "Leave it. You've had enough for now. Go down by the pool and swim it off."

"Well, Bobbie, I'm here on behalf of Mr. Conte," I brazened out, handing him a card with my "Joseph Russo" identity. "He informs me that you have something of his that he paid for. And he asked me to find out when you either plan to deliver it or return his money."

"Well, Mr. Attorney Russo," he said to me, extending the mirror, "you don't look like no Mafia tough guy to me. Would you like a hit?"

I declined. I don't do that stuff. Especially with rebel junkie motherfuckers pointing shotguns at me. All three of them took a snort. Their eyes looked like glass.

"I happen to know that our friend Pete is in the Mafia," Kelly said. He pronounced it Mayfia. "He's a member of the Genoveesy mob. I know all this because one of his men gave him up. His pal George told me everything. I got George stoned and he even told me that Pete could get killed if his bosses knew he was fucking around with this powder. So he's not going to get it. Or his money."

It occurred to me that the shit they were snorting acted like some kind of truth serum.

"So you tell Pete that he's fucked," Kelly continued. "And if he makes too much noise, I'll get George to drop a dime on him."

This fucking moron, I couldn't believe my ears. But to God's ears from this guy's mouth—he said it.

"Oh, so you really didn't get the stuff," I said. "You just bullshitted him. I told Pete that I thought it was a lot of baloney. I told Pete that no one as young as you could have a connection in the kitchen in Bogota. I told him. I told him."

I sounded like Gomer Pyle. But I was trying to draw the doper out. They were passing around a quart of Jack Daniel's, and so fucking stoned that if I could have grabbed one of the guns I could have whacked all three of them. But there were also the girls to think about.

"Let me show you something, Attorney Russo," this junkie Kelly said. "And I want you to tell Pete that you saw it."

He shoved me into the house. It was freezing from the air conditioning. In a room off the living room he pointed to stacks and stacks of what I took to be kilos wrapped in thick brown waterproof paper. Kelly ripped one open and showed me the coke.

"Now you can go tell Pete that this young kid does know what he's doing and is no bullshitter. And I want you to give him something for me."

"Yeah, sure," I answered, bracing myself for what I knew was coming.

"This!" he said as he whacked the barrel of the shotgun into my mouth.

I fell back on my ass, my mouth and nose a fountain of blood.

"Now get the fuck out of here and don't come back. Next time I'll kill you." All three of them were laughing as I stumbled to my feet.

Billy wanted to charge back in, guns blazing, when he saw my face. "It's not as bad as it looks," I told him. "I don't think my nose is broken. They were so fuckin' stoned, they didn't know what they were doing. Take me home. I want to change and wash this fucking blood off before I call Dominick.''

When we walked into the house, Bunny started to cry. "What happened?"

"Billy hit me," I said.

"Don't believe him, Bunny," Billy jumped in. "He got fresh with a girl, and she did this to him."

"That, I believe." She laughed, relieved that we could joke about it.

Two days later, around 4 A.M., our van pulled up to Bobbie Kelly's guardhouse. It was pitch black outside, and very peaceful.

Billy Ray was the lock expert. He had the wrought-iron gate opened in about a minute. I crept up to the screened porch. Soft music was playing. Inside, Kelly, his two friends, and the three girls were all passed out. All six were naked. Their mirror was piled with cocaine. There must have been at least a pound.

Ralphie stared at the broads' pussies while I glanced around. I put my knife through the screen and ripped it quietly. The sleepers didn't move a muscle. I whispered to Ralphie to go get the van. "We're going to load the stuff quickly and then get out of here."

"Gee, Joe, send one of the other guys," he answered. "I like this here girl."

I didn't believe this! Where did Dominick get this sick bastard?

Billy Ray saw that I was annoyed, winked at me, and volunteered to go fetch the van.

The people lying on that porch were so stoned and out of reality that they didn't bat an eye as we loaded 198 kilos of cocaine into our van. We were very quiet and professional. Dominick had sent good men. Ralphie excluded.

I told the guys to gag and handcuff Bobbie Kelly and dump him in the back of the van. I had some plans for him. He never even woke up.

* * *

The thing I think I most admired about wiseguys like Tommy A. and Little Dom was that they would never rob Peter to pay Paul when they could just kill Peter, then rob Paul. We were nothing if not thorough when it came to filling our pockets. That's why Dominick Cataldo had a Plan B for the rip-off artist Bobbie Kelly.

We'd stashed Kelly in Pete Conte's house in Homestead, south of Miami. Shackled to a cot, fed nothing but bread and water, it took him about a week to lose the shakes and sober up. That's when Little Dom unexpectedly flew in.

Pete met us in the driveway and looked a little shocked to see Dominick Cataldo sitting in my passenger seat. "Dominick, I didn't know you were coming. Joe didn't mention it. Is there anything wrong?"

"Nah, nothing wrong, Pete," Dom said. "Joe must have forgot to mention it. You didn't let that guy Kelly get away, did you?"

Pete hadn't, although he said that Kelly had been a major pain in the ass, screaming like an animal all week while going through withdrawal.

"That's good," I said. "What time is George showing up?"

"He'll be here in a couple of hours," Pete answered. "Do you guys want to tell me what's going on with my man George?"

Neither Dom nor I answered him. Instead, we told Pete to play along with a routine we had planned, and I brought Dominick into the house and introduced him to Bobbie Kelly. When Kelly saw me he started to tremble. That was a good sign. It meant he could remember things. I grabbed him by the hair and smacked him across the mouth with a thirty-eight pistol. I heard the cracking of his front teeth. He writhed in pain.

I lifted his head by the hair and saw a couple of teeth littering the floor. Blood was spurting from the gap in his mouth. I hit him again with the gun butt, on the forehead, just above the eye. Blood was seeping out from there now also.

"Okay," Dom said. "Let me finish him off. I'm going

to chop his hands off first. Then his head." Dom was gripping a meat cleaver.

I grabbed Dominick and yelled, "No, Dom, wait. Don't kill the guy. He don't deserve to die."

Pete chimed in. "Yeah, go ahead, kill him. Let Dom go, Joe. I got no use for this scum. He tried to beat me. Let him die."

It was my turn again. "Listen, Pete, hold on. If Bobbie here tells you a piece of information that your guy George told him, will you let him live? Because Bobbie knows you're a made guy. He told me so."

Pete looked stunned. Then he put two and two together, and it added up to George. Dom and I grinned. Then Dom grabbed the thirty-eight out of my hand and put it flush against Bobbie's forehead. I dove to push the gun away and as I did, Dom pulled the trigger and a loud "bang" echoed off the walls. I should have been an actor.

Dom and I wrestled over the pistol for a while as Bobbie begged for his life. Finally Dom turned to Kelly and said, "I want a ton of grass, you bastard. And I want a promise from you to deliver, or else I'll kill you right now, you cocksucker. And if you promise me now and then don't come through, I'll find you and kill you."

Bobbie naturally agreed to anything. I winked at the guys, who left the room as I uncuffed his ankle from the shackle.

"Bobbie, listen to me," I said. "I'm sorry I banged you on the head, but you had it coming. The only way I can save you from getting killed is for you to tell Pete about George. And you better make good on that promise to that other guy. He's dangerous."

Kelly was sobbing, crying with fright. "Are you sure they won't kill me? You're really not lying?"

"Bobbie, if you don't do what I just told you to do, I'll kill you myself."

Dominick and Pete returned, and Kelly told Pete everything about George. Pete listened without interrupting. When Bobbie was through singing, Pete turned to Dom and me. "What do we do with this guy now?"

Dominick assumed the Godfather role. "Pete, you pay Bobbie the balance of what you owe him, minus what this episode cost you in expenses. Bobbie is now our property. He belongs to me. As far as George goes, he's your business. I just did you a favor here. You clean your own house. *Capisci?*"

As Dom was speaking a car pulled up. George was a little early. Pete made arrangements to pay us our balance due that evening. We'd all meet up at the Tender Trap. Then George walked in, and his eyes nearly popped out of his head when he spotted Bobbie Kelly.

Pete bade us goodbye and put his arm around George. As we walked out I heard him speaking in Italian to George. "Come in, my *compare*, my right-hand man. Sit down. Have a cup of coffee. We have business to discuss."

We weren't out of the driveway before we heard four or five gunshots coming from the house. Bobbie put his head in his hands and started to cry. Dominick patted him on the shoulder. "Don't worry, Bobbie. You're with us now. No one can fuck with you. Not even the Pope."

Later, over cocktails—Kelly couldn't eat because his face was too fucked up—the doper saw the light. "You guys will have to give me a little time to get the grass. My last load got popped by the Coast Guard. You can check it out. But I got about ten kilos of coke left in secret storage at the house. I'm going to give you a key to show my appreciation for not killing me."

Dom and I nodded like he was our new best friend.

35
Tombstone Territory

OUT OF THE SEVENTY LARGE WE RECEIVED FROM PETE Conte, Dom handed me $45,000. And he took the five-kilo payment back north to sell in New York. I kept Kelly's peace offering of a kilogram. I kept a couple of ounces, passing it around to the broads. I didn't cut it or anything, and they loved me for it. The rest of the stuff I ounced out for sale. The powder was so good it sold for $2,000 an ounce. I made $60,000 from the kilo. I bought Bunny some jewelry as a present. Naturally that made her suspicious. You just can't please these women.

But every once in a while you have to keep the wife happy. Wiseguys always felt that this was easier to do in groups. That way, the women could keep each other company while we tended to serious business, like playing the ponies. We spent our money until our wallets were empty, especially at the track.

So, flush from the Bobbie Kelly cocaine boost, Little Dom came up with a plan to combine business with pleasure. He called and invited Bunny and me to join him and his wife, Clair, for the Saratoga racing meet in August.

Dom told us to come into New York on Thursday and he'd pick us up at the airport, adding, "Make sure you make it Thursday, Joey, because there's a horse running Friday and I'm told that it's going to win. *Capisci?*"

Dom and Clair met our flight, and we drove straight to Lake George, where we were all staying in a nice resort. Dominick's sure shot on Friday didn't even finish in the money, and Dom had bet him across the board. He dropped $15,000 and spent the rest of the day bitching about the jockey, threatening to chop off his legs.

We bet with both hands at the Lake George resort for five days. While we were there I met Allie LaMonte, Little Dom's capo in the Colombos. He had a hole in his throat and spoke with a little gargle out of a voice box. Every time one of the horses he bet lost he would rip the tickets in half, look up at the sky, and gargle out, "You Jew bastard." Allie was funny as hell.

On the drive back to the city we took the Taconic State Parkway. Near the Peekskill exit, while Bunny and Clair chatted in the back seat, Dominick nonchalantly pointed to the left and said softly to me, "Joe, there's Boot Hill.

"I think I got eight guys buried there," he added. "There's only one two-story job, though."

Clair must have overheard, because—looking around at the rolling hills and woodland—she asked what two-story buildings we were talking about.

"I was telling Joe that they're supposed to put up a housing project in this area, and they're going to be two stories high," Dom said. "Now shut the fuck up anyway, Clair. You're too nosy. Do you see us asking what you and Bunny are talking about? Pay attention to what Bunny is saying and don't nose in on our conversation."

"Don't talk to me like that, Dominick. I'm your wife, not one of the whores you bed down with. You never hear Joe talk to Bunny that way."

Dominick turned his head slightly to let Clair know he was serious. "Don't start, Clair. Remember your father and your mother. *Capisci?*"

I laughed to myself, knowing what he was threatening. But Bunny had no idea what Dom was saying.

"What has your mother and father got to do with this?" Bunny asked Clair innocently. I looked at Dom, and he was grinning.

"Oh, they got nothing to do with this," Clair explained. "It's just that every time my husband wants to stop arguing, or if I threaten to leave the bastard when he comes home with lipstick all over his shirt and shorts, he tells me he'll kill my mother and father. The lousy bastard."

I couldn't keep it in anymore. Even Bunny and Dom started to laugh.

"He wouldn't do anything like that, would he?" asked Bunny.

"You're fucking-A right he would," winced Clair. "You don't know my husband. That sweet baby-faced fuck. He's a killer, a murderer, and I know I'm going to pay for this."

"You just blew your allowance for the week, big mouth," Dom said to his wife.

"Oh, Dominick, honey, please. I was only kidding," Clair pleaded. "Right, Bunny? I was winking at you, wasn't I? Come on, Dom, you fuck, you know I need my allowance to play cards with the girls. Without it, they won't even let me in the game."

"Okay, if you keep quiet for the rest of the trip home I'll forget about it," Dom said. "But if you open your mouth one more time, it'll be two weeks instead of one without your allowance.

"How do you like the balls on her?" Dom added, turning to me. "She goes to a poker game and plays pot limit."

"Yeah, but I'm a good player," Clair said from the back seat. "I win a lot of times."

"Hey, Clair, what did I say? *Zitto!*"

"Oh, I'm only agreeing with you, my darling Dominick."

We all cracked up laughing, and I heard Clair whisper to Bunny, "I better shut the fuck up."

Bunny held my hand and kissed me the entire flight home. She was showing me how much she appreciated the good time we had had. I think I lost about $25,000 at the races. Dominick must have blown over $100,000. Easy come, easy go. Lake George was beautiful in the summer.

36
"I Wasn't Made with a Finger"

AUGUST '76 CAME AND WENT, FOOTBALL SEASON started, and I was getting wrecked. Not only were my own customers winning, but the four customers I was booking for Tommy A. were really winning big. This is how Tommy made me his Florida bookmaking partner:

"Joey, let these guys bet into you, and you keep the tabs. We'll split the winnings. But if they win, I'm out. I'm not your partner no more."

So it went, "belonging" to Tommy Agro.

So I got shafted. What's new? October. November. December. I took a major bath. I was tapped. And not only was I losing in football, I was also getting killed at the track. It was a godsend when Dominick called in

January of 1977 and told me he'd finally gotten rid of that coke.

"I let it go for three," Dom said. "So fly in and pick up your end before I lose it in the gambling joints."

My end came to $150,000. I flew to New York that morning. Dom picked me up at LaGuardia and we went to one of the lounges and had a drink. Under the table he handed me a paper bag stuffed with the cash. I went to the men's room and filled my money belt. I wore a jacket and an overcoat, so no one would notice. I'd made arrangements to fly back that night, so I invited Little Dom to dinner to kill four or five hours.

Walking toward his car, Dom said, "Joey, you have to do me a favor. Let's take a ride."

"Sure, Dom. What is it?"

"I have to go to the Taconic Parkway and dig a hole," he said. "I have this motherfucker in the car and I need a hand to put him in a hole. I'll do the digging. I just need a hand getting him out of the trunk. I can't just leave him in the streets, Joey. He was a made guy with the Lucchese Family."

I began backing away from his car. "Dom, you're kidding, right? You don't really have a body in the trunk, do you?"

"Hey, Joe, what the fuck's wrong with you?" he said. "Why would I tell you a story like that?"

Dominick opened the trunk of his car. There was a body all twisted up inside. The hole in the forehead had already formed a bloody scab. I felt sick. I had to get out of there.

"Joey, this guy's been in my trunk for three days now, and he's starting to stink. I need a hand. What do you say?"

He closed his trunk. I walked away. He followed.

"Dominick, I'm going to tell you like T.A. would say it: I wasn't made with a finger. What do you want to do, make another two-story job? Fuck you. Get someone else to help you. I don't want to know where your burial grounds are."

"Yeah, Joey, I guess I can't blame you," he said. "But

that's not what I had in mind, honest. I'll get someone else to help me.''

"Yeah, and get someone you don't like so you can leave them there, too.''

We took a cab to Manhattan, had a nice dinner, a few drinks. Later that night I flew back home. On the plane I began thinking about what T.A. had told me about Dom: *If Dominick knows that you know something about him that could put him in the jackpot, he'll whack you in a second without any grief at all.*

37
T.A. Gets His Button

IN FEBRUARY OF '77, SEVEN MONTHS AFTER WE'D scared the living shit out of him, Bobbie Kelly called. He had the grass he'd promised Little Dom. He said it was pretty good stuff, and I nodded sagely. To tell you the truth, I wouldn't have known good pot from sawgrass. Dominick and I made arrangements to rent a U-haul under a phony ID. I hired two of my crew to drive it to New York and fly back down. Dominick said he'd settle with me later.

He scored $200,000. Not the greatest price in the world for a ton of pot. Dom owed his Colombo Family compatriot John "Johnny Irish" Matera a piece of his share for some work Irish had done for him. I, of course, had to cut in Tommy, who was getting out soon. I figured half of one hundred large would make him happy.

"Joey, when are you going to come and see me?" It was T.A.'s voice over the phone from New York.

"Hey, Tom! When did you get home? I didn't know you were out. You should have called." It was April 1977.

"Bobby knew I was out. He came to see me. How come you didn't come with him?"

That fucking DeSimone. It would be just like him to have a calendar in his kitchen, marking the days until Tommy was free. Of course he never would have called me to let me know.

"Tommy, why the fuck didn't Bobby call me?" I asked. "But listen. Forget that. Why don't you come down here for a little vacation, and I'll see you then. I have a little surprise for you."

"Fuhgedaboudit, Joey, I'm not coming there. What, are you crazy? You come here."

"All right. Look, Tom, call Dominick. He's got a present for you. Meet with him, then call me back tomorrow and we'll make plans to meet, okay?"

I figured he'd be happy with the $50,000 from the marijuana. I wondered what that skinny fuck Bobby DeSimone had given him. Probably nothing.

Dominick flew down the next day. I picked him up in Miami, and as we were driving to the Castaways Hotel I mentioned that I didn't think two hundred large was the best price going for a ton of pot. Dom explained that Bobbie Kelly had fucked us, sold us shit.

"I'd like to break his fuckin' head," Dominick said. "But seeing how we got it for nothing, forget it. Joe, you had to see Tommy's face when I handed him the fifty grand and told him it was from you. *Minchia,* I thought he was going to have a stroke. He was so fuckin' happy. He told me to tell you that he's flying in tomorrow night and not to tell anyone."

"Good, Dom, that's good," I said. "Did he get his button?"

"Yeah, Joey. He got made with the rest of us, only I didn't know it till now. You are now working for a wiseguy."

I told Dom I had a problem with a guy in Queens. Bobby Anthony, who with his partner Rabbit had done that drug deal with me and T.A. back in '74. He owed me $5,000. I was having a hard time tracking him down. Anthony also owed T.A. some money, but that wasn't my beef. I knew he hung out at a certain bar—even though he was, mysteriously, never there when I called —and I wondered if Dom could maybe pay him a visit when he returned to New York.

"I know the kid." Dom surprised me. "His real name is Bobby Amelia. Or, was Bobby Amelia. You mean you don't know, Joey? Your friend Tommy had him whacked while he was in the can. Everybody knows it but you, I guess."

"That cocksucker Tommy, he don't tell me nothing," I said. It struck me that Tommy was just crazy enough to still be holding a grudge over the way Bobby Anthony had stood up to him on my front porch three years ago. I didn't mention that to Dom. "Too bad" was all I said. "I liked Bobby Anthony, despite the fact that he was a beat. But do me a favor, Dom. Don't tell Tommy that Bobby Anthony was holding five large of mine. Tommy'll try to bring him back to life for his cut."

Dom paid me my $50,000 and stayed the night. We had a nice time with a couple of hookers. He flew out the next morning as Tommy was flying in. T.A., fresh from the joint, had the run of the Diplomat Hotel. Everyone jumped at his slightest command. He was a wiseguy now. Tommy just wanted his respect, his recognition. That day, over poolside drinks, I thought I'd say something about Bobby Anthony.

"Joey"—he smiled—"would I do a thing like that? Just *zitto! Capisci?* And don't bring it up again. Now what happened with my customers with the football action?"

"Your people won forty-seven large for the season," I said. "I'm in the red. But I guess I'll have to eat that, right?"

"Now you're getting the right idea." Tommy smiled.

He said he was staying a week and he wanted to spend some time with me. He was, he said, very appreciative of the money Dominick had given him. "You did the right thing," he told me. Of course, I didn't mention the money Dom and I had scored off the cocaine while Tommy was in jail.

"Joey, did you hear?" Tommy asked. "I got straightened out."

"Oh yeah?" I said, pretending not to know what Dominick had told me.

"Yeah. They made me, Frankie the Hat—you know him, right?—and Nicky and Lenny got it, too. You know, Fat Andy's guys."

Frankie the Hat was Frank DeStefano. Nicky Corrazo and Lenny DiMaria were in a crew headed by Andrew "Fat Andy" Ruggiano, based out of Miami. They were all notorious Gambino soldiers.

"Yeah, Joey," Tommy continued, "someday you'll get yours. Just keep doing like you're doing and I'll see that you get it. I mean it. You're my main guy down here. So you do right by me and the Family and I'll do the right thing for you."

"Yeah, sure, Tom. I appreciate it," I said, although I really didn't understand everything that went into "getting made." I did know, however, that getting your button was what every guy working for a Family hoped to achieve someday. And to tell the truth, I saw that it had changed Tommy a little. It seemed to calm him down. Anyway, that's what I thought at the time.

"Joey, you have to expand yourself more," Tommy said.

"Tom, how many more fucking things do you want me to do? I got shylocking going. I got shakedowns. Bookmaking. Drugs. What the fuck is there left? I mean, I'm only one guy. I mean, I got a crew I use, but they're really nothing more than just a bunch of drivers. They never bring anything in, and they don't have the brains or the balls to bring anything down."

Tommy laughed. "Yeah, I know what you mean. But I want to meet your crew someday. Maybe not this trip but next time."

"Yeah, sure, Tom. There's only one guy you'll like. That Don Ritz. He's got a good Italian restaurant on Singer Island."

"Ritz!" T.A. shouted. "What is he, Jewish? You got a fuckin' Jew in your crew? *Minchia!*"

"No, Tommy, Don's Italian. He just shortened his name. I don't even know what his real name is. But he's a good guy. I got mostly greaseballs in my crew. Couple of Irish working for me in bookmaking. But most of the rest are wops."

"Hey, Joey, stop using those words, greaseballs and wops." Tommy was offended. "We're not those things. We're Italians. If my *compare* heard you say that, he'd chop your fuckin' head off. We're Italians, all right? And everyone else is a fuckin' Jew."

Jew, schmoo. What did I know from nationalities. As long as they earned, they could be Martians for all I cared. Yet most mob guys I knew were always so touchy about who was a true Italian and who wasn't.

Tommy stayed for a week. We spent a lot of time together. He was treating me real good, even though he was upset. He told me that as soon as he'd gotten out of the joint his *compare* had given him a hit to do. He had known the guy's family really well. On the drive to the airport he imparted one last word of advice.

"You see, Joey, in this thing of ours you have to do what you're told. If they know you can get close to someone who trusts you and there's no suspicion, then they choose you to do the job. I couldn't say no. It was an order from the top.

"Just keep your nose clean, Joey," he went on. "Do just like you're doing and you'll get far. Pay attention to what I'm saying, because you came up fast. And any time Jiggs or Little Dom or Johnny Irish or any other crew wants you to do a job, you let me know first. Understand, Joey?"

"Yeah, sure, Tip." I embraced him goodbye. I didn't realize until after he'd gone that it was almost five years to the day since I'd met him.

38
Gangsters in Love

THE '77 FOOTBALL SEASON MADE UP FOR THE LAST ONE. I did pretty well and Tommy was happy. But the big news that autumn was Jiggs dying at the racetrack. A heart attack took him as he sat in the grandstand. He was sixty-two. There was no wake or funeral. He'd requested that his body be cremated and the ashes tossed in New York City's East River. That's just what Sophie did.

Earlier in the season, my luck seemed to be turning. I had contracted a drywall job on Hutchinsons Island, three big condominiums. I got the job because they wanted to go non-union and I had connections through Chin Gigante, who was a Genovese capo at the time. He now runs the Family.

I made a deal with the builder: $35,000 per building—above and beyond my drywall fee—would prevent any and all wildcat strikes. There were five of us who split the bread: Chin, Jiggs Forlano, the union delegate, me, and—of course—Tommy Agro.

Once, the builder was a couple of days late with his payment. Three or four gunmen with rifles appeared at the construction site at night and shot the place up. No one was hurt, although they scared the hell out of the night watchman. The builder came running to me, and I assured him I'd look into the problem and that it wouldn't happen again. He never missed another payment.

I had my kid brother running the job for me. He was a good guy, would do anything for me. But I didn't want him to get involved in my kind of life. I wanted him on the other road, the right road.

The drywall job on Hutchinsons Island was still going strong, so when I got our next shakedown installment I gave Jiggs's share to Tommy Farese, the Colombo doper who was part of Johnny Irish's crew. After Jiggs died, Thomas DiBella, the acting boss of the Colombos, promoted Johnny Irish to capo. Rumor had it that Johnny put $500,000 in drug money into DiBella's hands. Most of that money came from Tommy Farese, who got his button from Johnny Irish in return.

When Jiggs was alive Farese had had to sneak around with the dope. Jiggs was against drugs personally, but he never enforced any rules, because Carmine "the Snake" Persico, the former Colombo head who had since gone to jail, was heavily into the dope trade. But now that Jiggs was dead, Farese came out into the open and began to move tens of tons of pot a month and God knows how much blow.

It was also around this time, late 1977, that I met a young lady and fell in love. Nena, at thirty-two, was fourteen years younger than me, and my wife would eventually catch us together in Nena's apartment about a year later. She must have been tailing me that day, because she burst in through the door, saw me sitting there with my pecker blowing in the wind, and that was that. Bunny was crushed. I had really done it this time. Bunny turned and, with tears in her eyes, left.

I chased after her. I begged and pleaded for a month. But it was no use. She told me to get out, and I went to stay at Nena's for a while.

Don't misunderstand me. Nena, a lovely blonde, was no slouch. And I cared for her very much. But I just couldn't get Bunny out of my mind. I'd hurt Bunny so bad. She was miserable, which only increased my guilt. And now my luck changed terribly. It seemed like everything I touched turned to shit. It was as if I no longer had Bunny as my lucky charm.

I was called before the grand jury investigating racketeering. The "G"—which was what we always called any arm of the federal government—had found out about the Hutchinsons Island payoffs. I didn't know how much they knew, but I realized once they didn't offer me immunity to testify that I was a target. Bob Sailor, my lawyer, had me take the fifth for every question.

To make matters worse, the winter of 1977 was also the season I had a falling-out with the Florida Colombos. I was delivering a cut of a drug deal to Tommy Farese at the Bridge Restaurant in Fort Lauderdale when I ran into Tommy's *compare,* Johnny Irish, in the parking lot. He told me Thomas DiBella just happened to be in Florida checking out his enterprises, and he wanted me to come inside and meet him.

I was hesitant. I didn't want any problems. I got along good with these guys from the Colombo *Famiglia,* and all I wanted to do was stay friends. I knew Johnny didn't care for T.A. that much, and I just felt that he had something else on his mind.

"Come on, Joe, you have to meet him," Irish insisted. "I told him all about you. How you and me and Tommy are all such good pals."

I went into the restaurant to meet Thomas DiBella.

"Tom, this is Joe Dogs," Irish began the introductions. "He's with that fuckin' animal Tommy Agro, but Joe belongs here. He used to be with our people, a long time ago in New York. How he wound up with that fuckin' T.A., I don't know."

"How do you do, Mr. DiBella," I said.

"Tom," Irish continued, "I'm here. You're here. Joe Dogs is here. And T.A. is in New York. See what you can do. Joe Dogs belongs with us. This is one guy I'll straighten out right away."

He meant get me my button.

Things were getting dangerous. I looked from Johnny Irish to Thomas DiBella and said, "Hey, what's the difference as long as we're all friends. It doesn't make any difference what *Famiglia* you're with. We're all friends anyway."

I was trying to fluff it off. I didn't want, or need, any problems with the Gambinos. But the protocol had been violated. You don't cross the line like Johnny Irish had done. He was wrong.

DiBella said, "Keep your nose clean, Joe. I've heard a lot of nice things about you. Let me see what I can do."

That night I cheated on my girlfriend and took my wife out. I missed Bunny. She said she missed me, too, but she'd had too bad a time of it. She would never take me back.

After dropping off Bunny I called Tommy A. and told him what Irish had done. What a mistake! T.A. reached out—as only T.A. can reach out, loud—and left word that Joe Dogs was part of his crew, and no one goes near me without consulting him first.

Now I was on the Colombo Family's shit list. None of them would have anything to do with me. And that really cut my earning power.

Things in Florida were falling apart. A week after Jiggs died, the shylock Jack "Ruby" Stein was discovered mutilated in the trunk of a car. He'd been in Jiggs's crew. In Ruby's breast pocket police found a list of all the juice owed to him from different customers. It led to a lot of investigations and arrests.

Ruby had been safe while Jiggs was alive. That's how strong and well respected Jiggs had been. Now that he was dead, punks felt free to cut Ruby Stein's tongue out. A Lucchese Family soldier was finally picked up and convicted of the murder. He did twelve years. I missed Jiggs.

Tommy and Nena hated each other. In fact, in T.A.'s eyes I lost a little respect for living with Nena.

"Why don't you go home and forget that fucking cunt," Tommy would hound me.

Each time I would explain to him that I'd tried to go home a million times, but Bunny wanted no part of me anymore.

"What the fuck do you want me to do," I screamed at him once. "And don't call Nena a cunt. You don't hear me calling your girlfriends cunts. And you got some nerve, to boot. How come you and Marian are divorced? Practice what you preach, Tip."

He hung up on me.

39
Unfinished Business

MURDERING OUR OWN WAS A FACT OF LIFE. NOBODY liked doing it, but it was the only way to maintain control. Nobody in the Mafia was really scared of anything else: not cops, not jail time, not even a beating. Everybody takes a beating. But, hell, there were some killings I just didn't understand.

On the last day of January 1978, I got a call from Stanley Gerstenfeld. He told me he had to see me. "Joey, you gotta do me a favor."

"Stanley," I said, "I'm not going to loan you a quarter. You're a beat."

"No, Joe, I don't want any money. I have to talk to you. When can I see you?" Stanley sounded very scared. I told him to come around to my house the following afternoon. He thanked me and hung up.

The next day Stanley was a no-show. I waited for him until early evening, finally telling Bunny to relay the message, should he call, that I was pissed off. I went down to Delray Beach to play cards.

The following morning Bunny shook me awake. Stanley was on the phone. I picked up the receiver and told that fucking suitcase how he had ruined my day.

"Joe, please," he said with urgency. "You're the only one who can help me. I have to talk to you. Can I come over now?"

"Sure, Stanley, come on over," I said. "Give me an hour to shower and get dressed. But listen, if you change your mind, call me and tell me. Don't leave me hanging here all day waiting for you."

I waited for two hours. Stanley finally called and said he didn't have to see me after all. "I'm going to the fights in Miami tomorrow," he said. "I'll see you Saturday at the track." He sounded a lot more relieved.

"Hey, Joe," he added before hanging up. "You want to come to the fights with us? I'm going with Robbie and another guy who hangs out with Freddie Campo."

I was throwing a party the next night for my sister's twenty-fifth anniversary, so I declined and hung up. That night I took Bunny to dinner at Papa Gallo's in Palm Beach. During dinner, Freddie Campo walked in, and we invited him to join us.

I mentioned Stanley's phone calls to Freddie. "He sounds like he has a problem," I said. "You know anything about it?"

Freddie gave me a stern look. "Joe, do me a favor and *fatti i fatti tuoi. Capisci?*" Mind my own business. So I didn't ask any more questions. Freddie was right, it was none of my business.

On Friday, February 3, I threw a party for my sister and her husband, Mario. We had about fifteen people over to the house. Everyone was gone by midnight. I helped Bunny clean up the mess and went to bed.

At about three in the morning the phone startled me awake.

"Yeah?" I said groggily.

"Joe, Stanley was shot to death tonight in a parking lot in Miami." Then there was a click.

I recognized the voice as Robbie's. So that's what Stanley wanted to see me about. He had an inkling. Yet they still conned him into going to Miami. Freddie's comment about minding my own business made sense now. Was I ever glad I threw my sister that party, because everyone in town knew I'd smacked Stanley around in Lord's. Poor Stanley, I thought, and went back to sleep.

40

"He Was Even Ratting On You"

IT WAS TWO WEEKS TO THE DAY SINCE STANLEY GER-
stenfeld got whacked in the Miami parking lot, an unusu-
ally cold February morning in '78. Bunny shook me
awake. "Joe, there's a guy at the door says he has to see
you. Looks like a cop."

Cops—the FBI, state dicks, IRS accountants, Alcohol,
Tobacco, and Firearm guys, the DEA, even local cherry
flashers; they were all plain cops to us—were no more
than a nuisance, like taxes (which I never paid anyway),
or locusts. They knew what I was up to, most of the stuff
anyway. I knew they knew. The trick was to keep them
from proving it.

"Tell him you made a mistake," I said. "Tell him you
thought I was sleeping, but I'm really not home."

"But, Joe, I already told him you were here. He's
going to know I'm lying."

"Tell him! I don't give a fuck what he thinks or knows.
Get rid of him. And don't take any papers from him. Tell
him to call Bob Sailor."

Sailor was my lawyer. I hopped from bed, dialed his
number, and cracked the bedroom door to eavesdrop on
Bunny and the cop. Bunny was great. She said she'd
made a big mistake, then slammed the front door in the
cop's face. He'd tried to hand her a subpoena.

My lawyer accepted the subpoena. We both showed up
at the state attorney's office about a week later. Freddie
Campo had disappeared. Word was he was visiting a sick
aunt in Connecticut. She must have lingered for a while,
because I didn't see him back in Florida for several
months.

A deputy state attorney by the name of Jack Scarola

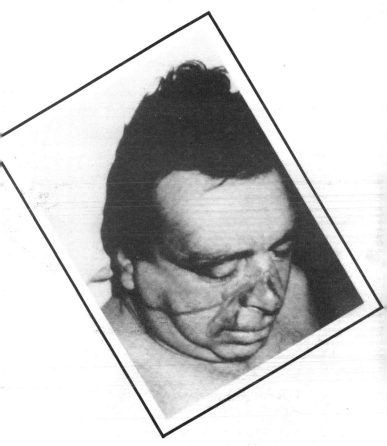

January 19, 1981. The FBI showed me this photo of myself just before I went to my first trial in 1984. It brought back memories of how mad I was. The photo encouraged me throughout the first trial in which I spent a total of twenty-eight days on the stand.

Outside of undercover club at 100 Broadway, Riviera Beach, Florida.

Downstairs at Suite 100. Picture of Bette Davis on wall. *(Photo by Howard Loth.)*

Upstairs at Suite 100.

March 1982, Suite 100. A lovely lady.

In this photo we posed for a photographer, Howard
Loth (now deceased). I'm between the two under-
cover agents in Operation Home Run at Suite 100.
On my right is FBI agent Richard McKeen, also
known as R. B. or Richard Bennett, and
Jack Bonino, aka John Marino.

Gennaro "Gerry Lang" Langello.

Mug shot of Carmine Persico, aka Junior, aka Snake.

Mug shot of Dominic "Donnie Shacks" Montemarano.

Mug shot of Frank Junior "Fingers" Abbandando.

MUGS

Thomas DiBella.

Mug shot of Alphonse "Little Ally Boy" Persico.

1992. Federal mug shot of Dominick "Little Dom" Cataldo.

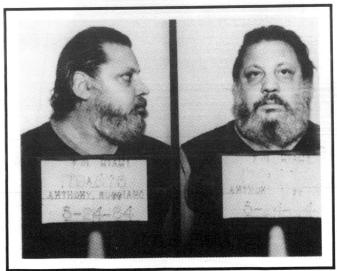

Mug shot of Andrew Ruggiano in 1984 after his capture from being a fugitive since October 1982 from Operation Home Run. Fat Andy was hiding with a motorcycle group to avoid being caught.

1982. Fat Andy outside Suite 100 talking with a friend.

March 7, 1981. Close-up of Frank Russo at the
Diplomat Hotel in Hollywood, Florida.

From left to right, undercover agent John "Marino" Bonino, Joe Blaze, Bobby DeSimone, Fat Andy with sunglasses and white shirt, and a friend.

July 1981. In the middle is Junior "Fingers"
Abbandando and Bob DeSimone to the right, looking
ambivalent about which car to drive.

SURVEILLANCE

July 1981. We are about to Leave Suite 100 in the
FBI's Cadillac, which was confiscated from a drug
operation. From left to right, Joe Dogs, Jack Bonino
and Joe Blaze.

1982. Myself and Joe Blaze entering Suite 100.

1982. From left to right, Geraldo Alicino and a general contractor who worked on Suite 100.

1982. Agro and I embracing. "I don't know if he's showing me affection or if he's feeling me to see if I'm wired." This is in Manhattan, outside of Lanza's restaurant. At this moment, I'm slightly apprehensive. A shot of scotch would probably relax me some.

1981. Agro and back of Joe "Piney" Armone.

grilled me. Some of his questions I answered. Some I didn't. I volunteered the information about Stanley's jumpy phone calls. I didn't mention Freddie, although Scarola did. I told Scarola about the middle-of-the-night confirmation of Stanley's death. I said I hadn't recognized the voice on the phone.

Finally I added that I had at least twenty witnesses who would swear I was home all evening the night of Stanley's demise. I was cleared and I left. Stanley Gerstenfeld's murder is still open on the Florida books these fifteen years later.

When Freddie pulled back into town we met at his place. I gave him a play-by-play of the state attorney's questioning.

"Your name came up quite a few times," I said. "Direct from this guy Scarola's mouth. He asked me how I knew you, how long I'd known you. The usual stuff. Wanted to know what you did for a living. Finally I told him that if he wanted to ask questions about me, I'd be glad to cooperate. But if he wanted to know about Fred Campo, then maybe he should be asking Mr. Fred Campo, or this fucking meeting is over."

Freddie was annoyed. "Those cocksuckers ain't got nothing better to do but start trouble."

"But, hey, Freddie, tell me why Stanley's gone," I said. "I mean, he was a pain in the ass, he was a beat artist, but I never thought he did anything bad enough to get killed."

"You don't know the whole story, Joey. He was a fucking rat. My connection in the sheriff's office told me who he was ratting to and what he was saying. Joe"—Freddie paused a beat—"he was even ratting on you."

"On me!" I yelled. "He didn't know a fucking thing about me. If he said anything about me it was either a guess or a fucking outright lie. But, shit, those fucking cops believe anything."

I was pissed. Freddie changed the subject.

41
The Feds Come Calling

"COME ON, NENA, HURRY UP. WE HAVE TO DRIVE ALL the way to the Diplomat to meet Tommy."

"Joe, if it wasn't Diana Ross performing, I wouldn't even go. You know how much I hate that big Mafia friend of yours."

It was New Year's Eve of 1980. Nena and I had been living together in a beautiful apartment in North Palm Beach. I'd decorated it with all new furniture and plush deep-pile rugs. Of course, I'd got all the furnishings on the arm. At least some people still respected me. But I wasn't earning any money. My luck had turned to shit, and my standing in T.A.'s crew had fallen. I was still his top dog, but that was almost by default.

At least I was still earning something—as opposed to the rest of those mopes like Skinny Bobby DeSimone. It had taken me nearly a decade to become the Gambino Family's right hand in South Florida, and I wasn't ready to give up the title. So I'd had a bad run for a year or so. So what? So had Jimmy Carter. Soon I'd be taking my cue from a new president, Ronald Reagan. The 1980s were here, and it was morning in the mob.

Diana Ross was great. Tommy had shown up with two broads, both young and beautiful. Nena behaved herself until the clock struck 1980. That's when Diana Ross came over to our table and kissed Tommy a Happy New Year.

"You let that nigger kiss you?" Nena asked. She was busting T.A.'s balls.

"Hey, Nena, *zitto!*" Tommy was pissed.

"What did he say, Joe?" she asked.

"He wants you to go over to him, he has something he wants to whisper in your ear." I laughed.

176

Tommy had quite a few drinks in him, and so did Nena. When she got up and approached him, he turned and hissed.

"Why don't you get your fat ass away from Joe. You have no class. His wife has more class in her pinky than you do in your whole body. Now, Joey, I want to be *solo*. Get her the fuck out of here and call me tomorrow."

We left with Nena bawling.

Nena had attended the American Airlines flight-attendant training school in Dallas. When she graduated, she was stationed in San Francisco. She was there when I had my heart attack, and she took a leave of absence to care for me. Although she was very good to me, we nonetheless had our problems. She wanted me to divorce Bunny and marry her. I couldn't see it. I had given up on Bunny. We were never getting back together. But I didn't want to marry Nena.

After I recovered from the heart attack, Nena got back with American Airlines, this time stationed in Chicago. Things seemed to work out. I missed her, all right, but while she was gone I just busied myself with other broads or my crew. On Sundays I had the entire crew over. I'd cook for them while we watched the football games. Then I'd have a girlfriend come in to clean up the mess.

In January of '80 the FBI went to my landlord and told him that he was renting to a member of the Mafia. My landlord asked me to leave. I rented a brand-new duplex up the street, and the FBI did the same thing. This landlord wasn't so easily intimidated.

Meanwhile, I was back to selling dope. Cocaine. I was hauling consignments by car to a buyer in Arizona. I'd leave on a Friday night, because those lazy bastards in the FBI didn't work weekends. I guess they thought La Cosa Nostra didn't either.

On one trip, in mid-February, I'd brought a lob from my crew named Aldo DiCuffa with me, more for company than protection. We left Aldo's lovely lady, Valerie, to house-sit my apartment. When we returned, Valerie told us the FBI had been around asking questions.

"Like what?" I wanted to know.

"Oh, the cute one, I think he said his name is Larry, he wanted to know where you and Aldo went," she answered.

I had to wonder how they knew that Aldo had accompanied me. My phone, I figured, must be tapped. And if that was the case, then they'd overheard the recent beef I'd had with T.A., which had turned into a wide-ranging conversation about Mafia mores. Tommy had invested $10,000 in one of my coke deals and the operation went south. My guy had gotten ripped off, and we'd all lost our money. It was an occupational hazard, although Tommy didn't see it quite that way.

"Joey, I don't give a fuck, you're responsible," he'd claimed. "You owe me juice on that ten large until I get it back. It was my *compare*'s money. If I tell him that story about a rip-off, he'd just come after you and hurt you."

"Listen, Tommy," I'd told him. "You go tell that fucking Gallo that he's going to have to try and hurt me, because I'm not paying juice on that ten grand. The guy that got ripped off told me he'll make good. He just needs a little time. So be patient."

That was not a word in Tommy Agro's vocabulary.

"Joey," he said in a low voice, "what are you, sick? If I told him that, he'd have a dozen guys at your house in a few hours. And if a dozen wasn't enough, he'd have two dozen. You fuckin' moron. And listen to this. I told Johnny Irish and Tony Black that I was gonna get you made soon. Very soon, I told them. And you know what they said? They told me I should wait awhile. They didn't think you were ready." Tony Black was a guy who Irish had secured a button for when Irish was promoted to capo.

"First of all, Tip," I replied, "can't I say something about Gallo without you getting all excited? You know I don't mean it. I'm just getting rid of my frustrations. And secondly, what's wrong with you? Are you so easy to con now? If Johnny Irish thinks it's too early for me to get made, how come he wanted to steal me from you and make me on the spot a couple of years ago?"

"You're right about Irish, Joey," Tommy said. "When

I asked him about that conversation he had with you in front of DiBella, he and Tony Black put their tails between their legs and left. They're nothing but punks. But don't say anything else bad about my *compare*. And don't ever mention his name over the phone. Don't worry, you'll get that thing. My *compare*'s standing behind me, so there'll be no blackball. Just don't fuck up. You're almost like me, eh, Joey?''

If my phone was tapped, the FBI had heard all that.

I was awakened, at eight-thirty the morning after I returned from Arizona with Aldo by a knock on my door. I peered through the peephole and spotted two guys. One was tall and skinny, with long hair. The other was stocky, with a mustache, and carrying a briefcase. I was sure they were dopers. I kept quiet, even when the skinny guy began yelling: ''Joe! We know you're home. We'd like to talk to you. Don't shoot. We're FBI agents.''

This I couldn't imagine. Even dopers didn't dress as sloppy as these guys. The tall, skinny guy bruised his hand on my door for fifteen minutes before both of them left. I got their plate number and called my attorney. He ran a trace on it, and it came back as belonging to someone in Tallahassee. Now I was sure they were dopers from a gang I'd recently had some trouble with. A Genovese Family dealer named Papo Tortora had sold me bad dope, and I'd refused to pay. There had been threats. I called a couple of guys from my crew, and they came rushing over with guns.

We waited. The phone rang.

''Hello,'' I said into the receiver, disguising my voice like a woman's.

''Good morning, ma'am,'' a male voice said over the phone. ''My name is Larry Doss and I'm an FBI agent. It's imperative I talk with your son. Will you please put Joe on the line?''

I continued with the falsetto. ''My son isn't home. Why don't you leave Joseph alone? He's a nice boy. He doesn't harm anyone.'' My crew was holding their stomachs, trying not to bust a gut.

''Yes, ma'am, I agree with you,'' the voice continued.

"But it's my duty to tell your son something of extreme importance to him."

I took the guy's phone number and told him I'd have Joe call him back. Then I called my attorney with the number and told him to find out where it went.

"That number goes nowhere, Joe," Bob Sailor said when he called back several minutes later. "I can't find anything on it, either in the reverse directory or through my sources. And when I called it myself and asked what residence I was calling, a voice asked me to whom I wanted to speak. When I made up a name, they told me I had the wrong number and hung up."

"Yeah, okay," I told Sailor. "I'll take care of it." I hung up and sent my crew home. Then I called the number myself.

"Is Larry Doss in?"

"Who's calling, please?"

"Tell him it's Joe Dogs."

"Joe, this is Larry Doss! I'm glad your mother passed on my message. She's a nice lady. Is she visiting you?"

"Whoa, slow down," I said to this Larry Doss. "Number one, who are you? And what's the idea of your telling my mother you're an FBI agent? What are you, fuckin' dopey or what? I told Papo that shit was no good, and that's the reason I sent it back. Now, do you want me to take this beef further?"

"Joe," the voice said, "I really don't understand what you're babbling about. I *am* an FBI agent, and I was there this morning with my partner Gunnar Askeland. We knew you were home, but we didn't know your mom was there. When did she get in? We've been on you twenty-four hours a day, but we didn't get a report that she'd arrived. Someone on the late shift must have dozed off."

"Well, listen, Larry, or whatever the fuck your name is," I said. "I called my lawyer and gave him your number. And he didn't come up with any FBI office."

"Joe," the voice replied, "Bob Sailor couldn't find his way home in the dark. Call information. Get the local FBI number. Ask for Larry Doss or Agent Doss. Remember my voice. I'll be waiting."

That was fair enough. I was kind of hoping it actually was the FBI. Who else would know my lawyer's name? I didn't want any shoot-outs at my house, especially with Papo's gang of dopers. My landlord had told me he didn't give a shit who I was as long as I paid my rent on time. But I wasn't sure if he'd overlook blazing guns.

I dialed the local FBI number, a girl answered, and I asked for Agent Askeland. I was trying a little strategy of my own.

"Hello?" It was a quick, brisk hello.

"Hi, Larry," I said.

"No, this is Gunnar. Who's this? Do you want to speak to Larry Doss?"

"Yeah, put him on," I said.

"Nice try, Joe Dogs," Larry Doss's voice said. Maybe they weren't so dumb after all. Agent Doss repeated that he had something very important to tell me, but he didn't want to speak over the phone. He asked if he and his partner could come by my place.

"No, come alone," I told him. "You don't need your partner. I won't shoot you. Just don't wear a bug. I'm going to frisk you thoroughly, and if you're wearing a wire I'll toss you out on your ass."

Fifteen minutes later a car pulled up in front of my apartment. Sure enough, the tall, skinny guy with the long hair stepped out. He walked in, shook hands, and took a quick glance around. He noticed the rifle and three pistols I had scattered about the apartment.

"You don't need all these guns for me, Joe," Larry Doss said as I was frisking him.

"They aren't for you, Larry. I'm expecting a little problem."

"So where's your mother, Joe?" he asked. "I hope I didn't alarm her this morning?"

I raised my voice to a falsetto. "My mother's in New York, Larry. I haven't seen her for a while."

He smiled, and we got down to business. Agent Doss told me that his sources had told him that Tommy Farese had put out a contract on me, and it was his solemn duty to inform me and offer protection. Would I help him?

Would I cooperate? I declined, telling him that wasn't my cup of tea.

We talked for a good forty-five minutes, and I even put away my guns. Larry Doss seemed like a nice guy, and he conducted himself like a gentleman. Before he left he even promised me he'd pull his surveillance team off. Of course I didn't believe him, although I thought maybe he'd pull them for at least a couple of days.

Agent Larry Doss didn't make any headway with me, although he did convince me of one thing. I wasn't worried about Tommy Farese, but I didn't want the "Eye" down my back. It was time for me to leave the state.

42
Running to the FBI

ON MARCH 1, 1980, I CALLED NENA AND TOLD HER I was coming to Chicago. I had about $30,000 handy, and a coke dealer in Arizona owed me another $70,000. I gave my daughters all my furniture and loaded up my Lincoln with all the clothes and personal items I could fit. The day after I met with Larry Doss, I drove nonstop to Chicago.

Nena's apartment was small but adequate. And she was ecstatic to see me. "Maybe you could start a business, a legitimate business," she suggested. "The two of us could begin a new life. You can divorce Bunny, and we'll get married. I'd like to have a baby before I'm too old."

That just proved how well she didn't know me. Nena was a good kid, but I didn't want any of the things she wanted. It was a shame, really. I once was a nice guy. But I'd changed so much. Now I was a heel. As if to prove it, I smiled and nodded and went along with her for the time being.

"Yeah, sure, honey, whatever you want. But first let

me ask you a favor. You fly to Arizona a lot, right? Let me call my friend Fred in Tucson. He owes me some money and maybe you could pick it up.''

She agreed to be my courier, although I had to swear that it wasn't drug money she was picking up.

"I'm a gambler and a shylock," I said in mock indignation. "But you know I don't deal in drugs. I'm ashamed of you for even saying that."

What a woman doesn't know can't hurt her.

I stayed in Chicago for the next few months. *Marrone,* it was cold. I went out and bought a nice cashmere coat, but even that didn't help any. But mostly I missed the action. Nena was gone on runs for days at a time. When she came home we'd fuck and—invariably—argue. It got old.

The phone rang one day while Nena was gone, working a three-legged flight. I picked it up and it was Agent Larry Doss.

"Hey, Larry, why don't you stop breaking my balls," I said. "I got the fuck out of Florida because of you. So why don't you leave me alone?"

"But, Joe, I want to talk to you," he answered. "Can't we meet somewhere. I'll fly anywhere."

I was so lonely in Chicago that I almost took him up on his offer. Almost.

"Larry, you're talking like a fag," I told him. "I'm a Gambino, not an FBI agent. Don't get confused. Why the fuck would I risk meeting and talking to you? Now stop this harassment. Don't call me anymore, or I'll get a lawyer. Leave me the fuck alone." I hung up.

What a pain in the ass, I said to myself, but at least he won't call me anymore.

The phone rang right back. It was Larry Doss offering me his home phone number, in case I ever needed to get a hold of him, "for whatever reason." *Marrone,* the guy was sure a dedicated FBI agent. I wondered if he loved his job that much or if he just really wanted to be part of my crew.

I was getting tired of Chicago. Those midwesterners just aren't my type. I couldn't put my finger on it; they just acted different. They were nice enough people, and maybe that was it. I was used to dealing with snakes and morons. After Nena picked up the $70,000 from Fred in Tucson, and despite the good times I had with her—and there were a lot—I told her I was thinking about leaving.

I just wasn't ready to settle down. Nena deserved much better than me. I mean, I cared for her a lot, but I don't think I was mature enough to handle the situation. She needed a nine-to-five guy. I slept during those hours.

One morning in late May 1980, Nena and I had an argument. Real bad. She was getting ready for a flight, and I didn't want her to go. I was tired of hanging around that place alone. I missed my friends. I missed my crew. I missed the street.

"If you go on that flight, I'm leaving and you can go fuck yourself," I told her.

"I don't want to leave, Joe, but I'm still on probation," she said. Then she reminded me that the reason she was still on probation was because she had taken the leave to nurse me back to health after my heart attack.

"You remember that, don't you Joe?" she needled me. "I'm not like those other girls you bounced around with. Now I have to go. Kiss me goodbye."

I didn't, and she left. She wasn't out the door before I was on the horn summoning one of my crew.

"Fly to Chicago right away, Ronnie. I want you to drive me back."

Ronnie flew in that day. I had all my stuff loaded into the Lincoln by the time I picked him up at the airport. We left from O'Hare, and drove straight to Singer Island, Florida. I got a room poolside at the Best Western Sea-Spray Inn. I paid the desk clerk for a week. I wasn't in the room five minutes when the phone rang.

"Hello?"

"Joe! You just got back, huh? How was your trip?" Agent Larry Doss asked.

"Fuck you," I said and hung up the phone.

43
Ripping Off the Eye

LARRY CALLED BACK THE NEXT DAY, AND I AGREED TO meet him on the beach. One thing you have to understand about the mobster life: We were always talking to feds. Nobody ran from them. It was kind of an unwritten rule throughout the *Famiglias:* If the Eye approached, tell them what they want to hear, just don't tell them nothing.

There wasn't a wiseguy worth his button who wasn't polite and blandly accommodating whenever the G came around, from Joe N. Gallo to Tommy Agro to me. Plus, in this case I wanted to see what the feds had to say about the South Florida Colombo crew, the ones who allegedly had a contract out on me. I knew Larry Doss had been bullshitting when he said Tommy Farese wanted me whacked. But it wouldn't hurt to find out exactly what kind of game he was playing.

As we walked along the sand, Agent Doss popped the big question. "Joe, why don't you become my confidential informant? It won't go past me. I'll benefit by it. And I'll pick up all your living expenses."

"Fuhgedaboudit, Larry," I said. "I'm no stool pigeon."

"Think about it, Joe," he pressed. "If you help me, you got carte blanche. How about right now. Do you need some money? Could you use a thousand?"

I looked at the guy. He wasn't a bad guy. He was just doing his job. Squeezing me. The vibes were right for him. The Colombos were on my ass, T.A. was getting shorter and shorter with me. I wasn't earning. You might say it was a vulnerable time. I asked him to give me a couple of days to think about it. "I'm sure I'll hear from you," I added.

* * *

It was good to be back in Florida. I was in my old stomping grounds. I knew all the players, and I knew all the broads. Nena called, crying. But I convinced her that Chicago wasn't the place for me.

"Wait one year, and then we'll get married," I lied to her. "In the meantime, you come down here and see me once a month, because you fly for free, right?"

All I was thinking about was myself. I got a little shylocking going, a little bookmaking. It wasn't all that hard to pick up where I'd left off, although where I'd left off wasn't the greatest place in the world. The heart attack had really slowed me down.

But Nena did come to visit me occasionally. And when she did our routine never varied. We'd go to bed, satisfy our carnal cravings, and then begin to argue. We'd accuse each other of infidelities and then lie to each other and make up.

I didn't tell Nena that I was taking money from the FBI.

The Eye was picking up my hotel tab every week. The telephone bill alone averaged between $200 and $300. I signed for everything at the pool, in the gift shop, at the restaurant, and then I would meet with Agents Larry Doss and Gunnar Askeland and tell them a bunch of things they already knew. I told them nothing about the Gambinos. Well, next to nothing.

I would fly to New York occasionally to see Tommy and pay him the juice on his $32,000 I still had out on the street, and the feds would reimburse all my expenses. I would tell them who I met, where we ate, what we talked about—to a point. Frankly, most of the time I would have to embellish Tommy's moronic conversations. I didn't lie about anything. I just told them things I didn't think were important. Larry and Gunnar ate it up.

There were times when I gave them solid information. For instance, the latest bars and clubs where T.A. was hanging out. I once informed them that his new in-spot was the Manhattan nightclub Regine's, and sure enough T.A. was visited there by a Brooklyn Agent named Andris "Andy" Kurins. Kurins sent word back to Larry and

Gunnar that my info was good. And in exchange for these tidbits I lived and I ate and I drank for free. The FBI didn't even tail me anymore, an added bonus. I had no problems. I was a CI.

Of course, I was going through money fast. I'd returned from Chicago with most of the $70,000 Nena had picked up in Arizona. But that was almost gone. I was paying juice to T.A. every week, almost all of it straight out of my pocket. The people to whom I'd shyed out loans were not paying their interest. But that wasn't T.A.'s problem, as he was quick to remind me. And so soon after the heart attack I didn't feel like breaking heads.

We were in a recession. And the economy affected even the mob.

The '80 football season rolled around, and I got hit real hard from the start. It got to the point where I was doing so bad that I began relying on my FBI money to pay off my customers. I was still having a problem with Papo the doper and his Genovese crew, and at one point Tommy flew in with part of his Brooklyn crew when we thought there was going to be a showdown. We waited with guns. We were going to kill them. But they never showed up.

Tommy left and the FBI picked up his bill. I never told them why he'd been there. The SeaSpray Inn's Top O'Spray lounge and restaurant had been packed every night because a wiseguy was staying there.

By October 1980 I was down to about fifteen large. I'd gotten wrecked booking some NFL preseason exhibitions—I was stupid to list them—and I felt a decided financial pinch.

By November I was barely making ends meet even though the FBI was still picking up my hotel bills. I got pinched for pistol whipping some smart-ass in a bar, and had to lay out $5,500 bail. I held back T.A.'s juice payments for two months.

And by December I was running out of little treats to lead on the FBI. Since I'd refused to give them anything important, I wouldn't see them. I tried to make a deal with the manager of the nearby Colonades Hotel to kick back half of the FBI payments on a suite, but he wouldn't go for it. So when the Eye cut off my hotel expenses completely, I moved in with a broad named Donna, a bartender I knew from DeCaesar's, a nearby ribs joint with delicious food, and I mean delicious.

December came and went, and again I held back Tommy's juice. T.A. was calling all my usual hangouts, desperate to find me, but I was embarrassed. People weren't paying me, and I couldn't pay him. I didn't return any of his messages.

In January 1981, Donna and I moved into a cute little apartment in Riviera Beach. I was still calling Nena and telling her how much I loved her. She arranged for me to meet her in Hawaii, and I was happy, for my luck finally appeared to be changing. I won $35,000 at the Palm Beach Kennel Club—more than enough to pay back Tommy and to throw him a few thousand extra for his troubles. I figured I'd do this when I returned from Hawaii. I never made it there.

PART THREE

The Sting: Operation Home Run

44
Kicks and Punches and the Clanging of the Pipe

I ANSWERED THE PHONE IN OUR APARTMENT ON JANU-
ary 19, 1981, a date I'll never forget. Don Ritz, who
normally stuttered, sounded even more excited and nervous than usual.

"Joe, he's here! T—, T—, T—, T.A. is looking for
you! He's with two guys and he asked for your number
but I told him I didn't have it. He took Ronnie out somewhere, probably to get him to talk. And, Joe, you know
Ronnie. He'll sell out his own mother."

Ronnie Gerantino, part of my crew, the guy who'd
driven me back from Chicago, was all mouth and no
balls. I found out later that he'd been working as a confidential informant for Agent Larry Doss for the last couple
of years. He was the reason Doss knew I was back in
Florida so quick. He was also the guy who'd told Doss
the bullshit about Tommy Farese having a contract out
on me. Ronnie had nothing to tell him, so he made up the
story.

But even without knowing all that, right then I rued the
day I'd hired him. I only kept him around as a go-fer. He

191

was nothing like Don Ritz, or Aldo DiCuffa, or even Tony Micelli, another guy in my crew. If there was one guy in my crew who was going to rat me out, it was Ronnie.

"See if you can get to Ronnie and tell him to keep his mouth shut," I ordered Don Ritz. "I'm leaving tomorrow for Hawaii. And I want to leave with no problems."

Don warned me to "be prepared" before hanging up, and I dialed Larry Doss's number. I told the agent Tommy Agro and two thugs were in town looking for me. I told Larry I didn't know whether I should meet them or not.

"Get out of the apartment if you're afraid," Doss said.

"I'm not afraid, Larry," I lied. "I just want to get the fuck out of here tomorrow and see my girl from Chicago and then see Tommy A. when I get back."

"Joe, I don't understand why you're dodging him," Larry said. "You've been his right hand down here for ten years. Call me if you need me. Call me anytime." And then he hung up.

I hadn't told Larry I had some of Tommy's money shylocked out on the street. And I certainly hadn't told him I was in arrears on my juice payments. He didn't even know that I was going to Hawaii, or about the fact that I'd won thirty-five large at the dog track.

Around noon I answered the phone again. It was that motherfucker Ronnie Gerantino. "Joe, Tommy's here and he wants to see you. He has a couple of guys with him. Here he is."

"Joey," Tommy said, "come over here right away. I have a couple of guys I want you to find some construction work for."

"Why don't you bring them over to my place, Tip? I only live right across the bridge. Ronnie will show you the way."

"Nah," Tommy answered. "Come on over to Don Ritz's Pizzeria. We'll be waiting in the kitchen. And hurry up. I ain't got all fuckin' day. I have to go to Miami. So make it fast."

"I'll be there in a half-hour," I told him before hanging up. "I want to straighten you out anyway, and I have a present for you."

I sat for a few moments in deep thought. There was really nothing to be apprehensive about. I was, after all, a proposed member of the Gambino Crime Family. Tommy was my mentor. Why should I worry about $7,000 or $8,000 in back juice? My paranoia subsided. I convinced myself that all was well. There was, however, no harm in watching my back.

I called Larry Doss and told him I had spoken to T.A., and that everything was going to be all right. "I'm going over now," I added. "I'll be going in through the kitchen door. Just for the hell of it, why don't you and Gunnar try to cover me?"

He agreed, and then I called Nena, who was aware that I owed Tommy juice. "I'm going to see him now. I'll pay him what I owe him, and I'll call you this afternoon. It's only one more day, but I can't wait to see you, honey, I miss you so much. If you don't hear from me today, it means Tommy killed me."

It was a joke. Nena didn't find it so funny.

"Don't talk like that, Joe. If something did happen to you, I wouldn't know how to reach you. I can't see why you can't give me your number—unless you're living with a woman."

"Nena, I've told you, there's no incoming calls to this line. Can't you believe me for once in your life?"

I was a scumbag to the end. She told me to be careful. And she told me she loved me.

I grabbed the cash out of my freezer, where I kept it wrapped in tinfoil. I figured I'd pay T.A. the $8,000 juice, throw him a $5,000 peace pipe, and pay off $15,000 of the principal I owed, leaving me with a $17,000 debt. I left $10,000 in the freezer for the trip to Hawaii.

Singer Island was the fancy part of Riviera Beach, reached by bridge across the Intercoastal Waterway. I was there in fifteen minutes. I wore dress slacks and a silk shirt. The cash was in my back pocket, two stacks of $10,000 and one stack of $8,000.

I parked in the rear of Don Ritz's Pizzeria. As I opened the screen door to the kitchen I saw Tommy A., dressed in an expensive plaid sportcoat and an open-necked shirt. Tommy was always an extremely sharp dresser. Behind him was a bigger guy, Italian-looking and husky. To Tommy's left—my right—stood another strong-looking Italian guy.

I hadn't noticed the FBI outside. But I knew they'd be there. They were probably just well concealed.

I stuck out my hand to T.A., and moved to embrace him. He grabbed my hand hard and uttered what I seem to recall as "You motherfucker." Out of the corner of my right eye I saw an object that looked like a baseball bat or a pipe coming toward my head.

I sort of felt myself falling, as if it wasn't me, and I remember kicks and punches and the clanging of the pipe and the thrust of both a pipe and a bat and feet and fists to my head, face, and body.

After a while I felt nothing.

45
"Get Me My Money Right Away"

TWO DAYS LATER I WOKE UP IN A DARK ROOM. I FELT no pain. I could vaguely see. I saw a shadow hovering over me. It was like a blue ghost. Then I saw more blue ghosts. In a moment I could focus. The closest shadow was my daughter Sheryl. Behind her in a row were Bunny, my mother, Molly, and Donna. Eventually even Larry and Gunnar hove into view.

There was also a guy in a black robe. Hey, I know, it's a priest! I wondered why he was praying. Was I in heaven? Doubtful. Was I dying? How did I get here? What the fuck happened? I couldn't think, but I had to think. To remember. In the background I heard everyone crying. Bunny said to the priest, "Let me kiss him good-bye."

Suddenly the phone was ringing somewhere. Far away. No, not far away. In the room. Right next to me. A nurse appeared out of nowhere. "I'm sorry," she said to the huddled group, "but he's passed away."

I shot up to a sitting position. Everyone came rushing over. The priest said, "God has answered your prayers." I think he said this to my daughter.

The nurse screamed into the phone, "He's alive!" She handed the receiver to me. There was a bandage over my right ear. I pressed the receiver to my left.

"Joey?" The word was harsh, angry.

"Tommy? Tommy! Did you do this to me?"

"Shaddup, you motherfucker. You better get me my money right away!"

I lay there thinking. I don't know how long. Everyone was making a fuss. The priest began praying again. He had beads in his hand.

The doctor walked in and said it was "a miracle."

I stayed in the hospital for five days. Thinking. And crying.

How could my good friend do this to me? We were so close. There wasn't anything in the world I wouldn't have done for Tommy Agro. And he did this for $8,000? After all the money he'd made with me? I couldn't believe it. Me! Joe Dogs! His right hand down in Florida!

I didn't deserve this. Why hadn't he killed me? Why leave me like this, like a vegetable? I cried and cried for four or five days and then checked myself out of the hospital and went to Donna's.

I don't know who took me there. I don't remember much from that time. I stayed at Donna's and started to deteriorate slowly. I lost thirty pounds. I vaguely remember calling Nena. She had gone to Hawaii without me. She said she was glad I was alive.

Donna took good care of me. She was in love with me. I didn't reciprocate. I loved Nena. Or I thought I did. But it was Donna who nursed me back to the point where I could at least get up and walk around the apartment. She did this with ham and cheese sandwiches and canned chicken soup.

My mother dropped in to say goodbye, she was flying

back north. And then Larry and Gunnar came by with an offer they were sure I couldn't refuse.

The FBI agents thought they had compromised me, and that was the reason for the beating. I set them straight, and told them about the back juice. They were angry with me for not having told them before. "Maybe we could have gotten the money from the Bureau," Larry said. It was too late now.

Gunnar said that they had been outside of Don Ritz's, "but we didn't know what was going on until the ambulance arrived. Tommy and his guys must have left through the front door."

It didn't matter. This was my fault. I hadn't been straight with the Eye. Had I told Larry about the juice payments, this would never have happened. I pondered my options. I didn't want to go full-scale with the FBI. What I'd been doing as a confidential informant had been dangerous but peripheral. Now they wanted me to be a part of a wide-ranging operation concentrating on the Gambinos and the Colombos. I needed more time to think.

I called Bunny and pleaded with her to take me back.

"I'll be a good husband," I cried. "Please give me another chance. I can't stay here. Poor Donna loves me, but I can't love her back. Please take me back. I'll never cheat on you again."

"Oh, honey, don't cry," Bunny begged. "After all, I'm only human. But I've made a new life for myself. I'll be glad to take care of you for a while, to help you get back on your feet. I'll put my life on hold. But after you're well, I'll expect you to leave. I still love you in a lot of ways, Joe, but I've fallen in love with somebody else. He was there at my side when I needed him. I hope you understand, Joe."

What a bastard I was. It must have been agonizing for Bunny to tell me these things. I'd hurt her so bad. And here I was doing the same things to Donna and Nena.

"That's okay, Bunny, I'll take care of myself," I told her. "Thanks for being honest, and I wish you the best of everything. Let's always be friends. And I'll always love you."

I was in a lot of pain. In the hospital they'd pumped me with morphine and Darvon, and they'd given me pain-killers to take home. But I refused to eat them. I needed all my senses to build up a hate for T.A. and the Gambinos.

The injuries I'd received would scar me for life. My head was the size of a balloon. My nose was busted—not broken, but split open and crushed. I had a bump on my forehead the size of an orange. My teeth were cracked and broken. My right ear was partially severed. When they found me, it had been dangling from my head. I had broken ribs and swollen balls and cuts and bruises all over my body. I saw double for a full year because of the concussion.

I found out later that Don Ritz's wife, Marilyn, had walked in on the beating. She saw me splayed out on the ground, unconscious, Tommy kneeling over me with a meat cleaver upraised in his hand. One of his goons was holding my right arm extended. Tommy was going to chop off my hand. But Marilyn Ritz's terrified scream sent them scurrying out of the kitchen. She saved my life, and my hand.

Tommy began calling me at Donna's every day, always with the same threatening tone. But I was a vegetable. Finally, seeing no other alternative, I called the FBI.

46
Getting Even

LARRY AND GUNNAR HELPED ME DOWN THE STAIRS AND into a car where their supervisor was waiting. I told the three feds that I was ready to cooperate full-scale with their ongoing La Cosa Nostra investigation.

Gunnar Askeland was dubious. "Joe, you're finished

with those guys. You'll never get back in their good graces."

"Oh no? Gunnar, you don't know how wrong you are."

I turned to Doss and said, "Larry, you make those juice payments for me every week, and I'll get Tommy for you. I'll get all three of them."

I knew that to the Eye, Tommy A., his thugs, even me, were just means to an end. Bait, you might say. And that end was the big boys. Gallo. Persico. Castellano.

Gunnar tried to convince Larry that using me was a waste of time. Larry ignored him and had me sign papers stating that I would be willing to record all conversations with any and all organized crime figures. I also signed a piece of paper stating that I would testify to any evidence that I received in the course of an investigation. I told myself I was volunteering to be a cooperating witness. To the rest of the world I'd just become a stoolie.

Larry called the following day, and we met. It was hard for me to go far, because I couldn't drive. So I hobbled down the block, Larry and Gunnar picked me up, and I began my new job.

Larry wanted me to start taping T.A.'s calls. I told him that would be tough, because Donna would see the recorder, and word of something like that always leaks out. He agreed. Donna was a doll, and she treated me great. And even though I cared for her, I knew it was too late. The FBI gave me a pile of cash, and Larry and Gunnar began taking me around to look for an apartment.

They read the ads for me and drove me to different places. But they wouldn't go in. I went in alone and talked for myself, and I was turned down at two places because I looked like a mook. My head and face were still swollen, I had to cock my head at a forty-five-degree angle to clear the double vision, and my speech was thick and slow. I was also having trouble breathing, as there was a bone chip lodged in my nasal passage.

I wouldn't have rented an apartment to me, either.

The third place we tried was a condo in Lake Worth. I'd come full circle in Florida—out in the boondocks, about six miles south of Palm Beach. I went in, introduced myself, and decided to use a different approach. I told the rental agent I'd been in a terrible car accident and I'd just gotten out of the hospital. My wife and I were splitting up, I said, and I needed a furnished apartment immediately.

An hour later I'd signed a lease on a second-floor one-bedroom apartment for $650 a month. It was the middle of February 1981.

The FBI wanted me to move into my new place that night. But I needed a few days to sneak out on Donna. Two days later, while Donna was at work, I enlisted my daughter Sheryl and her husband to help me move. I felt like a heel. But it was time to start getting even with Tommy Agro.

I couldn't do anything alone, so Sheryl helped me get set up in my new place and did my grocery shopping, and when she heard me talking nice to T.A. over the phone she was sure I had brain damage. She didn't know that the FBI had installed a recorder on the phone in my bedroom. I taped every conversation. I'd let no one but Larry and Gunnar and Sheryl into the apartment.

Larry and Gunnar would call every morning, asking if the coast was clear. Then they'd come over. Even Sheryl wasn't allowed in unless she called first.

The FBI had given me $1,000 to send as a token to Tommy. This made the motherfucker happy.

In early March, as Sheryl was straightening up, she happened to ask what had happened to all that money I'd won at the dog track. "Holy Christ," I said, the light bulb going off over my head. I'd completely forgotten about the stash of cash in Donna's refrigerator. Then I recalled the money I'd had in my back pocket the day of the beating at Don Ritz's joint.

Tommy must have taken it, I figured, along with the gold watch, diamond ring, and gold chain that had been missing from my unconscious hulk when they discovered me. But I still had Donna's key. And I knew she was at work. "Sheryl, take me to Donna's right away," I said.

On the drive over I told Sheryl about the cash, and she

assured me that Donna wasn't the type to take it. But when we arrived at Donna's twenty minutes later, her front door was open and the landlord was standing on the porch.

"Who's going to pay for this mess?" he demanded.

The apartment was empty, and the walls were smeared with black-painted graffiti. "Fuck Joe," and "Hate Joe," and "Love Hate" were written all over. If Donna was the artist, she must have been one angry lady. I went into the kitchen and the refrigerator door was open. It was unplugged. The freezer was empty. The landlord told me Donna had been gone for six days. Someone had taken my money, and I knew it wasn't her. She took only her clothes. The furniture, which was hers, was still there.

"Who's going to pay for this?" he repeated.

"You know what you do, Frank," I told him. "You have the place painted, and in exchange keep the furniture. And if I hear one more word out of your mouth I'll blast *you* all over the walls. *Capisci?*"

I felt some of my old strength returning.

Don Ritz had opened up a new restaurant in West Palm Beach called Don Luigi's. He was partners with an attorney from Utica, New York. And Don had a problem. A Colombo wiseguy everyone knew as Donald Duck had brought a couple of thugs into Don Luigi's one night and beaten the hell out of Don Ritz with a blackjack. Don called me the next morning.

"Sure," I said, "this is all T.A.'s fault. Now the fucking Colombos are making a move because they think I'm weak. Let me call that *sciallo.*" That fucking jackal.

I called Tommy in New York and explained what was going on with Donald Duck and the Colombos. I taped the conversation. I taped every conversation I had, even Don Ritz's, but one.

"Tell Don Ritz to carry a gun and blow their fuckin' heads off if they come back," Tommy said. "Tell your whole crew to carry guns, and not just to make their belts tight."

But my crew was scared, and I didn't blame them.

They weren't messing with kids. The Colombos were bad motherfuckers.

The next day, March 5, Larry and Gunnar came over to listen to my tapes. They mentioned that Tommy sounded annoyed and suggested I try to goad him into flying off the handle.

"Antagonize him, Joe," Larry said. "Generate some conversation. You know him. You can make him nuts. Maybe you can get him to say something he'll be sorry for later."

Don Ritz called again with a Colombo update, and at 1:30 A.M. on the morning of March 7, 1981, Tommy called me. I told him that the night before, Johnny Irish, Freddie Campo, Pasquale "Checko Brown" Fusco, and Robbie had all eaten dinner at Don Luigi's. They'd been asking a bunch of questions about me. Wanting to know if I was still attached to T.A. Later that same night, I told Tommy, I'd taken a cab to Joey's Restaurant and Disco in Riviera Beach and run into the same crew.

Freddie Campo, the former free agent, had been cozying up to the Colombos since failing to collect his race-fixing money from Tommy years before. He'd finally seen the wisdom of aligning himself with a *Famiglia*.

"I sent them over a drink, and they didn't even acknowledge it," I reported. "You'd think they'd have sent me one back."

"I wouldn't have sent them my cock," T.A. said.

"Well, Tip, I hate to say it, but you brought this on yourself."

It wasn't hard to trigger Tommy Agro. All you had to do was insinuate that he was at fault for something. I had pulled that trigger.

"Me?" he ranted. "I'm at fault? I got people that will eat the fucking eyes out of your fucking head. You dumb bastard! And they're as loyal as a motherfucker. With balls the size of cows. All I have to do is tell them to load up, be in this place at this time, and they'll walk in and blast everybody. No fuckin' hesitation. No nothin'. And don't look for nothin' beside it. No questions asked. They'll blow you up. You think you got something going? You got nothing going!

"You think I'm easy? You think I'm where I'm at today because I'm easy? What I've done, you haven't dreamt of, my friend. Why do you think people fear me? Because I was a hard-on, you fuckin' moron? You think I got where I was because I was a jerkoff in the street? You're easy, you motherfucker. The most wrongest thing you ever did was fuck me. People fear me, you dumb fuck. You're only alive today, my friend, because Don's wife walked in. Not because we stopped. You wasn't supposed to walk away no more. And I'm gonna even enlighten you more better than that, while you're having these fuckin' hallucinations. I missed you three times. I was there looking for you two other times before this, you dumb motherfucker."

The tape is a classic. Tommy Agro had incriminated himself—the dumb fuck had admitted everything. I stretched out on my bed and smiled as he went on raving for another twenty minutes. He ended his harangue by promising to fly in the following night to let the fuckin' Colombos know who ran Don Ritz's place.

I wanted to play the tape back after he hung up, but I didn't dare touch it. I didn't know too much about tape recorders, and this was one screed I didn't want erased by mistake. I supposed it could wait until morning.

"Did you hear from Tommy A.?" Larry asked expectantly, brandishing his portable tape recorder. He and Gunnar had arrived at my place around ten-thirty. It was payday. I was doing this for $500 a week plus expenses —or about the amount I used to throw away in tips in one night.

"Oh yeah," I answered nonchalantly. "We talked for a while early this morning. Why don't you give it a listen."

Larry collected the tape while Gunnar pulled out a Form 302, the kind they used to write up their intelligence reports. I handed Larry the two tapes, the one from Don Ritz and the one from the rabid Tommy A. After listening to the first, Larry mentioned that "Don seems kind of scared. I know I'd be if what happened to you and Don happened to me. Wouldn't you, Gunnar?"

Gunnar nodded dutifully. The two FBI agents played

as a team. Larry's role was to be in charge, Gunnar's was that of the agreeable yes man. I went along with their charade. It didn't make any difference to me. They were both nice guys who I sensed didn't know too much about organized crime. But they both tried hard, and that counted for something with me.

They put on Agro's tape. I walked into the kitchen and began brewing coffee. After twenty minutes of small talk between me and T.A., Gunnar Askeland turned and said with exasperation, "Joe, does he say anything relevant during this conversation?"

"Yeah, I think so, Gunnar. It gets better about five minutes from now."

You had to see the look on the FBI agents' faces when Tommy began ranting and raving and admitting what he'd done to me. Then he admitted that the beating had been planned for weeks. Larry was so elated he jumped around the apartment like a jackrabbit. Gunnar came over to me and stuck out his hand.

"I'm sorry for doubting you, Joe," he said. "You did a great job."

"We can nail him with this," Larry added. "Premeditated. Conspiracy. He's going to be one sorry wiseguy."

They packed up my tapes and instructed me to call them at home, no matter the time, if and when T.A. reached out for me. After they left, Sheryl called and asked if I needed anything. I told her Tommy was coming down and I was concerned.

"Don't see him, Dad. He'll hurt you again," Sheryl said. "Is there anything I can do for you?"

"Yeah, honey," I said. "Come on over and clean my apartment."

47
È Pulito, He's Clean

TOMMY CALLED AT MIDNIGHT.

I was now in the habit of pressing the "record" button whenever I picked up the phone. I always made sure there was a fresh tape in the machine. The only person I didn't tape, I wouldn't tape, was Little Dom. It was part of the deal.

"I'm here, Joey, at the Dip. Come and see me tomorrow."

"I'm hurt, Tip," I whimpered. "I'm hurt bad. Please don't hurt me anymore. I didn't do anything wrong. Can't it be over? Can't we start fresh?"

My begging was not a facade. I was really afraid. I dreaded facing him so soon. It had been seven weeks since the beating, and my head was still a mess. The scars from the stitches were still raw.

"Joey, I'm not gonna do nothing to you," Tommy said. "I didn't come here for you. I came here for that Don Ritz thing. I swear on my daughter Kimmy, Joey! I won't do that no more. Believe me, it's all over. I'll never do that again. I really did come here for Don. I've had guys down here for three days now, in case there's a problem."

"You have your guys with you?" I asked.

"Joey, they're not here for you, believe me. Would I tell you they were here if I was gonna hurt you, you dumb fuck?"

"Okay, Tip," I said. "I'll be there around noon, by the pool. It takes me longer to drive now because it's hard for me to see."

I hung up and called Larry. "Don't go anywhere until

Gunnar and I see you," he told me. "We'll be there at nine in the morning."

I had problems sleeping that night. I was trying to convince myself that everything was going to be all right. I wasn't doing a very good job. I kept visualizing being beaten with bats and pipes by a mob of guys. I must have fallen asleep sometime around six. The telephone woke me at eight. Larry and Gunnar were on their way.

I made coffee as Larry and Gunnar listened intensely to my conversation with T.A. After it ended, they pleaded with me not to go.

"We can't cover you good at the pool," Gunnar said. "It's the season, and the place will be mobbed. Don't be foolish. You've done enough."

They sure sounded as if they really were concerned for my safety. It didn't matter.

"Look, guys," I explained. "If I don't go to see him, chances are he comes to see me. It would look too suspicious if I don't go. It'll start him to wondering."

Larry and Gunnar wouldn't buy it. They offered to take me to their homes to protect me. I finally convinced them that I had a feel for Tommy's voice, and I knew everything was going to be all right.

But I didn't really.

On the drive down I-95 to the Diplomat I watched Larry and Gunnar through my rearview mirror. I had to steer with my head cocked at an angle in order to see. It took me an hour and a half. I drove like an old lady. The valet parking attendant recognized me and there were no charges. I noticed he charged Larry and Gunnar.

The Olympic-sized pool was packed with tourists. Tommy's cabana was at the south end, near the wading pool. My stomach sunk when the first guys I saw were Paul Principe and Frank Russo, the two sluggers who'd helped Tommy beat me to a pulp. They were staring at me. I slowed down, looking for Tommy.

I became even more nervous when I saw Checko Brown, the Colombo soldier, talking to Fat Andy Ruggiano, the Gambino capo. Bobby DeSimone was there, fresh from a short prison stretch. I stopped in my tracks and started to tremble. I didn't know whether to run or what. I was frozen to the pavement. Tommy came hurrying over.

"Joey, don't worry, relax. Didn't I tell you we wasn't going to do that no more?"

We embraced.

"What are they doing here?" I asked, motioning to Checko and Fat Andy.

"Everybody at the pool is with me," Tommy said. "Come. Sit down. Take off your shirt. Get some sun."

It was an odd request. Checko was fully dressed. So were Fat Andy and DeSimone. Tommy and the two thugs were in bathing suits. Then I realized. They were expecting a wire. All six stared at me as I pulled off my Ban-Lon.

Everyone seemed to relax a little. We made small talk for about twenty minutes. Though I noticed that the conversation still wasn't going anywhere, as if they were afraid to talk about business.

"Christ, it's hot," I said. "I wish I'd brought a suit."

Everyone in the area heard me, and it loosened things up.

"Tommy, don't you have an extra suit in your room?" Fat Andy asked. "Come on, you're about the same size as Joe Dogs."

I was insulted. Tommy had a good five inches on me.

Anyway, Tommy didn't. But Paulie Principe did. Checko Brown walked me to Paulie's hotel room, and I wondered what the agents were thinking—if they were even still there. I started to get my balls back. I wanted to kill every one of those guys.

Checko found the swimsuit, and I got naked in front of him. Unless the wire was up my ass, they knew I was clean. When we reached the pool the crew looked at me, then to Checko.

"È pulito," Checko said. He's clean. What the fuck? I wondered. Did he think I didn't understand him? I mean, did the fucking moron think I was Japanese or something because my eyes were still swollen?

But everyone came closer to me after that—except Paulie and Frankie, who remained in the pool. I'd made the right move. Business could now commence.

"Joe Dogs, I was telling Tommy that you said Don Ritz was with you, and to leave him alone," Checko began. "Remember that time I wanted to break his head and you stopped me? Remember?"

"Yeah," I answered.

"Well, I told Tommy that this recent stuff, no way we were involved," Checko said, lying through his teeth.

"Oh, we believe you," Tommy interjected. "Why shouldn't we believe you?"

That was good enough for Checko Brown. He stood, kissed everyone on the cheek, and left.

He wasn't past the pool before Tommy was calling him a "fucking liar."

"Didn't I tell you he'd deny everything," T.A. ranted. He was looking at me, filling me in. "I went to see the Colombo *Famiglia* underboss Gerry Lang yesterday. I told him what that fuckin' pimp Johnny Irish and Checko did to Don Ritz. We had a sit-down. That's why Andy's here. I told Gerry Lang that Don Ritz is with Joe Dogs, Joe Dogs is with me. So that makes Don Ritz with me. Whatever happened between Joe Dogs and me is nobody's fucking business."

"Of course he's a fucking liar," I said. "Did you see his nose start to grow? It was growing like Pinocchio's grew when he told a lie. You know Pinocchio, don't you, Tommy?"

"No, I don't. Who the fuck is he with?"

"Forget it," I said. "I thought you knew him."

Fat Andy was laughing, and said, "Tommy, he's fucking around with you."

"Fucking-A, Joey." Tommy was exasperated. "I'm down here trying to take care of business, and you're fucking around."

Fat Andy changed the subject before things got out of hand. Andy was a big sloppy guy. You'd never think he was a wiseguy. What with the double chins and the bulging eyes and all the polyester. But he was always so quiet that when he spoke he commanded a world of respect.

"Joe, you know what I have in mind?" he asked. "I'd like to start a private club in your area. Do the people up your way like to gamble with cards? You know, black-jack and poker?''

"Yeah. Why?'' The people up my way? Christ, the guy lived an hour south of Palm Beach. You'd think he was talking about Alaska.

"Well, Tommy tells me that you and that guy Freddie Campo got a cop on the pad,'' Fat Andy continued. "And I was thinking maybe he could help get us a private-club charter, a bring-your-own-bottle club. Maybe this cop can kind of make sure that nobody bothers us.''

Tommy, Fat Andy, and I discussed the idea for over an hour. T.A. and Fat Andy told me to reach out for the cop and to do it quickly, as they wanted to get started. They both walked me back to Tommy's cabana, where I got dressed and started to leave.

"Joe, why don't you come back down tonight and see the show with us,'' Fat Andy suggested. "Air Supply is in the big room.''

"Yeah, come on back down and we'll talk some more,'' Tommy agreed.

I told them I'd like to bring along my daughter and her husband. Not only was Sheryl a big Air Supply fan, but I still couldn't see well enough to drive at night. No problem.

On the drive home I didn't see the agents, so I assumed they had left. I decided not to tell them about the swimsuit ploy unless they saw it. Now that Tommy and Fat Andy wanted to start up a club, I wasn't sure where this investigation would go. I didn't mind helping the FBI for a little longer, as long as I was still fucked up physically. But by Tommy coming down and flexing his muscles, I realized I'd be able to go back on the streets with the same respect, if not more. Maybe I could figure out a way to revenge myself on Agro without working with the feds.

But what about those papers I'd signed? Here, I thought, I had a problem. I had many possibilities to consider. Little did I realize at the time that the evidence I'd gathered poolside at the Diplomat would ultimately lead to one of the biggest and most successful undercover operations in the history of organized crime.

48

"You Should Have Shot Me, Tommy"

THE COP ON THE PAD THAT TOMMY AND FAT ANDY referred to was named William "Boone" Darden. He was the chief of police in Riviera Beach, Florida. Freddie Campo had had Boone on his payroll since God knows when. Boone protected Freddie's bookmaking operation and—for the right price—was usually available with the kind of small-talk, cop-talk information you spent like money.

When I returned to Lake Worth that afternoon, I called Larry Doss. I told him I needed money because I had to go back down south again. I also advised him to bring his pad and pencil. He would definitely want to write up a Form 302. The agents' handwritten Form 302s would later be typed at the FBI office in the event any investigation led to trial. They are considered evidence.

Larry arrived, and I told all. I also insisted that I was comfortable taking my daughter and son-in-law back down for the show. What I needed from him was enough money to pick up the entire tab. "Let's blind them with greed," I said. He was all for it and handed me $1,000.

"Try to bring me some change," he said on his way out.

When the maitre d' showed us to Tommy's table, everyone stood and embraced. There were Tommy and some Chinese broad, Fat Andy, DeSimone and his wife, Betty, and Joe "Piney" Armone's wife and daughter. Armone, T.A.'s capo, was nowhere to be seen. The thugs Paulie and Frankie arrived just before the show.

We ate. We drank. We listened to Air Supply. And when the check for the evening arrived I wrestled

Tommy Agro for it. He threatened to break my jaw. I told him he didn't hit hard enough. That brought a smile to Tommy's face. Our tab came to $470. I gave the waiter $600 and told him to keep the change.

Tommy noticed and gave me a wink. "I see you're back in action," he whispered.

"Hey, Tom, I'm dealing in the babonia," I told him. "You know the money that's in that dope. I'm just starting to get on my feet. But don't say nothing to Fat Andy. *Capisci?*"

"Joey, I don't tell anyone anybody's business. Just be careful and don't get caught, because this club Andy's talking about is going to be a good thing—especially if you can get to the cop. He's an eggplant, isn't he?"

He meant black. "Yeah, but I'm pretty sure he's with us."

After the show, Tony the maitre d' had our table waiting in the Tack Room. We were all talking and having a good time when Tommy suddenly asked me to take a walk.

"Where?" I said, a little apprehensively.

"To my room, Pip. I want to talk to you alone."

My daughter caught the drift of our conversation, came over, and said, "Daddy, Michael and I are really tired. We want to go now."

"Wait ten minutes more, darling," Tommy cut in. "I want to talk to your father for a while."

"I'll be right back," I told Sheryl, leaning over to kiss her cheek. Then Tommy and I excused ourselves and left for his room.

"Does your daughter know about our falling out?" he asked as we walked to his first-floor suite.

"Nah, are you kidding?" I lied. "She never would have come tonight. She thinks the Colombos did this, and you're here to straighten things out."

We arrived at T.A.'s suite and he poured me a Scotch over ice. I wondered whether he'd planned on this meeting, since he had my brand of Scotch sitting on the bar.

"Nah," Tommy said. "That fuckin' petunia I'm with drinks Dewar's White Label. I don't know how any of you can drink that shit. It tastes like medicine."

"It's what you acquire a taste for," I told him. "Some people like black broads. Some people like white. I notice that you're always with dark broads."

"Joey, my broad isn't black. She's a Chink. What, are you color blind? She's red."

"Red is what she ain't, Tommy. But she ain't white either. I suppose that's what all you Sicilians are used to. After all, it's only a short swim to Ethiopia."

"Listen, you fuckin' suitcase, there's something I want to tell you," Tommy said. "But you have to promise me it doesn't go any further than this room. Because if it does, it'll make me look bad, and I'll have a bad taste in my mouth."

"Who would I tell?" I asked, throwing up my arms. "You see how quiet I am. Even to Andy, and he's a capo in our *Famiglia*."

"That's good, Joey," Tommy said. "Because Andy's a goodfellow on Neil's side. You know? The under. Now don't misunderstand me. Fat Andy may be here, but I'm closer to Paulie."

Tommy was referring to a rift that had developed in the Gambino Family between the forces of Boss Paulie Castellano and those allied behind his underboss, Aniello "Neil" Dellacroce. A couple of years later Dellacroce's people, led by John Gotti, would declare war, whacking Big Paulie. I knew all about this intrigue. But for Tommy I played dumb.

"You got me all confused now, Tip," I said. "I thought we were all one big happy Family. So who are we with? And where do I belong? I thought Paulie was the boss and Neil was the underboss. What are there, two Families in one? Gambino Seniors and Gambino Juniors? I don't know what the fuck you're talking about."

Tommy laughed with me for a moment, but suddenly his face turned serious.

"Joey, I didn't want to hurt you the way I did," he said. "It wasn't my fault. My *compare*, Joe Gallo, made me do it. It wasn't me or the money you owed me. He just used that as an excuse to get to you. I swear, Joey. It wasn't me."

"But why did Gallo want to hurt me?" I asked. "After

all the money he made with us on the dope? On the race-track scam? And what about that beating I gave that guy in Naples for his little fucking bitch?"

"Stop, Joey! Stop right there! I told you once before never to talk like that about my *compare*. That's the reason. That guy you fucked up, the zip with the sister. You fucked him up too much. You weren't supposed to hurt him that bad. That girl, Sophia, left my *compare* over that. It's been eating at him ever since, and he blames you."

I was flabbergasted. This happened to me all because of a cunt! It couldn't be. Tommy had to be lying.

"But what about the proposal that you told me about, the proposal to get me a button?" I asked. "Was that all bullshit? I mean, Gallo had to okay it. You were supposed to be my mentor. And Gallo was your mentor. You even brought me to your capo, Joe Piney. I don't understand.

"That's why I wasn't too worried about the back vig that I owed," I continued. "You knew I'd catch up. For eight months after my heart attack I paid you out of my pocket for guys on the street who weren't paying me. Did you know that? No, you didn't. Because I was too much of a fucking man to come crying to you and get someone else hurt."

"I know, Joey, I know," Tommy mumbled. "What can I say except that my *compare* wanted you *morto!* It's a good thing Don's wife walked in. You would have been either dead or with no right hand."

I said, "You should have shot me, Tommy. You should have killed me. I didn't deserve to be left like this. I've been nothing but loyal to you for ten years. And look at me. I'm fucked up. I look like a freak. I can't even eat without cocking my head. I don't even feel the liquor I'm drinking. All this because Joe Gallo blames me for his cunt! You wouldn't have done this to Bobby. You feel too sorry for him. That's what you told me, anyway."

The mention of DeSimone's name triggered something in T.A. His face looked like a fist.

"Bobby! Bobby! You know why I feel sorry for Bobby? Because I was the one that whacked both of his brothers. That's why! Remember the guy, Bobby's brother, he worked for you once? The guy that once bought me a watch?"

"Yeah," I said. "Anthony DeSimone." Back in the early '70's I'd gotten Bobby's youngest brother a no-show job on one of my construction sites. I didn't know it at the time, but the Gambinos and the Colombos both had a contract out on Anthony. He ratted some of them out to feds in New York. Tommy now explained to me that he'd lured Anthony DeSimone back to New York under the pretense of a sit-down and whacked him.

"And then a couple years later I had to whack the other one, Tommy," T.A. went on.

"Tommy DeSimone, that fucking nut!" I blurted out. "The real suitcase? The one we met at Bobby's house when we were all playing pinochle, and he started throwing darts at us because he was losing?"

"That's right," T.A. said. "Remember I told you he had a problem with some good people? And he was claiming to be around me? Well, he ended up with a Lucchese crew, Paulie Vario's, and then he whacked a wiseguy in our Family. He whacked Billy Batts. So, Vario and the Luccheses had a sit-down with Neil Della-croce, and Gallo came to me and told me that I had the contract, because I knew him very well. That fucker John Gotti had me set up to do this. Me and that motherfuckin' Gotti never got along. Batts was part of Gotti's crew, and my *compare* told me Gotti went to the under, to Neil, and said, 'Give this to T.A.' Gotti wanted him nailed as soon as possible. 'Let that bigmouth Agro do it' is how I hear he said it.

"Joey, listen to me, Pippie," he continued. "In this life you do what you're told. They pick the closest people to whack one another, and if you don't do it it's bye-bye for you. *Capisci?*"

Tommy looked pathetic. We went back to the Tack Room, and Fat Andy gave me his home phone number.

"Call me as soon as you find out about the cop," he said.

But I wasn't paying that much attention. I couldn't

take my eyes off Bobby DeSimone. I felt so sorry for the poor bastard.

I had two more Scotches and didn't feel a thing. Fat Andy and T.A. talked as if nothing had ever happened between us. I invited the crew to Don Luigi's the next night for dinner. I would cook. Tommy and Fat Andy wanted to hit Joey's Disco and a few other joints afterward with me and the crew. It was an exercise in muscle flexing.

I decided not to tell the FBI about the conversation in Tommy's room. I wouldn't lie to them. I just wouldn't tell them.

That fuck Gallo is mine, I thought. No one else's but mine.

49
Poison in the Sauce

"CHRIST, LARRY, I DIDN'T KNOW YOU AND GUNNAR worked weekends. Do you get time and a half, or double time?"

I was handing Agent Doss his $400 change from my night at the Dip.

"I have to cook for them tonight," I said, and Larry asked me what kind of cover I needed. None, I told him. We would only be in Don Ritz's. I was safe there.

Tommy showed up at Don Luigi's with Fat Andy and the crew in tow. I looked at DeSimone in a different light now. But Principe and Russo still gave me the creeps. Don Ritz got everyone seated in a private room in the rear of the restaurant, and I headed off to the kitchen to prepare my famous caponata, one of Tommy's favorites. While I was cooking, Don Ritz joined me. He looked nervous.

"Christ, Joe, I can't believe these guys," he stuttered.

"They come down here, beat you, leave you for dead, and then they want you to cook for them. I wou—, wou—, wou—, wouldn't do it."

I laughed to myself. Don was a real nice guy. He had a heart of gold and he ran a good restaurant. All he wanted to do in life was make good pizzas.

"Yeah, Don, that's just how they are. I hope they like the caponata, because they didn't like the fettuccine I made. They almost killed me over it."

"I don't know how you can fuck around like that," Don said. "Don't you hate them?"

"Nah. Why should I hate them? By the way, Don, do you have any arsenic? I'm going to kill the whole group."

"Joe, quit fucking around," he said. "I just got this joint. My partner and I stuck a lot of money in here. If you want to whack them, please do it somewhere else."

Don's stuttering became even more pronounced when Bobby DeSimone walked into the kitchen.

"Joey! Joey!" DeSimone said in his fag voice. "I was telling Tommy that you make the best caponata I ever tasted."

"I'm glad you like it, Bobby. But listen, this ain't my joint, so you can't hang around back here. You'll get in the chef's way."

As DeSimone was walking back out, I said loud enough for him to hear, "Don, hand me that shit I wanted to mix into the sauce."

A light bulb went off over Bobby's head. He half turned, looked at me, and continued out.

"Wh—, wh—, why did you say that?" Don asked. "Now he's going to tell them there's poison in the sauce."

"Fuck 'em." I said. "Let them sweat a little."

I spooned the sauce over the perciatelli and told Don to serve it to the crew while I washed up. He brought it out and walked back in smiling three or four minutes later.

"They want you to eat with them," Don said without a stutter. "They're waiting for you before they start."

I walked out of the kitchen with a grin. "C'mon, fellas, dig in."

"After you," Fat Andy insisted. "Here, let me put some on a plate for you, Joe. I mean, after all, you did all the cooking and we want to show our appreciation. Honey? Honey, bring Joe Dogs a nice Scotch. Dewar's, isn't it, Joe?"

Andy filled my dish and told me to dig in while he and the other guys filled their plates. I took a couple of healthy bites and licked my chops. Everyone stared.

"Aren't you guys going to eat?" I asked as I filled my mouth again. They started eating, and the compliments began rolling in.

We got around to discussing Chief Boone Darden and what he could do for the club. Fat Andy and Tommy told me not to let it die. There was, they said, plenty in this for everyone. Tommy gave the waitress a fifty-dollar tip, thanked Don for the drinks, and invited him to go bouncing with us. Don, saying he had to lock up, declined.

We hit a couple of joints and ended up at Joey's Disco. Tommy wanted people to see me with him. The Colombos wouldn't be around anymore. Al Capone got his point across. You can't fuck with the Gambino Family. You can try, but you won't get away with it.

At home that night I lay in bed wondering what to do. I didn't know whether to remain on the Eye's payroll or chase Larry and Gunnar altogether. I definitely wanted to get even with Tommy and Joe Gallo. I didn't care if Tommy had gotten an order from the *consigliere* to kill me. He should have brought it higher, to Neil Dellacroce, or even Paulie Castellano. Gallo was a love-sick old fuck. Castellano would have squashed the contract.

Finally I decided that I couldn't leave the FBI. They'd been good to me. They'd helped me get over the worst part. I'd have to have been a real prick to boot them now. I figured sooner or later it would come down to me pointing my finger at Tommy Agro from the witness box. What the hell, the feds would find me somewhere safe to live.

But what if they couldn't protect me? Guys had gotten whacked in the Witness Protection Program before. I was in limbo. I decided to wait another week before making a decision.

50
"Your Closest Friend Will Whack You"

LARRY AND GUNNAR CAME OVER THE NEXT MORNING. Larry pulled out a Form 302 and told me his West Palm Beach superior had teletyped a request for more money to their Washington headquarters. They wanted to expand our undercover operation. When I told them about Fat Andy's club idea, and Chief Darden, Larry seemed to get nervous. This was big stuff for two guys operating out of an office in the Florida backwater.

Neither one of them could sit still. Larry, in fact, was running around like a chicken with its head cut off. I liked Larry, and I liked Gunnar. They had become my buddies.

"Joe," Larry said, "if this thing goes all right with headquarters and we start getting into this undercover operation big time, you're going to have to start taping Little Dom Cataldo."

"No, Larry," I told him. "No fucking way. I told you before, and I'll tell you again. Dominick is my friend. I won't record him. Everyone else, yes. But we shook hands on this decision and I want you to stand by your word. I'll keep mine. Dominick does not go on tape. Not by me, anyway."

"Okay, Joe. That was our agreement. But I think you're making a big mistake. Remember what even Tommy A. said: 'They pick the closest people to whack one another, and if you don't do it it's bye-bye for you.'"

"Dom's not like that," I argued, ruing the day I ever mentioned Tommy's line to the feds. "He's my friend."

"Well, Joe, I believe Tommy A.," Larry said. "But if you're too blind to see, if you can't read the handwriting on the wall, then I feel sorry for you."

What the hell did Agent Larry Doss know? Sure, Dom was a killer. But I didn't want to tape him. I wouldn't tape him. At any rate, I decided to play it by ear for a week or so. But I continued to tape Tommy and about ten days later Larry told me that the Eye had approved money for an undercover sting. The feds wanted me to generate some conversations with Boone Darden.

After a long night of thinking, I came to a decision. I decided to go all the way with the FBI and leave the Mafia for good.

51
Wired

I'D BEEN WORKING FOR THE FEDS FOR TWO MONTHS TO the day when I called Police Chief Boone Darden and made my first appointment with him. We set up a meet at Joey's Disco.

I was wearing a Nagra body recorder. It was a rather large, bulky, and out-of-date recorder for an investigation like this. But it was all the West Palm Beach office had. If this was rural Ocala, where they have no organized crime but a lot of horse farmers, then I would have been supplied with the most modern, sophisticated equipment. That was the way the "empty suits" in the Eye worked. They got everything bass-ackward. I was to find out later that both the Manhattan and Brooklyn offices had the same problem. The joke was that the agents on Guam always got the best equipment.

Joey's Disco had a roof deck, and on the afternoon of March 23, 1981, Boone Darden sat up there as if he owned the place. Waitresses hovered about him as he sipped his beer. I extended my hand to shake, and when we clasped, a smile creased his face. I'd palmed three hundred-dollar bills. Talk about coming cheap! Boone took them as if he'd been taking bribes all his life. He probably had.

We made small talk over a couple of dozen clams. Finally I got to the point.

"The boys down south want to get a charter club going up here, Boone. You know, little poker, little blackjack. Bring your own bottle. Private. But we won't do it unless we're in your good graces. *Capisci?*"

"I understand, Joe. Tell you what, let me think it over for a week. There's an election coming up, you know. City Council. I want to see who's getting in and who's getting out. I don't foresee any problem if one certain friend of mine gets in. And to tell you the truth, this town needs something like that. A little action. And I can help. But give me a week."

"Sure, Boone," I obliged. "You understand that you can earn from this, too. We aren't the type of people who eat alone. You know that, right?"

"Oh yeah, I know," Boone answered. "You're good people, and you and Freddie been friends for a long time. Joe, I'm glad you called. As long as I'm chief I'm sure we can work something out."

After he left I said, for the benefit of the Nagra, "That was Boone Darden." I gave my name, the time, and the date. I had a couple more drinks, paid the check, and left. I saw the agents following me home. Gunnar unhitched the Nagra. Larry took a Form 302. Then they both left.

By April of 1981 the undercover sting was well under way. I had lunch with a Palm Beach county official who offered to help us set up our club. This guy did favors for his friends, and I was now one of them. T.A. was greasing him for a license for an illegal bingo joint, and I was the go-between. He was a typical double-talking politician, and in my opinion the tapes I made of him were worthless. But the FBI liked them. They seemed to get a special hard-on when they thought they could nail a public official.

In the middle of April I took a few days off to visit Nena in Washington, D.C. She had flown there to visit her mom and dad, who worked for a senator. We stayed at her mom's, I cooked several Italian dinners, and her parents seemed to like me.

Back in Florida, I met with Freddie Campo, who was angry with me for approaching Boone without his say-so.

"Boone is with me," Freddie said loudly, and I thought of the Nagra spinning under my shirt. "He's been with me for a long time. And I'll kill to protect what's mine."

"Okay, Fred, take it easy," I told him. "I meant no harm. He did mention your name, but never said anything about having to get your okay. But look, no problem. I'll tell Fat Andy what you said, and then he'll ask your permission."

After I left Freddie I had to laugh. I couldn't wait to tell Fat Andy. It's too bad I couldn't play him the tape.

The agents met me at my apartment, removed the Nagra, and took down a Form 302.

"You better not tell Fat Andy what Freddie said," Larry warned me after listening to the tape. "We both know Andy will hurt him."

"Fuck him!" I said. "He's standing in our way, so the best way to take care of it is to tell the truth, and whatever happens, happens."

Larry was dubious, but Gunnar agreed. That night I got word to Fat Andy about Freddie.

Throughout the spring of '81 I met every two weeks with Bobby DeSimone to deliver T.A.'s juice payments. Bobby was Tommy's conduit. I was not yet totally back in Tommy's good graces, and if I wanted to talk to T.A., I would have to call Bobby first and tell him to have Agro call me. It was a three-ring circus until sometime in June, when Tommy finally realized that without Joe Dogs he would have nothing going in Florida. Or so I made him think.

At any rate, the day I taped Freddie I met with DeSimone and told him to pass on Freddie's message to Fat Andy.

Bobby must have told the Gambino capo right away, because I got a call that night from Andy instructing me to meet him at the Thunderbird Hotel in North Miami the next night, May first. Larry and Gunnar were nervous. It was the Nagra's—and my—first big test.

"We'll have Miami agents to cover you," Larry instructed. "Your code name will be Bob Jackson. If you have any problem, any at all, try and get to the men's room. An agent will follow you and ask if you're Bob Jackson. If there's a situation, tell him yes. If you're all right, tell him no. *Capisci?*"

"*Capisco*," I answered. "And, hey, Larry, don't be learning too much Italian. I won't be able to talk about you."

They wired me up, and I drove down I-95 to Miami. Christine Lee's gourmet Chinese restaurant, off the lobby of the Thunderbird, was our meeting spot. I walked in at half past eight. I really didn't feel nervous at all.

Fat Andy was at the bar with Bobby DeSimone and three sluggers from his crew, Joe Blaze, Gerald Alicino, and Frank "Junior" Abbandando. I had a couple of drinks and we all relaxed. After a while, with the music so loud, we moved to a table to eat.

DeSimone, the little big man, was acting like he had a hair up his ass. "Joey, tell Andy what Freddie says to you! Go ahead and tell him, Joey!"

Fat Andy shot a disgusted look at DeSimone.

"Yeah, go ahead, Joe, tell me," he said. "Tell me before Bobby has a stroke."

I related my conversation with Freddie Campo. Fat Andy seemed especially intrigued when I got to the part about Freddie killing to keep what was his.

"I don't fuckin' believe this," Fat Andy finally said. "You mean to tell me that he's telling us that he owns this cop and we have to get *his* permission to talk to this fucking eggplant? Can you believe where this guy's coming from? Okay, Joe, this is what you do: Wait a few days, because I have to go back to New York. Then go to this cocksucker Freddie and tell him I'm coming down to talk to him. Make plans to meet somewhere. Then we'll set him straight."

"But, Andy, he's close to Johnny Irish," I warned. "Johnny's been grooming him."

"I don't give a fuck if he's close to the Pope," he spat out. "I want to hear this cocksucker tell me to my face not to go near *his* cop. Now let's eat. I'm starving."

While we were eating I was so relaxed that I even took my sports jacket off. After dinner I went to the men's room. Joe Blaze followed me in. He had to go, too. I was finished, washing my hands, when some guy tapped me on the shoulder and said, "Excuse me, but you look like a guy who was my sergeant in the army. His name was Bob Jackson. Is that you, sir?"

I smiled and said, "You know, I was asked that once before. But I'm sorry, it's not me."

Out of nowhere, Joe Blaze piped up with "Yeah, I know the guy he's looking for. Come to think of it, Joe, you do look a lot like him."

Yet again I wondered where the mob gets all their intellectuals.

I had another drink, picked up the tab, and on my way out Fat Andy instructed me to start looking for a site for the club. He was sure, he said, that Boone Darden was going to play ball.

"That Freddie, he's in a lot of trouble," Gunnar said in Italian. We all laughed.

"Where did you learn to speak the Italian?" I asked.

"Larry and I practice it every day. Not bad, huh?"

Actually it wasn't. I definitely was spending too much time with the FBI. Little did I know.

"Joe, the Justice Department prosecutor assigned to our case wants to meet with you," Larry said. "We can have lunch here and talk. What's a good day for you?"

"Sometime next week," I said. "Nena's flying in on May fifth. She's making a service stop."

"Damnit, Joe, I hope she doesn't know what you're doing," he said. "Why does she have to come now?"

"Hey, Larry, I don't mind working with you guys. But my little head don't understand these things. You know what I mean, Sonny Boy?"

They both laughed and left.

52
Bagging My First Boss

I CALLED FREDDIE CAMPO AND TOLD HIM I HAD TO SEE him. "How about Thursday?" I asked. "Same place and time? *Capisci?*"

"Can't do it," Freddie said. "Not this week or next."

"Hey, Fred, Andy told me to make an appointment with you. What am I supposed to tell him? What, are you a big shot all of a sudden? I need a reason here, Freddie."

"Joe, I got to go to New York with J. from down south here. You know who I mean?" he asked. I did. Johnny Irish. "There's a big important meeting up there. Everybody's going. Everybody in the C. *Famiglia*, right? I'll call you when I get back."

Freddie was trying to impress me with his closeness to the capo Johnny Irish and the Colombo Family. What he didn't realize was that the information he'd given me— after I'd passed it on to the feds—led to the rearrest of the Colombo boss Carmine "the Snake" Persico for parole violation. A warrant was issued on the Snake for attending a Commission meeting at Fred DeChristopher's house on Long Island. Persico ran, but he couldn't hide.

Freddie called on his return, and I asked him how his trip had gone. He didn't want to talk about it and sounded very solemn. Hah!

53
Operation Home Run

WHILE FREDDIE WAS GONE, LARRY AND GUNNAR TOLD me that a supervisor from the Eye's Fort Lauderdale office was coming in to oversee our operation. His name was Tony Amoroso, and he gave our sting a name. Operation Home Run. It was an appropriate tag, considering how Agro's sluggers had gotten the whole ball rolling.

Tony came for lunch one day, and I was immediately impressed. He was a good-looking guy, about five eleven and one eighty, and he carried himself with an air that said, Don't fuck with me.

"Tony, it's nice to finally see an Italian." I smiled when I met him. "I thought all the agents were Irish."

"Well, then you'll like me even more after this," Amoroso replied. "Because I'm bringing in an agent from out of state to work with us. He'll be here tomorrow night. Talk to him. Tell him what these guys from New York are like. Be honest with him and, most important, see if you can work with him. I want somebody undercover with you."

I invited everyone back for a veal dinner the next night. The guy Amoroso brought in was an agent named Rossi. He was Italian, all right, but he looked about sixteen years old. He was professional, and he was anxious, and as we wolfed down our meal I gave him the lay of the land.

"These aren't just kids or bank robbers we're dealing with here," I explained. "They're hardened criminals and killers. If you think for one minute that if they find out you're an FBI agent you're safe, forget it. They'll chop you up and then grind up the parts so no one will ever find you. They'll flush you down the toilet, and your friends here'll be burying an empty casket."

Then I played for Agent Rossi Tommy Agro's infamous "I'll eat your fucking eyes out of your fucking head" tape.

"What's wrong, Agent Rossi, don't you like my veal? You look a little pale. Do you want to lie down?"

Agent Rossi didn't pass the screen test. He'd never be able to hack it. He knew it. We knew it. No hard feelings.

Next up was Agent John "Jack" Bonino out of the Chicago office. He showed up in the beginning of May '81. I prepared veal marsala with a linguine marinara. I also made a nice tomato salad and homemade Italian garlic bread. Larry and Gunnar advised me to drop the flushed-down-the-toilet bit.

"It's unsanitary, Joe," Larry told me. "Tell him instead that they're going to chum him for bait."

John Bonino appeared to be a little more sure of himself, more worldly, than the baby-faced Agent Rossi. He carried himself like he belonged. He ran to over six feet, with a nice trim body. I could see right away that the baby dolls were going to love him.

John seemed to enjoy the meal. He raved over my veal. I warned him about the Gambinos, how they were sure to react when threatened. I explained the dangers of going undercover against the mob. Then I played him Tommy's tape.

After the reel spooled out I looked at John. I was searching for some kind of reaction. There was none.

"You've heard the tape, John," I said. "You see how they are. If you have any questions I'll be glad to answer them the best I know how."

"Well, Joe, there are one or two things I'd like to know," John Bonino said. "If it's not a problem, I'd like to have your recipe for the veal, and the marinara sauce. I've never tasted better veal marsala."

I looked at Larry and Gunnar and then back to John. "You're going to be just fine," I told him. "We'll get along great."

We finished dinner and shot the shit, and Larry and Gunnar left. John was going to be spending the night at my apartment. John and I drank the same Scotch and smoked the same brand. And to be perfectly honest, he intimidated me a little. Not a lot, but a little, like he had me hoping I'd grow up to be just like him. The ability to act like a wiseguy was in there, you could see that, but you could tell he wasn't programmed for it.

What John possessed wasn't exactly "guts," it was more like "uncommon valor," something the Mafia knew nothing about. It was something I didn't have. Oh sure, I had balls, and I had a feel for the mob. But I always knew their next move. I knew what to expect. Bonino didn't. And that took more courage.

"John, what do you say we go out for a couple drinks? It's never too early to start getting introduced around."

Agent John Bonino and I hit the Yacht Club first, and I introduced him as my partner.

"John and I are starting a private club in Riviera Beach, and I want you to join," I said to anyone we bumped into.

Everyone liked John, especially the ladies. A half-dozen baby dolls must have asked me if the guy was married. My cover story was that he was separated. I didn't know what else to say. John and I had a lot of details to cover. The next day I checked him into the SeaSpray Inn, and the two of us put our heads together about the questions that were bound to arise.

"They'll be curious, John, especially the nobodies," I explained. "The wiseguys won't ask you anything. They'll ask me, though. And then they'll tell some go-fer like Bobby DeSimone to go around my back and casually start up a conversation with you. Our stories better match, and you have to be prepared at all times. The nobodies aren't easy to fool either. Sometimes they're more of a problem than the wiseguys. And if the nobodies suspect anything, and I mean anything, they'll buzz the wiseguys' ears. *Capisci?*"

"*Hai capito*," John said.

By mid-June John and I were an item. All the Florida regulars were used to seeing us hang together. We had yet to face the test from New York. One night John and

I were sitting in the Top O'Spray lounge when Boone Darden ambled in.

"Give me a couple hundred," I whispered. "And watch this fish."

Boone came over and I introduced the undercover agent as John Marino, an old friend from Chicago. "He's going to be my partner in that club we talked about. Boone, let me buy you a drink."

I tried to slip Boone the hundred-dollar bills. To my surprise he waved them away. "Thanks, Joe, but I can't take the money. You have to check with Freddie first. He don't like me talking to no one but him."

After Boone left, John wondered if he'd spooked the chief.

"Don't think so, John," I said. "We're having a little problem with Freddie. Fat Andy was supposed to straighten him out, but he's been hung up in New York. We're going to have to have a meeting soon, though. It should be all straight by the time you get back from Chicago."

John was scheduled to leave the next day. He was flying back home to pick up his wardrobe, say goodbye to his wife, and establish a phony background—credit, address, former jobs—in case anybody ever got around to checking up on him. He was planning on returning in about two weeks.

"Hurry the fuck back," I told him when we parted.

"Joe, do you always curse like that?" he asked.

"Fuck no!" I responded.

54
"Johnny Irish Has a Big Problem"

DURING ALL OUR RUNNING AROUND I'D MET A NICE lady, a hairdresser. Believe it or not, our relationship was strictly platonic. She was from Utica, New York, and had been separated from her husband when we first met. But they'd patched things up and were now back together. At any rate, she had introduced me—via telephone—to a friend of hers in Utica named Brooke Johnson. I'd gotten to know Brooke quite well over the phone.

Brooke said she'd like to meet me, and seeing as how I had a little time on my hands with John back in Chicago, I decided to fly up to New York. Surprisingly, even Larry Doss agreed that I owed myself a little "holiday," although he cautioned me that the Eye wasn't going to pick up this tab.

I took a flight to Syracuse. Brooke and my hairdresser friend picked me up and drove me to Utica, and I checked into the Holiday Inn. Ironically, I was to find out later that during my stay I was surveilled by the local feds, who teletyped a bulletin to the West Palm Beach office that a "Joseph 'Joe Dogs' Jannuzzi [sic] has arrived in Utica and we have him under surveillance for a possible drug purchase or sale."

It was a joke. Work with them in Florida, have them try to bust you in New York. I had a tail everywhere I went.

The second night in I called Little Dom, who said he was heading for Lake George, and suggested that I grab my girlfriend and meet him. So Brooke and I, who had hit it off pretty well, drove to the resort hotel in Lake George where Little Dom was staying with his girlfriend Lorraine.

I hadn't seen Dominick for a while, and it was a happy reunion. Brooke raised her eyebrows when Dom pulled out a peanut butter jar filled with cocaine. He drew some lines on a glass table and handed me a straw.

"Nah, Dom, I don't do that stuff. It's bad for your heart, and I have a bum ticker anyway."

So Lorraine snorted some, and Dom snorted some, but Brooke politely declined, explaining that she'd once had a bad experience with the stuff.

"Come on, Joe," Dominick said, looking back and forth between Brooke and me. "The girl probably thinks you're a cop. Here, take a line. Come on."

So I snorted a line. But Brooke still refused. We went to the lounge for a few drinks, and after taking that snort I began to feel nauseated. I excused myself and went to the men's room to upchuck. When I returned, the girls were gone. Dom said they'd been in the ladies' room for quite a while.

"I bet Lorraine turns her on," he said. But I didn't care one way or the other. It was her nose and her business. To me the stuff was good for one thing: making money.

"Listen, Joe," Dominick said quietly, "I've been meaning to ask you, are you still friendly with that girl Nena, the one whose parents work in Washington?"

I told him we were still friends. "Why?"

"Well, you know I have to go into the can in October." Dom was going in on a weapons charge. "After my kid's wedding. You're coming, aren't you?"

"Yeah. Go on."

"Well, remember you said that Nena's father worked in the Senate Building, for either a senator or a congressman?"

"So?"

"So I was thinking, Joe. Maybe Nena's people got some connections to get me a soft prison, because it's federal time I gotta do."

"Gee, I don't know, Dom. I suppose I can ask."

"Yeah, Joey, ask. And if they can, I'd like to go to Louisville. I think that's the name of the joint. Better yet, Joey, give me a call when you get back down to Florida, and I'll get you the exact name of the prison. It's either Louisville or Allenwood. One of them country clubs. I'll say either number one for Louisville, or number two for Allenwood. Joey, will you remember that?''

"Gee, I don't know, Dom, maybe I should write it down," I said sarcastically. And Dominick told me to go fuck myself before clamming up, because the girls were coming back.

Brooke was talking a mile a minute. She must have taken a hit. Both Dom and Lorraine were laughing at her. While these guys were enjoying their blow I kept wondering if it would be kosher to ask the FBI to do a favor for Dom. They knew how close we were, and I knew Nena's people couldn't help at all. I don't even know where Dom got the idea that they could.

On one of the girls' many trips to the bathroom, Dom leaned across the table and told me a secret. "My friend Johnny Irish has a big problem. He led the FBI from Florida to where the boss was on Long Island. Now the Snake is really pissed off. Johnny's got a big problem, Joey, but don't say nothing to nobody. Fuck him. Just see if you can help me out."

"Who am I going to talk to, Dominick?" I asked. "Irish and his whole crew hate me, thanks to that motherfucker T.A."

Little Dom was saying that Johnny Irish was probably not long for this world. My heart bled.

Brooke and I had a nice time in Lake George. And as we left I told Dom I'd see about that thing. Brooke talked like a jackrabbit all the way back to Utica, and when we got there she fucked like one, too. I really liked her. She was a natural blonde.

The next day my hairdresser friend drove us to the airport, and I kissed both girls goodbye. Then I boarded my plane back to West Palm.

Larry and Gunnar showed up at my apartment early the next morning to ask me if I had a nice time and to tell me how comical it was that the FBI was onto me in Utica.

"They put out on the teletype that you were there to

see Joe Falcone," Larry said. Falcone was a button in upstate New York.

"Nah, I didn't go," I told them. "Joe sent word that he wanted to meet with me and invited me to his home. But I knew that I was being watched, and I didn't want to put heat on the guy. I sent word that the next time I'm in town I'd be over."

"You should have gone," Larry said curtly, holding out his empty pad and pen.

"Why, Larry? You told me the Eye wouldn't pay for the trip, anyway. Besides, I was busy with a nice young lady. I wasn't working. But while you got your pad out, write this down. Little Dom told me that Johnny Irish has a problem because you guys pinched the Snake for violating parole. He was consorting, and you know you got him with information that Freddie Campo gave me and that I related to you.

"Remember?" I added with a smirk.

"Where did you see Dominick?" Larry sounded surprised.

I told them about Lake George. And then I asked for a favor.

"It's an unusual favor," I said. "Little Dom's been sentenced. He reports to prison in October, after his son's wedding in August. Dom wants to get into a certain prison. I told him that I'd try. Larry, it will make me look real strong to the whole mob if I can do this. Do you think you can try?"

"Where does he want to go?"

"Either Louisville or Allenwood. They're both federal pens."

"No, really, Joe?" Gunnar said with sarcasm. "We didn't know that."

"Let me talk to Tony Amoroso," Larry said. "It's up to him. I'll let you know tomorrow. In the meantime, call Dom and ask him which one he prefers. Start generating some calls. Start earning your money."

They both left. And I picked up the phone.

55
I've Been a Good Boy

"It's number two," said Little Dom. That meant Allenwood.

"I can let you know in a day or so, Dom. I hope I can do something for you."

"I appreciate your trying, Joey," Dominick said and hung up the phone.

Tommy called me that afternoon, wanting to know where I'd been. I figured that this would be as good a time as any to try to get his phone number.

"I went upstate New York."

"How come you didn't get in touch with me?" he asked.

"Because I don't have your phone number. How am I supposed to get in touch with you? I called your manager Bobby's line, and all I got was busy, busy, busy. But I called Little Dom, so I had a nice time with him. He came to Lake George with his girlfriend."

"You should have told Little Dom to reach out for me," Tommy screamed. "He knows how. And Bobby ain't my manager."

"Hey, Tommy, I didn't go to New York to stay on a line making a bunch of phone calls. I went there to have a nice, relaxing time with a young lady. I would have liked to have seen you, and had a nice time with people from my own *Famiglia*. But you're like Ronald Reagan. To get you I got to go through six million channels. *Capisci?*"

"That fuckin' Bobby," T.A. muttered. "His kid is always on the phone. I told him to get two lines."

The thought crossed my mind that maybe now Tommy would kill Bobby, too, going for the DeSimone trifecta.

"Here, take my number," Tommy finally said. "If you have to reach me, call direct. But never talk on my phone. I'll go out and call you back. Do you hear what I said?"

I did. But I wasn't through busting Tommy Agro's horns.

"Maybe you better check with him first," I said. "Or did you do that already?"

"Check with who, Joey?" T.A. said calmly. "What are you talking about? I don't understand what you're saying."

"With Bobby. Maybe you should check with Bobby before giving out your number."

"Hey, Joey, how about I come down there and rip your tongue out of your mouth?" T.A. said before slamming down the phone.

Larry called later that afternoon. His supervisor, Tony Amoroso, had given us the okay. He'd try to get Little Dom into whichever prison he preferred.

"Where does Dominick want to go?" Larry asked.

"To Allenwood."

"That's a real country club, Joe. Mostly for politicians."

"See what you can do, Larry. As T.A. would say, don't let it die. And speaking of that, Tommy called, and finally gave me his home phone number."

"What made him do that?" Larry asked.

"Because I've been a good boy," I said. "He told me I was no longer on probation. I taped the call. You can listen to it."

I was beginning to realize that this job wasn't as easy as it had sounded. In fact, working for the Eye was a nerve-racking experience. Making calls, generating conversations, taping calls, and especially wearing that body recorder to meetings with guys who would sooner whack you than ask your name. It took its toll. Thank God Bonino was joining the operation. I was sure he'd take some of the weight off my shoulders.

56

Johnny Irish Is "Gone"

JOHN BONINO RETURNED FROM CHICAGO IN LATE JUNE
with a lot of luggage. Together we rented him a beautiful
apartment on the northern tip of Singer Island, right off
Palm Beach. It was on the ninth floor of a lavish condominium. We were now separated by about eighteen
miles, but John had done the right thing getting a place
close to the mob action. At the time I'd taken my place
in the boondocks, I needed to be safe and secure. But
now that I was back in the Mafia's good graces I felt
abandoned. Yet, I couldn't ask the agents to move me. It
was too expensive. Nonetheless, I pouted because John
had a nicer pad.

A few days passed as I gave John time to get organized.
In the interim I stopped by my hair salon on Singer Island
to get a haircut.

I was outside my hairdresser's building, walking to my
parking spot, when I spotted the car driving past. Johnny
Irish was in the front passenger's seat, Tony Black was
sitting behind him, and a knockabout named Skeets was
driving. I thought nothing of it at the time.

Later that afternoon John Bonino and I began discussing strategy. The first order of business was getting
John some new clothes and new shoes. He dressed like a
cop. I'd been covering for him by telling people that he'd
left his wardrobe in Chicago, but now that he was back it
was time to drop the Timberland moccasins and Hyde
Park Oxford button-downs.

"Fine, Joey, we'll discuss it further tonight. Larry and
Gunnar are bringing Tony Amoroso down for some of
that fine veal marsala of yours."

"Oh Christ," I said. "I forgot about that. Come on and come shopping with me and we'll talk."

At the supermarket I gave John a few pointers on how to act like a mobster. The don't-fuck-with-me swagger. The jewelry. The moronic stare.

"I don't want to sound pushy," I told him. "It's just that you're a good guy and you're basically here to protect me, and I don't want to get whacked. So if you think I'm overdoing it, tell me, and I'll do it even more. *Capisci?*"

"*Hai capito,*" he answered.

John was smart. He was patient. He paid attention. And most important he took me with a grain of salt. That night I told Tony Amoroso that I'd begun priming the wiseguys for John.

"I've been telling them I have a partner going in with me on the bottle club," I explained. "As far as they know, John's an old babonia partner of mine."

"Huh?" said Amoroso.

"Babonia, drugs," I said. "That's how John supposedly got all this money to invest with me."

"You should have gotten the okay from Tony before you went around with that story," Larry interjected.

"Hey, listen, Larry," I said, a little annoyed. "I talked it over with John. Neither of us could figure a better cover story. All of a sudden John appears with money? It's kind of hard to explain. I just hope the dope story works. Larry, it's John's and my asses hanging out there on the line. Not yours. We need some leeway. We have to make some decisions ourselves. We're out there in the streets! Not you and Gunnar! I mean no disrespect by this, and I don't want you to think that I'm trying to run things. But John's an agent, he's one of you, and he's capable enough and intelligent enough to make some decisions."

There was a bit of a silence before Tony Amoroso cut the tension. The drug-dealer angle was a good one, okay by him.

"I'm certainly not going to argue with three Eyetalians," Larry said, and we all broke up. The ringing phone quieted us down.

"Hello?" I pushed the "record" button on the nightstand in the bedroom.

"I didn't think you were home. You usually get the phone on the first ring."

It was Dominick. Once I heard his voice I stopped the tape from recording. A mistake.

"Did you find out anything about that thing?" he asked.

"As a matter of fact, Dom, I just got word about twenty minutes ago," I said. "I was going to call you tomorrow. You're going up to where you wanted. Where you said. You know, number two."

"You sure, Joey? You sure?" Little Dom couldn't believe his good fortune. "That's great, buddy. Are you really sure?"

"Yeah, yeah, I'm sure, Dom. You'll get your confirmation in the mail, sometime in July."

"You gave them my address, Joey?" He was always suspicious.

"No, Dom, I didn't give them your address. But I'm sure they already got it. They sentenced you, didn't they?"

"Oh yeah, sure, Joey. I wasn't thinking. You got me all excited. Thanks a million, Joey. I owe you one."

We continued to small-talk, with Dom telling me to expect an invitation in the mail to his son's wedding. Then out of nowhere he asked cryptically, "My friend Johnny, down south there, you know who I mean?"

He meant Johnny Irish. "What about him?"

"He's gone, Joey. Gone."

"Are you kidding me, Dominick?"

"Hey, Joey! Would I kid about something like that? My *compare,* you know, Donny, he told me about six o'clock tonight that he was gone." Dominic "Donny Shacks" Montemarano had taken over Little Dom's crew after Allie LaMonte died in '79.

"Dom, he's got to be mistaken," I said. "I saw him with Tony Black and Skeets driving around Singer Island late this afternoon, about four o'clock."

"Hey, Joe, what the fuck is wrong with you?" Dom

said. "I don't give a fuck if you saw him at five-thirty. He's gone. *Capisci?*"

"Look for that prison confirmation." I hung up.

I walked back into the dining room, and Tony immediately mentioned that I looked a little pale.

"That was Dominick Cataldo," I said soberly. "He called to tell me Johnny Irish is dead. He got whacked this afternoon."

Larry jumped in. "I thought you told me you saw Irish with Tony Black this afternoon."

"Yeah, I saw him," I said. "With a guy named Skeets, too. It must have happened after that. Dom told me all about this in Lake George, and I told you. You have it all in that Form 302, if you bothered to write it down."

"I don't imagine that you taped Little Dom?" Gunnar asked. "Did you?"

"Nah, goddamnit, that's why I'm pissed off. I should have taped him, just to let you hear it."

"That's evidence out the window, Joe," Larry said. "You know that, though. Well, I'm not going to preach to you. You know how I've felt about taping Little Dom. We had one argument about it. I don't want another."

Once again, I found myself in the middle of an unsolved murder beef. Like Stanley Gerstenfeld's, nobody was ever indicted for whacking Johnny Irish.

"Did you tell Dom he was going to Allenwood, Joe?" Tony Amoroso asked.

"Yeah, I told him. He was real happy. He must have thanked me a dozen times. He also told me he's sending me an invitation to his son Sammy's wedding August eighth."

"That could be dangerous, Joe," Larry said. "Doesn't Tommy have some kind of affair coming up around then, too?"

"His daughter's wedding. That's the end of July," I told the four agents. "T.A. hinted around that he wanted me up there, but I don't think I'm going to that one. If he sends me an invitation, I'll send a gift. But I'd like to go to Dominick's. There'll be a bunch of heavy hitters there, and I'm sure that getting him into Allenwood is going to make me a big man with them."

"Why don't you bring John with you?" Tony suggested. "I'd like for him to get to know some of the wiseguys."

"I don't know. It might look strange." The thought of bringing a stranger to a mob wedding didn't thrill me. "I don't think I can take him to the reception, but maybe I can angle a way for him to hang out with me before and after the wedding. John and I can figure out what to tell Agro and Little Dom, I suppose. What do you think, John?"

John, who had been sitting quietly and listening throughout this whole discussion, responded by walking across my living room and picking a daisy out of a vase. One by one he pulled the petals from the flower. "Eenie, meenie, miney, moe . . ." When he'd pulled the last, he said, "That settles it. I go."

"Goddamnit," Larry exclaimed. "I just don't get it with you Eye-talians. Give me another Dewar's."

Over coffee and dessert everyone agreed that John needed new clothes to fit his new role. Larry advised John to follow my leads, but also to use his own judgment in a pinch. "And if Joe gets out of hand," Larry added, "shoot him."

Later that night I met Freddie Campo for drinks. I wanted to see if there would be any discussion about Johnny Irish. But no one mentioned the late Colombo capo. Freddie did, however, tell me that he'd ordered Chief Boone Darden to do whatever he could for our private bottle club.

"Maybe I can buy in for a piece of the action?" he added.

"Fine with me, Fred," I told him. "I'll mention it to Fat Andy. I know he still wants to sit down and talk with you. I'll tell him that you're here trying to help us."

"Good, Joe, good. But listen to me, I told Boone to help you. But he has to get my okay first on anything. *Capisci?*"

"Yeah, okay, Fred."

I left, and as I walked to my car I spoke into my stomach. "I just had a meeting with that banana-nose Fred Campagnuolo, aka Freddie Campo, in the Howard Johnson's lounge in West Palm Beach, Florida. It is June 29, 1981. This is Joseph Roberto Iannuzzi, Junior, signing off."

I always postscripted the Nagra recordings that way. It aggravated Larry Doss a little. That's why I did it.

57
Meet My New Partner

THE FOLLOWING DAY WAS PAYDAY FOR TOMMY A. It was also time I began figuring a way to get Agent John Bonino, code-named John Marino, into the middle of things. So I called Bobby DeSimone and told him my car wasn't working.

"It's in the garage, Bobby. I'll mail you the juice."

"But, Joey, Joey, that will take three days and Tommy needs the money now," he whined. "And what if it gets lost in the mail. I don't trust the mail. How about that partner of yours? Can't he drive you here?"

It didn't take a rocket scientist to bait Bobby DeSimone.

"I don't know, Bobby," I said. "I'll ask him. But I hate to take advantage of his good nature."

An hour later I called Bobby back and told him we'd see him at two the next afternoon, July first.

I told John to wait in the car as we pulled up to Bobby DeSimone's house in Hollywood. It would look suspicious if I handed Bobby the money in front of a stranger, new partner or not. "Let Bobby invite you in."

Once inside, I handed over T.A.'s vigorish and gave Bobby a progress report on the club.

"John's rented a building," I told him. "It's a nice

place, but it needs some fixing up. There's plenty of parking and everything. It's two stories, so we have the gambling upstairs and the bar downstairs. You'll like it, Bobby. Wait till you see the joint."

"I gotta be honest with you, Joey," Bobby said. "I called Tommy in New York and told him about you and your new partner being all kinds of pals all of a sudden. And he didn't like it too much. He told me to be careful."

"Hey, Bobby, you're the one who asked if John could bring me here," I reminded him. "I didn't ask you. And he don't know from Adam what I'm doing here. He doesn't ask questions."

"How long you known this guy, Joey?" Bobby asked. "We've known you for ten years and you've never even mentioned his name before. All of a sudden, boom, he's everywhere. It don't smell good."

"Look, Bob, I have to eat, all right? I owe that animal in New York a bunch of money and he wants his juice every week. Where the fuck do you think I'm getting this dough? John's indebted to me, he has a lot of bread, and he wants to be close to me. Besides, he's got very good babonia connections. As far as anything else goes, forget it. You and Tommy and Fat Andy don't ever have to meet with him. In fact, why don't you call Fat Andy right now and tell him about your suspicions. And while you're at it, you can tell him to forget about the club.

"Those guys want everything for nothing, and then they want to question my judgment, too? Fuhgedaboudit. I'll do my own thing. I'll pay Tommy off and do whatever the hell I want to do. So long, Bobby. I'll be in touch."

I made it as far as the kitchen door.

"Joey, Joey, wait a minute. Let me at least meet the guy."

"Fuck no!" I exploded. "I don't want you to get diarrhea and shit all over the house after we're gone. Just deliver my messages. I'll tell John to cancel the lease. The poor guy's been sitting out there in the heat all this time. You have no class, Bobby. You should have invited him in."

With that, Bobby went to his front door and yelled for

John to come in. He introduced himself. "My friends call me Skinny Bobby, and you have that privilege. I didn't know you were sitting out there. Joe should have invited you in. He's got no class."

Bobby was smiling. Like I said, it didn't take a rocket scientist.

John immediately won Bobby over with his charisma. I was astonished. John didn't come on strong, but he played his role perfectly. When Bobby would ask him a question about, say, something to do with the club, John would inevitably begin his response with "Whatever Joe says, I'm behind him one hundred percent."

On the ride back north I congratulated John and described at least one end of the conversation I was sure was taking place as we drove.

"I can hear Bobby on the phone," I said. "He'll be all excited, saying, 'Tommy! Tommy! I checked him out. He's a nice guy. And Joe didn't even want to introduce me to him. Wanted to keep him in the car.' Et cetera.

"Okay, John, now we've gotten a mope to run with the hook. Next we do nothing and let them come to us."

John and I had bought a lot of nice clothes, but we still needed shoes. On the way home from DeSimone's we stopped in the Bally's at Boca Raton. I purchased three pair, black, brown, and blue. John bought two pair. The shoes were on sale, yet the bill still came to over $900. When we told Amoroso he nearly swallowed his coffee cup.

"Jesus Christ, the pencil pushers in accounting will have heart attacks when they see this bill," he kind of sputtered. "And you say they were on sale? No one in the Bureau spends this much on shoes in a lifetime."

"Fuck 'em if they can't take a joke, Tony," I said. "What do they think, it's easy out there?"

Larry Doss, always on my case about my filthy mouth, could stand it no longer. "Joe, the way you talk is just terrible. And while we're on the subject, you have to stop using the word 'nigger' over the phone. They're going to be playing those tapes in court, and the prosecutor we drew on this case is a black man. How is it going to look? You'll embarrass him."

Tony Amoroso rode to my defense. "Leave him alone, Larry. If Joe wasn't the way he is, we wouldn't have a case going. He wouldn't know these guys if he was an altar boy."

58
"We'll Blind Them with Greed"

THROUGHOUT JULY OF '81 I REACHED OUT FOR TOMMY Agro several times. He always called right back. Bobby DeSimone and I were on the phone every day. I made calls to Freddie Campo, as well as to Chief Boone Darden. I was generating a lot of conversation. I was—as I reminded Agent Larry Doss—earning my money. I had to get all the players to start talking to each other. I was on a roll. Now was not the time to stop.

In fact, things were moving faster than I'd expected.

In mid-July John took another ride with me to DeSimone's juice bar. Dumb, gullible Bobby had actually suggested I bring him along. While we were there, Bobby cleared the way for John to meet Fat Andy. We were to gather the following night at the West Palm Howard Johnson's, and from there John was to show the Gambino capo the spot he'd selected for our club. We needed Fat Andy's approval before signing the lease.

The next evening I introduced "John Marino," my old babonia partner, to Fat Andy Ruggiano and his slugger, Joe Blaze. Bobby beamed at the far end of the booth as John gave Andy the cover story we'd concocted. He told him that the drug business was getting dangerous, what with all the crazy Colombians running around with automatics, and the nightclub business was something he'd always had a hankering for.

"If Joey here can get that police chief for you to watch out for the gambling end upstairs, I'm really just interested in the nightclub side of it," John said. "I have a lot of good ideas, and if you like them, Andy, I'll put one hundred percent effort into it. But I want to hear your opinions, your ideas, too. And if you don't like the place, Joe and I will look elsewhere."

"Let's go see it," Fat Andy grunted.

The site was only a few miles away, and on the drive, with Fat Andy, Bobby, and Joe Blaze following, John asked me how he'd played.

"Everything went fine, John. Fat Andy's a naturally cautious guy. But we got that lob Bobby on our side now. Unbeknownst to him, he's working for us. I'll bet he's singing your praises back there right now."

John wasn't quite convinced. "I don't know, Joe. Andy seemed awful quiet. Do you think maybe he's uncomfortable?"

"Nah, Andy is basically a quiet person," I said. "Not a bigmouth like Agro. But he's sharp. And he's notorious. But if Fat Andy likes you, he'll go to the wall for you. Just keep charming him, John. We'll blind them with greed, the cocksuckers."

Fat Andy was impressed with the size of the building we'd chosen in Riviera Beach, the downscale section of Palm Beach County. We talked in detail about where the bar would be, where we'd put the lockers for club members' bottles, how the tables would be set up. A general contractor I'd worked with stopped by and walked Andy through his recommendations. When we got upstairs, Fat Andy was in blue heaven.

"It's going to be beautiful," he gushed. "Here we can keep the gamblers away from the people downstairs in the lounge. No interference."

"I just hope the gamblers don't get too loud and drive away the drinking crowd," John said.

"Don't worry about that," Joe Blaze piped up. "If anybody gets out of hand I'll just take 'em for a ride."

From the empty site we all drove to the Palm Beach Yacht Club to celebrate. Fat Andy, suddenly a casino designer, held forth about where he wanted the blackjack tables, the roulette wheels, how to set up the poker games. I mentioned to Andy that Boone Darden could smooth the building permits right away, as long as we didn't get any interference from Freddie Campo and his *compare*, Johnny Irish. I wanted to see Fat Andy's reaction. He didn't disappoint.

"Johnny Irish won't be any problem," Fat Andy said. "You'll never have to worry about him anymore." Bobby DeSimone sat there smiling and nodding, so I assumed he knew about the whack, too.

From the Yacht Club we drove to Papa Gallo's Restaurant in Palm Beach for a celebratory dinner. While Andy and I discussed paying off Boone Darden, John schmoozed Bobby and Joe Blaze. We had an exceptionally elegant meal before driving back to the Yacht Club for more cocktails.

Fat Andy was loose, having a good time. He talked about T.A. in a positive light and, when talking to me, referred to Agro as "your friend." If the proposal for my formal indoctrination into La Cosa Nostra went through, Agro would thereafter be addressed as "our friend." Such were the idiosyncrasies of life in the Mafia. They could try to whack you one day and propose you for membership the next.

After the crew left, John and I moved to the bar, and he informed me that DeSimone had interrogated him in what we were both sure Bobby assumed was a subtle manner.

"He wanted to know where I was from, how I met Joe Dogs, on and on," John related. "Finally he said to me, 'John, you are with us now. There is nothing in the world that we can't do. You have the strongest group of people around you. In return for this, you never do anything on your own.' Then Bobby began threatening Freddie Campo, and even Don Ritz. Before he left, he gave me his phone number."

"I wonder what he's got against Don Ritz." Christ, the guy'd never hurt a flea. "It must be something I don't know about. But the bottom line is, Fat Andy likes you,

John. He's not one hundred percent convinced, but as far as first meetings go, yours went well. Tommy's going to be the tough one to convince, though.

"And don't sell Bobby DeSimone short either, John," I continued. "I fuck around and call him a fag and a dummy, but he'll whack you in a minute. Oddly enough, I feel sorry for the guy. Agro's always screaming at him. But Bobby can never be made, because of his two brothers. He's treacherous, but I still feel sorry for him."

I hadn't ever told the Eye about Tommy A. whacking Bobby's brothers. The feds knew they were dead, of course, but I'd piqued John's curiosities with my talk of feeling for Bobby, and he tried to press me on it. I told him it was personal and changed the conversation. There was only so much I was going to report to the FBI.

59
A Mafia Wedding

OVER THE NEXT SEVERAL WEEKS JOHN WAS BUSY OVER-seeing the construction of our bottle club. Boone Darden sent a steady stream of building inspectors around, and we dutifully paid them all off.

I spoke on the phone a lot with both Dominick and Tommy. T.A. I taped. Little Dom I didn't. I was trying to get a feeling from them about bringing John to New York for Sammy Cataldo's wedding. I mentioned to Dom that my new partner was flying in with me, because he had to see his *compare* in New Jersey. "While he's in the city you can meet him, Dom. He's a nice guy. You'll like him."

"That's fine with me, Joey," Dominick said. "But I got to tell you, I don't know if your friend will like it."

"I don't give a damn if T.A. likes it or not," I said. "He doesn't have to meet him anyway. And, Dom, you don't have to meet him either. He's just going to Jersey on business, and we're flying together.''

"Calm down, Joey," Dom replied. "I don't care. You're my friend. If he's with you, he's welcome in my house. You know that, so stop talking like an asshole.''

"Joey, I don't understand. Why didn't you give Bobby the two thousand to bring to me. He's on his way here for my daughter's wedding and I want the dough.''

It was the last week in July. Tommy Agro was on the line. The FBI had suggested that I mail T.A. a partial payment of the principal he'd shylocked out to me. They wanted the postal receipt for court and trial purposes. Things were coming to a head.

"Listen, Tip. I asked Bobby to stop by my place to pick it up on his way to New York. He didn't want to. He said it was out of the way. I only live one fucking mile off I-Ninety-five. Maybe he's got a problem. He wanted me to tell John to bring it to him, but I don't want John knowing our business. I mean, you never even met the guy. And I'm busy as a bastard with the club, what with meeting with Freddie and the cop and every fucking friend of theirs who's got a hand out. I mean, Tip, I think I'm going to move into a phone booth.''

"What do you mean a phone booth, Joey? What are you talking about?''

"That's where Clark Kent goes all the time.''

"Clark Kent? Who's he, Joey? I thought we were talking about Bobby.''

"Forget it, Tip." I laughed. "I'll wire the money Western Union. And I mailed back your invitation with a gift for your kid. Sorry I couldn't make the wedding." I hung up.

On August 7 John Bonino and I sat in the Palm Beach County Airport waiting to board our flight to New York.

"So, John, did you call your wife and tell her you were going to New York to meet some of the heavy wiseguys?" I asked.

"No. Why? I don't tell my wife anything about what's going on with us. She don't want to know, anyway.''

"Well, I was just thinking, John. I have a strong feeling we're going to get whacked. You know how good my hunches are. I'm usually right on the money, and I have a hunch that this is it. I think you should call her and at least say goodbye."

I searched John's face for some kind of reaction to my put-on. I saw none. He either knew me too well or had stainless steel balls. Probably a little of both.

We flew first class. To the dismay of the FBI, that is the only way I travel. Somewhere into our first hour and first Scotch I asked John to let me see his return ticket. He handed it to me with a puzzled expression. He frowned even more when I removed his ticket from his folder, replaced it with my return ticket, and put his in my breast pocket.

"What are you doing, Joe? Why the switch?"

"Fuhgedaboudit, John."

"No, really, Joe, you don't do things for no reason. What the fuck did you do that for?"

"Hey, John, you cursed! That's not like you."

We went back and forth for almost an hour. By the time we were preparing to land, John was so uncomfortable I had to give him an explanation.

"Look, John, you have your ticket with my luggage receipts and I have yours, right?"

"Right. So what does that mean?"

"It means," I explained, "that in my suitcase there's a loaded thirty-eight. I wasn't coming to New York without a gun. Just in case. But you're an agent. If they find it, you just tell them who you are. If they find it on my ticket, I'm in big, big trouble. *Capisci?*"

"You cocksucker." John smiled. "I'm going to keep that gun and throw it away. You're not coming back with it."

"All right, John, keep cursing. You're beginning to sound like me."

After we landed John remembered that he hadn't brought his FBI credentials along on the trip.

"Don't sweat the small stuff, John. They got phones in New York. Just call headquarters."

As it turned out, we picked up the luggage with no problem.

"Joe! Joe Dogs! Over here!"

It was Dominick's brother-in-law Tito. Dom couldn't make it, so he'd sent Tito to pick us up. I made the introductions and the three of us proceeded to Little Dom's house. On the way, Tito gushed with gratitude about what I'd done to get Dom into Allenwood Federal Penitentiary. The entire *Famiglia*, he said, was in my debt. It made me feel like a million bucks.

Dominick and John got along great. There was no pressure, as I wasn't working Little Dom. This was a pleasure trip. About eight of us went out for a nice Italian dinner, and Dom and John fought over the check. John won, and it annoyed Dom a bit.

"Joey, you shouldn't let your friend do that," he said. "I'm no cheap fuck, Joey! I'm not like your friend and all the bambinos."

"You mean Gambinos," I answered.

"Call them whatever you want," Dom said. "To me, they're the bambinos. We do all their fucking dirty work. Now come on, let me get you guys set up at the Riviera Hotel. And tell your friend John there that if he puts his hand in his pocket one more time I'm going to chop it off."

While we were at the Casbah having a drink, John mentioned that he had to rent a car to drive to New Jersey. Dominick would hear nothing of it. He offered— no, demanded—that John take his.

"Thanks, Dom," John said. "I'll be careful. I haven't had an accident for a week now."

"I don't care if you demolish it," Dom said with a smile. "I'll get another new one the same day."

John and I dropped Dom at home and went back to the Riviera. I warned John not to do any talking in Little Dom's car, as it could be bugged by another agency. John left, and Dom sent a car to pick me up for his son Sammy's reception. It was being held at a joint called Le Mans, in Brooklyn.

I assumed the FBI was covering the affair, taking pictures and whatnot, so when I got out of the car I turned and waved. Dom and a few of the wiseguys standing with him near the entrance started to laugh.

I said a hello to the guys I knew and Dom introduced me to the rest. I handed Little Dom an envelope with a card and five hundred-dollar bills. And then we all headed for the open bars and buffet. Dom, naturally, had done everything up right. There was everything a hungry and thirsty gangster could possibly want. And then some.

I milled around for a while. There must have been over three hundred guests mingling. Then suddenly, a half-hour into the party, I spotted Tony Black and Checko Brown. Skeets was standing behind them. They saw me and snubbed me. I expected that from those guys.

Dominick ambled by, hugged me, and asked if I was having a nice time.

"Yeah, sure, Dom," I replied. "Except I seen that fuckin' Checko and Tony Black over there, and when they saw me they ignored me."

"Oh yeah?" Dom said. "I'll straighten out those punks right away. Joe, I had to invite them because they're from my *Famiglia*. That fuckin' Johnny Irish gave a button to anybody that made him money. But these guys ain't shit. Come on."

I followed Dom across the dance floor, protesting all the way. "Don't say nothing to them, Dom. Don't ruin a nice party. They don't bother me. And I don't like them anyway."

It didn't matter. We were interrupted on our journey by Donny Shacks, Little Dom's capo.

"Donny, this is my friend Joe Dogs," Dom introduced me. "He's the one I told you about. He's responsible for getting me into Allenwood."

"Joe, all of us really appreciate what you did for Dominick," Donny Shacks said. "If there's anything I can ever do for you, just get in touch."

Dominick, listening to our conversation, decided that there was something his capo could do for me right now. Nodding toward Tony Black and Checko Brown, he said, "See those two punks over there, Donny? They gave Joe a hard time in Florida, and now they're acting like ass-holes up here. Go straighten them out for me, okay?''

Before I could react, Donny Shacks was huddled with Checko, Tony, and Skeets. I saw him pointing at me as they nodded their heads up and down. They apparently came to some kind of agreement, the huddle broke, and Checko nearly trotted my way. "Joe Dogs!" he yelped, embracing me in a bear hug and kissing both my cheeks.

"I didn't know you were here," Checko continued. "We could have flown in together. That was a wonderful thing you did for Dominick. Come down to Miami once in a while."

Tony Black said basically the same thing, and I was elated. This cleared the way from any interference in our club from down south.

After the reception, Dom and I drove his wife, Clair, home and went on to the Casbah for reception number two. Just the guys. Oh, there were girls, but they weren't wives.

At one point Little Dom left to call home, and when he returned he thanked me profusely for the gift to his son and new daughter-in-law.

"You're welcome, Dom," I said. "The kids can use it. They're just starting out." Just then a sight at the bar caught my eye. "*Marrone*, there's three *melanzanes* over there with two white broads!"

"This *is* New York, Joe," Dom answered. "But I still don't like those fucking eggplants coming around here. It started about two years ago. First there was one. Then another. Before you knew it, the place was overflowing with niggers. The white people were afraid to come in.

"So you know what happened, Joe? One day they found a dead eggplant in the lot next door. Then a couple of days later they found two more. They got the message, the black bastards. But I guess these two don't have Western Union.

"Petey!" Dom yelled to one of his sluggers. "Do me a favor and go and tell those bastards to get the fuck out of here. Them and the two tramps with them. Tell them it's a private party. Tell the bartender I'll chop his arm off if he gives them another drink."

I watched Petey grab another gorilla and saunter toward the bar, his arms waving and his fingers pointing to our table. The black party with the white ladies smiled nervously and left.

"Thanks, Petey. What did you tell them?"

"Aw, nuthin'. Just that if they didn't get the fuck out we was gonna have charcoaled niggers for brunch tomorrow. Big Jake there insisted they finish their drinks. But for some reason they didn't want to."

Soon after, John walked in. It was about two in the morning. Dom ordered the bartender to fix him a drink, but John demurred and offered to buy the entire party a round.

"No can do, John," I told him. "Dom will take care of it."

John smiled. "Just like Chicago," he said, then turned toward Dominick. "Dominick, I sideswiped a car in Jersey and took off. I don't know if they got your plate number."

"No matter, John," Little Dom replied. "That plate will only come back to some dead guy. As long as you didn't get hurt."

"I'm only kidding." John smiled.

"I know, John," Dom said. "I wasn't made with a finger, you know?"

We kept drinking, the place was packed, and Dom caught me yawning at about four in the morning. So he dragged me into the men's room and shoved a teaspoon half filled with cocaine under my nose. I was in no mood to argue. I snorted the spoon's worth, and it did wake me up.

"Go out there and tell John to come in and take a hit," Dom said. "This is good shit."

"I don't know if he does it, but I'll ask."

Out in the lounge I relayed Dom's request to quick-thinking John.

"Tell him I already snorted a couple grams and I'm coked out," he said. "In fact, I'm going to bed. But I want to say goodnight to Dom first."

I told Dom, who approached John and seemed surprised when the agent handed him an envelope. "Here, Dom," John said. "This is for Sammy and his wife." There were two hundred-dollar bills in the card.

"This isn't necessary, John. You don't even know us," Little Dom protested.

"That's all right, Dom," John said. "Whoever's a friend of Joe's is a friend of mine. *Capisci?*"

What a sweet move that was. John retired to our suite —Dom had gotten it for us—and Dominick questioned me about him a little. He seemed satisfied with the answers I gave him. But Dom mentioned that word on the street was that Tommy A. was concerned about the new guy I was bringing around.

"Dominick, did John seem nosy or pushy to you?" I protested. "Tell me one thing about him that you didn't like."

"What's not to like, Joe?" Dom answered, shrugging his shoulders. "But that's me. Tommy's paranoid, because of what he did to you. He told me that his kid Bobby DeSimone and even Fat Andy both thought John was all right. But you have to answer to Tommy, not to me."

The party broke up at five in the morning. Not used to the babonia, I was wired to the gills. Not feeling sleepy, I decided to break balls. I grabbed the house phone and dialed our suite.

"John? It's me. Joe. Come down to the lounge! It's an emergency!" I hung up.

A minute later John came barreling into the bar. His hair was mussed, his shirt was unbuttoned, and he was carrying his shoes and socks in his hand.

"John, have a drink," I said.

"What's the emergency, Joe? What's wrong?"

"Nothing. I'm just lonesome. Sit down. Let's talk."

John cursed me up and down. Then he settled onto a stool and ordered coffee with a Scotch chaser. We stayed awake all night, talking, until I was interrupted early in the morning by a call from Tommy Agro. "Come to my house, Joey," T.A. commanded. "And don't bring that guy you call your partner. Come alone."

60

"He's Going Bye-Bye"

I GOT TO T.A.'S KEW GARDENS MANSION AND WAS shown into the living room by one of Tommy's geisha girls. Tommy's wife, Marian, was now his ex-wife, and Tommy kept the house stocked with exotic broads. Although I'd only had time for a shower and shave, I felt fairly revived. When T.A. met me we kissed and embraced. Together we moved out to his veranda.

"Here's twelve hundred for four weeks, Tip," I said, handing him his juice. "I know the last week isn't due yet. But I'm here already, so take it."

"Yeah, thanks, Joey," Tommy said. Then he got right to the point. Tommy Agro was not as dumb as he looked. "Listen, who's this guy you brought up here with you?"

"He's a good friend. His name is John Marino. He's from Chicago. And I know him longer than I know you. What's on your mind, Tip?"

"What's on my mind is you're sure he's all right? I mean, you don't have any illusions that you think you can bring a cop in and try to infiltrate us, do you?"

"Look, Tom, in all due respect, I didn't come here to be insulted. I told you who he was. If you'd like to check him out, be my guest. It would give me great pleasure to get an apology from you. John is my partner for babonia. I earn off the guy. He's indebted to me for something I did for him back in seventy-seven and seventy-eight."

"Oh yeah?" Tommy probed. "And what was it exactly that made you such a big shot with him?"

"Hey, Tip, are you kidding me? What are you, wired? Is this placed bugged? Does Macy's tell Gimbels? You should know better than to ask me something personal like that."

T.A. smiled. He knew I was right. "So this guy's your dope partner, huh? Well, let me tell you something, and I'm only going to tell you once. The boss, Paulie, he's put out the word. No more drugs. He just had three made guys from Neil's side of the *Famiglia* whacked for dealing in that shit. They were all with that cocksucker Gotti's crew.

"So, Pippie, don't make me have to tell you again. No more! Understand? Find some other way to earn. And if that guy John continues to do it, you're going to have to answer for him. So tell him, *'Finito!' Capisci?* Don't let me find out different."

"Shit, Tip, and I was just starting to get back on my feet," I said, adopting a conciliatory tone. "Listen, if you want me to chase John, I will. He'll understand. The only thing is, though, we're building the club and he's putting up all of the cash only because he wants to be close to me. He kind of worships me, like the way I kind of did when I first met you. But if you want me to chase him, Tip, I will, because I'm with you."

"Nah, you don't have to chase him," Tommy said. "But don't bring him around me. I don't want to meet him. Fat Andy likes him. That's fine. Put him with Andy. But you belong here. *Capisci?* You aren't going anywhere. But tell that guy if he fucks with drugs, he's going bye-bye and you're the one who's gonna send him off. Are you listening to me, Joey?"

"Yeah, Tip, yeah. John'll do whatever I tell him. Now listen, I don't know if Little Dom told you, and I didn't want to discuss it over the phone, but I got him into Allenwood. He got his confirmation the other day."

"That's very good, Joey," Tommy said in a tone that let me know he already knew. "Dom's a friend of mine, even though he's over there. I'm glad you could help him out."

We spoke for ten more minutes and then Tommy had his driver take me back to the hotel. I was dead tired now, but we had a flight to catch. John dragged me to the airport, and a couple of Scotches pulled me through. I even made a dinner date with the first class flight attendant. What the hell? You only live once.

61
A Prison Travel Agent

THE FBI WAS HAPPY WITH THE WAY THINGS WERE
going. Larry and Gunnar had rented a safe house in
West Palm, and we used it to plot our strategy. John was
working hard setting up the club, although I never really
showed my appreciation to him, because I was beginning
to feel that I was in over my head. I didn't want to keep
working with the feds, but there was no way to get out of
it. I was locked in. I'd made my own bed, and now I had
to sleep in it. It was a fitful time.

Fat Andy had finally had his sit-down with Freddie
Campo, and he'd made Freddie understand in no uncertain terms that the cop Boone Darden was to cooperate
with us in any manner we wanted. The highlights of August and September 1981 were another meeting between
Freddie and me and a sit-down I attended with Police
Chief Darden. Dominick called constantly, thanking me
for his prison assignment.

"I'm having a going-away party October first," Dominick told me. "Why don't you try and fly in?"

I told him I'd see if I could arrange it, but the feds
vetoed the idea unless John could tag along. That was
impossible. One coincidental trip had been feasible. But
a second was out of the question. It would arouse too
much suspicion. I couldn't make Tony Amoroso understand that.

"Tony, this isn't ABSCAM, where you're dealing with
a bunch of political fags," I argued. "These are wiseguys. They use real bullets in their guns. We're talking
organized crime!"

I embarrassed him and pissed him off, but I didn't care.
Most of the shots Tony called were straight and true.

This would have been a bad one. Not everyone's perfect. I told Dom I couldn't make it.

On October 1, the night of Dom's party in New York, John and I were in Palm Beach meeting with Bobby DeSimone and my "friend," the Palm Beach county official. We talked about getting an illegal bingo operation going. My friend never committed himself, and DeSimone finally scared him away by mentioning that his kid was doing a stretch for possession. The guy didn't like the word "drugs."

Later that night, as I was unhooking my Nagra, the phone rang.

"Joey, you got my money, you hump?"

I just loved Tommy Agro's sophisticated sense of humor.

"Nah." I laughed. "I'm broke."

"Listen, that's not why I called," Tommy continued. "You know that thing you did for Little Dom?"

"Yeah?"

"Well, I got this friend of mine that I want you to do the same thing for him."

"Who?" I asked.

"Never mind who, Joey. Just do it. Dom's going to call you tomorrow and he'll explain to you. He'll call you from outside, and then you go outside and call him back. *Capisci?* You talk pay phone to pay phone."

"Who is this thing for, Tom?" I was insistent.

"It's someone very close to me," Tommy said. "Dominick will explain everything tomorrow. Don't talk about it now. He'll call by two in the afternoon."

"How come you're not at Dom's party?" I asked.

"I am, I'm here, that's where I'm calling you from," T.A. said. "Let me go now. But, Joey, make this thing your number-one priority. Do this before you do anything else. It's important."

I had to hurry myself. I was late for an appointment at the Yacht Club with Freddie Campo. I was doing about forty-five, fifty miles per hour in my Lincoln when the Chevrolet ran the stop sign. I smashed into its passenger side. The Chevy flipped up into the air. My Lincoln was like a tank. At the hospital, I was interviewed by a cop and released. I didn't have time to stay in the hospital. It was too bad. I could have made a bundle off that accident.

Freddie was gone by the time I reached the Yacht Club. My daughter Sheryl picked me up and took me home.

The next morning I told Larry about the call from T.A., and he reported it to Amoroso. Later that day Tony himself called, ordering me to tape Dominick.

"You've got to do it, Joe," he said. "He's the one who got himself involved with Agro. We'll just see what they have to say."

I told him I'd do it just to get him off my back. But in truth I had to think about this.

By three o'clock, when I hadn't heard from Dom, I called him myself. I woke him up, and he wouldn't talk over his phone. He wouldn't talk over mine either. He was too hung over, at any rate, and when I told him about my accident we decided to speak the next day. I had to get a portable tape recorder from the Eye.

The following morning Larry arrived with the portable recorder, and I went to the pool area of my complex, where there was a pay phone. There was no one around, so I didn't have any trouble. I'd decided to tape Little Dom.

Dominick told me that the Colombo *Famiglia* boss, Carmine "the Snake" Persico, was currently being held in the MCC, the Manhattan Correctional Center, and he wanted to either remain there or be transferred to the Danbury, Connecticut, prison.

"He wants to stay near New York so he can run the Family," Dom said, referring to Persico throughout our conversation only as the *Serpente*. "He's going to be moved, and he doesn't want to go far. If you do this, Joey, you can write your own ticket."

"I'll see what I can do, Dom, but this one's going to cost you. Yours was a return favor. I'd done something hard for that politician, and he owed me. But the next one's not free."

"Don't worry about the money, Joey. They got barrels

of it. There won't be a problem. Just do it," he said and hung up.

I gave the tape recorder to Larry. He turned it on, and nothing moved. "Shit," he swore. "I forgot about batteries."

The phone rang at nine in the morning. It was October 8.

"I have a collect call from Dominick Cataldo. Will you accept the charges?"

"Yeah, yeah. Dominick! How are you? How is that Allenwood joint?"

Little Dom proceeded to tell me how elated he was to be there. The atmosphere, he said, was pure country club. And the food was delicious. He wanted to know about that favor for the Snake, and I told him I was flying to Washington the next day to see my connection.

I was following FBI Supervisor Tony Amoroso's orders. Tony had himself flown to Washington that afternoon for instructions. Operation Home Run had become the top priority with the FBI's Organized Crime Division. Or, as Amoroso had put it, "We're playing ball in the major leagues now."

On October 20 Dom again called collect.

"It's going to cost your friend forty large," I told him.

"*Minchia,* Joey, that's a lot of bazookas," he said. "I mean, your connection's not getting him out of jail, you know?"

"Hey, Dom, this is what he asked for. You want me to see if I can chop it for you? You're the one who told me that we're playing the game with barrels of money."

"Yeah, Joey, but it ain't my money," he said.

"Dominick, I mean, am I going deaf here or what? You're the one who said, quote, There won't be a problem, unquote. Remember?"

"Yeah, Joe, I know. But I'm in here. I can't tell those cheap fucks what to do. See if you can chop it in half for me. I'd like to be able to tell my friend Donny that this will cost him twenty dollars."

"Yeah, okay, Dom. Call me tomorrow."

"If I can, Joey. I'm in a prison, you know," he said and hung up.

Not ten minutes later Tommy A. called and I related my conversation with Dom.

"Forty thousand dollars!" he screamed. "What is your friend, crazy? How come it cost so much?"

"Tommy, I don't know. You know that Dom's was a favor. This time the guy wants to get paid or he'll move the Snake somewhere up near the Canadian border. Dom told me at first that money was no problem. Now he wants me to chop it in half. Should I do it, or what?"

"Yeah! Chop! Chop it all. That's a lot of money, Joey. They expect it for nothing, like Dom's. That's what he told them, that it wouldn't cost a dime."

"Well, Tommy, they're wrong. I told Dom up front that it was going to cost. And if he said any different, he's a liar."

"Sure he's a liar," T.A. said. "He's sitting in that country club nice and safe and he don't want to know a fucking thing. He got me involved in this, and now he wipes his hands clean. That little fuck."

While Tommy was bitching I came up with a plan. I decided to throw it out without consulting the feds.

"Listen, Tommy, let me be honest with you," I said. "My guy really only wanted twenty-five large. I added the other fifteen large as I figured we should earn from it, since they're not our *Famiglia*. I was going to give you the fifteen to knock my loan down."

"Hey, Joey, I don't want nothin'. The guy, the *Serpente,* is close to me. So see if you could chop it more. See if you could chop it all."

"Okay, Tip, I'm flying there tomorrow. I'll let you know tomorrow night what my friend says."

After I hung up I sat there wondering what I'd gotten myself into. I mean, who needed all this work? Although I did like the idea of the FBI putting something over on the mob.

62
"Why Choke the Guy?"

NOVEMBER 10, 1981. THE NAGRA WAS DIGGING INTO MY ribs. Bobby DeSimone and I were driving south to Fat Andy's hangout, Christine Lee's restaurant in North Miami. The FBI had come up with a plan to have Fat Andy shylock a loan out to John. More evidence, they said. The net was tightening. I was driving south to negotiate the terms.

"You know, Joey, I knew the next day when Johnny Irish got whacked," DeSimone said. "Tommy told me."

Bobby went on and on, incriminating T.A. as the tape recorder rolled under my silk shirt.

Fat Andy was surprised, maybe a little wary, when we showed up without John. Behind him, standing at the bar, I saw Joe Blaze and Gerry Alicino. I explained that John had had to fly to Chicago, where one of his kids had taken sick. They all passed on condolences. It was good to hear that they liked John.

"So how's the club coming?" Fat Andy asked. "Did you get the permit yet?"

The club this, the club that. It was all these guys ever talked about. Soon they would all be peering out from behind bars at Club Fed.

"Not yet," I answered. "But Boone Darden says next week for sure. Now listen, I got a business proposition for you. I told John that I could get him a shylock loan. He needs it for the club. This way, you can earn, too. But I don't want you to choke the guy."

"How much does he need to finish?"

"I think he could do it for twenty-five large," I said.

"You're standing for the guy, ain't you Joe?" Fat Andy asked. "He's with you, right?"

"Yeah, yeah, I trust him with my life," I answered, turning to DeSimone. "No, Bobby, not with my wife. With my life."

"That's all then," Fat Andy said. "As long as you're speaking for him, he can have the loan. I'll only charge him two points a week. Why choke the guy? Then you got to worry about him paying. Two points is enough. When does he want it?"

"As soon as possible."

"How about if we do it around the middle of next month."

"That's fine," I agreed. "I'll tell him. Let's eat now. I'm hungry."

We had dinner and drinks, and on the ride home Bobby talked and talked. I didn't know how anyone could yap so much.

That November I got the okay from Tony Amoroso to move into the same condominium as John on Singer Island. I rented a two-bedroom on the eleventh floor, facing the ocean. John had spurred his fellow agents, saying he needed me close to him for security reasons. Tony also got headquarters to underwrite surgery on my face. My nose was still all fucked up. On the undercover tapes they could barely make out what I was saying. I sounded like a frog. The nose had to be completely rebuilt.

Dominick called collect the day after my meeting with Fat Andy. I was fast becoming a prison travel agent. Besides the demands from Snake Persico's loyalists, there was Tommy's *compare,* the suave Gambino *consigliere* Joe N. Gallo, who wanted his kid moved to a cushier prison. Joe Gallo, Jr., had been popped in New York selling heroin, and he was doing a tough eight-year stretch in Attica, a state-run hellhole in the boondocks of New York. "I want to get him away from the niggers," Gallo, Senior had been heard to say. "He got no one to protect him up there." The task had fallen to me.

To this day I think about the irony. Gallo's compassion for his son would set into motion a series of events that brought down the entire hierarchy of the nation's strongest Mafia Family. I would indeed get my revenge on Tommy Agro and Joe N. Gallo.

I told Dom I'd managed to chop the $40,000 "travel fee" in half. "It's the best I can do."

"Okay, give me a couple days," Dom said. "I'll get my brother to go to Donnie and get it."

"Just make sure it gets done," I said. "My connection wants his money, and now I got Tommy's *compare* on my ass, you know, for his kid. I don't want that fuckin' animal T.A. to start on me again. So get it to me as soon as possible and I'll give it to my guy."

"Give me three or four days, four tops," said Dom before he hung up.

"I have a collect call to anyone from Dominick. Will you accept?"

"Yeah, operator." It had been five days since we'd last talked. "Yo, Dom, I haven't heard from your brother yet. My guy wants to get moving soon. What's up?"

"You should be hearing any day now, Joey. Don't worry. I won't let you down. How do you feel? How'd the surgery go?"

"Fine, Dom. I hope I hear from your brother soon, because this connection of mine won't do the thing for Tommy's you-know until we get yours done."

"Yeah, look, Joey, I got to run. My brother will be in touch with you soon."

This was feeling more and more like a runaround.

On November 20 Tommy called to say he'd gone to the Gambino underboss Neil Dellacroce to complain about the Colombos and their delaying tactics. He said he didn't like the fact that they were fucking me around on the money. But I knew that he was only afraid that they'd blow the deal for Gallo's kid.

"We had a sit-down with my *compare* and their under, you know, J., plus the little guy's friend." He meant Joe N. Gallo, Colombo underboss Gennaro "Gerry Lang" Langello, and Little Dom's capo, Dominic "Donny Shacks" Montemarano. "You should get the money the first week of December."

I caught T.A. up with club business. We'd finally, I said, gotten the building permits. And then I warned him that if I didn't get the dough soon, my "connection" was threatening to ship "the Snake" to the moon. Tommy swore it was coming.

Oddly, Boone Darden and Freddie Campo had been no help whatsoever in acquiring the various building permits we needed to get the club moving. That big nose Campo must have told his police chief to back off when it came to the building inspectors. They took our bribes, all right, but in fact it was John who got the permits the old-fashioned way. He applied for them and kept squeezing the bureaucracy.

63
"My *Compare* Wants This for His Kid"

ON DECEMBER 3 I RECEIVED A CRYPTIC CALL FROM Agro. "Joe, fly in right away. I got to talk to you." He hung up.

After a meeting with the agents, I flew first class to New York while Larry and Gunnar sat back in coach. Tommy picked me up at the airport and threw my luggage in his trunk. I was carrying the Nagra in a briefcase I kept with me. It was rigged so that if I pressed a button near the lock it would begin recording. As we drove to the Riviera Hotel Tommy began talking, and I pressed the button.

"That Johnny Irish got whacked because he brought the FBI to the Commission meeting. That's why he got whacked. Persico got put back in the can because of him." Tommy was trying to show me how subtle he could be. It was warning, a hint, a sniff. I didn't answer.

"Anyway, that's not why I brought you here, to talk about Johnny Irish. I needed to see you because my *com-*

pare, Joe, wants this for his kid,'' he said, thrusting a piece of notebook paper in my face. ''Can you read it?''

''I'll look at it when we get to the hotel. It's too dark in the car. Is this your handwriting?''

''No. It's my *compare*'s. You copy it all down, and then I'll throw his away. It's a list of prisons. Where he wants the kid to go. In order. I don't want you to give your connection anything with my *compare*'s handwriting on it. I don't want to take any chances.''

We pulled into the hotel valet and the bellhop began hefting my luggage.

''Joe, why don't you give him that to take to the room?'' Tommy lifted his chin toward the briefcase.

''I got some important papers in here,'' I said. ''I want to keep them with me at all times.''

We headed for the lounge, and Tommy started in with a Gallo sob story. How the *consigliere* was sick at heart that his kid was trapped in Attica with a bunch of niggers. How he needed to get him out of the state pen and into a federal facility. How I just had to do this for the old man.

After a few minutes I excused myself and went to the men's room. In a stall I copied down all the information on the note, waited a few moments, and flushed the toilet. I put the original in my wallet, and the copy in my jacket pocket. When I returned to the lounge I took the copy out of my pocket and asked, ''So this is where he wants the kid to go?''

''Yeah,'' Tommy said. ''Where's the one with his handwriting?''

''Oh, I didn't know you wanted it. I flushed it down the toilet. I'm sorry, Tip.''

''You did that?'' he said. ''That's good, Joey. I was going to do the same thing. Let's have another drink here and then head for the Skyway to eat. We'll call Dom's brother Joey and see if they got the twenty thousand yet.''

At the restaurant Tommy told me I looked like a businessman walking around with my attaché case. The next day I met with the FBI agents and told them I was comfortable enough in New York, no one was planning on whacking me. They decided to leave while I stayed on. They took the briefcase and the evidence with them.

"What if Tommy asks you what happened to the attaché case?" Gunnar asked before leaving.

"I'll tell the asshole somebody stole it."

I stayed in New York for two more days. I felt good. I felt like partying. I'd gotten something good on Joe N. Gallo. Finally.

64
Shylock

"WHY DO WE BOTH HAVE TO WEAR NAGRAS? CAN'T just one of us wear it?"

It was the week before Christmas 1981. We were at the safe house in West Palm. Me, John, Larry, Gunnar, and Tony Amoroso, planning our trip to Fat Andy's house to pick up John's $25,000 shylock loan.

"It's because if you and John are separated we'll still get all the conversations." Larry looked like shit.

We drove John's Cadillac south. Larry and Gunnar followed at a distance. I felt like breaking balls.

"John, listen to me. I have this feeling in the pit of my stomach that I don't like. I have a strong feeling that something's wrong. I don't think we should go in there wired like this. They're going to search us and whack us. I think this is it, John."

He looked at me seriously, and I thought I had him. Then John stuck out his hand.

"Well, Joe, then let's shake hands now in case we can't later. It was a nightmare working with you, and I hope I don't have to do it again in a new life, if there is one. I don't think we have to worry, though. Larry and Gunnar will be outside taking pictures."

"But, John, while they're out there we'll be inside getting chopped up for bait."

"I don't care, maybe a mermaid will eat me," he said. "Now shut the fuck up. I'm scared to death. Now are you happy?"

Fat Andy met us in his driveway, surrounded by his crew. I introduced John around to some of his sluggers. Sal Reale was a made member of Fat Andy's gang, and Ronnie "Stone" Pearlman was a rich Jew who was only an associate. Junior Abbandando, who was discounted by the manicurist because he had only nine fingers, was there, and, of course, Bobby DeSimone lurked in the background. Gerry Alicino was in the kitchen cooking.

We all went into his dining room. Gerry was making pasta, and Andy told us there was more than enough to go around. We talked about the club, the different prices for building materials, how John already had the trim done upstairs. Finally Fat Andy and Sal asked me to join them in the bedroom. They wanted to ask me some questions about John.

"Joe, how well do you know this guy John?" Sal Reale began. "We're giving him the loan only because of you. You understand that, don't you? Your friend Tommy said that you're tops with him. So that's why we're doing it." Sal was a rich hump with connections all over New York, especially with the cops. He had all these civilian commendations from the NYPD to prove it. I didn't need his shit.

"Well, if Tommy said all those nice things about me, why are we in here?" I asked. "Did you bring me in here to read me the riot act? I feel insulted, Andy. Look, forget about the loan. I can get it somewhere else. You're still a partner, Andy. See you at the club."

I turned for the door and felt a hand on my shoulder. I almost shit in my pants, and I was sure the rivers of sweat pouring off my body were going to short-circuit the Nagra. It was Fat Andy's paw.

"Joe, don't feel insulted," he said. "Sal didn't mean no harm. He just asked you one little question, that's all. Come on, shake hands, and let's all get something to eat. Give Joe the money, Sal. We only got ten thousand now, but we'll have the other fifteen anytime after next week. I forgot to tell these guys that you needed twenty-five. It's my fault, although they usually have that much on them."

Sal and I shook hands and laughed. "*Marrone,* what a hothead," he said as he tried to hand me the ten large.

"Do me a favor," I said. "Give it to John. It'll make him feel respected if you were to hand it to him and make the arrangements with him about the other fifteen large."

"Okay, Joe."

So Sal walked out and gave John the money. They made plans for the delivery of the balance sometime next month.

On the drive home Larry and Gunnar pulled up abreast of our car, and John waved the $10,000 and flashed a big smile. We arrived at the safe house together, and the FBI agents got down to the tedious task of copying down the serial numbers from each shylocked hundred-dollar bill.

I kidded that at least they hadn't paid us in tens and twenties.

65
"I Put Three or Four in His Head"

THREE DAYS BEFORE CHRISTMAS ROBBIE CALLED. He wanted to make plans to meet me at DeCaesar's Restaurant in North Palm Beach to straighten out my football bets for the week. I was splitting a bookmaking sheet, Freddie Campo was my partner, and Robbie was our writer and collector. My customers would call Robbie, give him the code name "Blue," and he'd take down their bets. If the callers gave him the code name "Red," he knew they were Freddie's clients.

Larry had given Robbie's phone number to a dozen or so FBI agents, who would each call in and tape their conversations. Half would bet one team, say, for a hundred apiece, while the other half would bet the other team for the same amount of money. That way the only thing the feds lost was the 10 percent vigorish on the bet.

I invited John along to meet Robbie at DeCaesar's. I couldn't track down Larry or Gunnar, and my Nagra was on the fritz, so we arranged for John to wear his. On the way to the joint, John told me to try and get Robbie to open up and talk about the murder of Stanley Gerstenfeld three years before.

"I'll do what I can, John. He likes to brag about it anyway. He's an egotistical bastard and he might try and impress you."

Robbie was in a good mood when we met, and after paying me my winnings I sprung for drinks all around. As we were eating and talking I brought up the subject of the late Stanley Gerstenfeld.

"You know, Robbie, Stanley had a hunch that something was wrong, because before he went he kept trying to reach me," I began. "In fact he did reach me and wanted to talk to me, but we never got together. I think he knew what was coming."

"He didn't know a fuckin' thing," Robbie said. "When I put the bag over his head, *then* he knew he was going. I put three or four in his head, and one in his heart so he wouldn't bleed all over the car."

"Oh, does that stop the bleeding?" I asked, playing dumb.

"Yeah, Joey. You're putting me on. You know it does."

This entire conversation took place in front of John, who did the right thing by just sitting there nice and quiet and listening. We got the whole thing down on tape.

During the ride back I mentioned to John that deep down Robbie was nothing less than a maniac. "Did you hear him say he wishes he was Italian?"

"More Italians like him we don't need," John answered. "We need nice quiet ones, like Tommy A."

The holidays arrived and John went home to visit his family in Chicago. I spent Christmas with my daughter

Sheryl. John returned January 2, 1982, and the two of us headed out to our hangout, the Palm Beach Yacht Club. Our club was finished and looked absolutely beautiful. Upstairs, the blackjack tables had arrived the previous week. We'd ordered cushioned chairs. The rug was a thick plush. Downstairs, there were lounge tables, a dance floor, and a bandstand, all situated around a mahogany bar. Couches lined the wall. Thick drapes covered the windows.

We discussed sending out opening-night invitations. Our goal was the third week of January. We had yet to receive the building inspector's final certificate of ownership.

Fat Andy called two days later. He had John's $15,000. John and I drove to the safe house to be wired, and I began kidding Larry Doss about his haggard appearance.

"When I first met you, Joe," the FBI agent said, "I didn't smoke, I had no gray hairs, and I only drank once in a blue moon. But since this fuckin' investigation started, I drink excessively, my hair's turning silver, I curse like a motherfucking sailor, and I'm keeping Philip Morris in business."

It was the kind of effect I had on people.

Again Fat Andy met us in his driveway. Sal Reale had the money, all right, and he wanted to meet us at a deserted boathouse across the way from the Castaways Hotel on Collins Avenue in Miami Beach. During the drive I went through my usual ritual of trying to scare John. He told me to go fuck myself.

Everything went smoothly. Sal tried to lay some big-man bullshit on us about John being fortunate to get a special two-point juice rate. And he said that if it took John longer than three months to pay back the principal, the vig would jump to three points a week. John, naturally, agreed, and Sal handed him the $15,000. We left, advising Sal that the club would open January 15, in eleven days.

66
"Do I Look Like an Agent to You?"

TOMMY CALLED EARLY ON JANUARY 11. HE WAS AT THE Diplomat, and he wanted me pronto. I told him John and I had a meeting with Fat Andy down that way around noon, so we'd both stop by afterward.

"Don't bring that John around me," Agro warned. "I don't want to meet the guy."

I had to give Agro this: He was the only one out of all the wiseguys we were cornering who smelled a rat.

"Okay, Tip, I'll leave him by Andy's."

But then Fat Andy called. He, too, had made plans to meet with T.A. He wanted us at his house an hour earlier for an update on the club.

I arrived at the safe house late. John was already wired. It would take too long to wire me. We decided to go with just John's Nagra. On the trip to Miami I had an idea, and ordered John to pull over at a pay phone.

"Andy, it's Joe Dogs. Listen, there's been an accident on I-Ninety-five. The traffic's all backed up, and we're going to be late. Maybe forty-five minutes, an hour, I don't know. We ain't moving."

"That's too late, Joe," Andy said. "You know what you do? Come straight to the Dip. I'll be there with your friend. In the Tack Room."

"Okay, Andy, but Tommy doesn't want me to bring John around him. I got the guy in the car with me. What should I do? Leave him sit in the parking lot?"

"Nah! For what? Just tell Tommy I told you to bring him in. Don't worry about it. I don't know why the guy's so worried."

I skipped back to the car. "Let's go. You're finally

going to meet Tommy Agro. At the Dip. But first we have to stop for coffee and kill an hour."

John was amazed. "How the hell did you swing that?" he asked.

"Does Macy's tell Gimbels?" I smiled. Later over coffee I told him how I'd done it.

As we entered the Tack Room, Bobby DeSimone grabbed John and pulled him aside. I kept walking to the table where Tommy and Fat Andy were huddled. The ubiquitous Joe Blaze hovered in the background.

"Hey, Tip," I said as I embraced my *compare*.

Tommy was his usual charming self. "Hey, Joey, I thought I told you not to bring that friend of yours around here."

"Tip, Andy told me it was okay! Ask him."

Fat Andy jumped in. "Tommy, I told Joe Dogs to bring John here. Listen, he's a good guy. You should meet him."

Tommy looked back and forth between us. You could almost hear the gears grinding in his head. I was waiting for smoke to billow from his ears. Finally, "Okay, Andy, if you say he's all right, then that's good enough for me. Bobby's talking to him now. When he gets through, I'll meet him."

I looked from Tommy to Bobby and shook my head. They had to be the two worst actors in the world with this limp-dick, too-much-television, good cop/bad cop routine. I mean, here was Bobby over in the corner throwing questions at John, and Bobby was perhaps the dumbest mobster in the world. Well, maybe not the dumbest. If Bobby's IQ was somewhere in the low double digits, you could halve that number for Joe Blaze.

"So what's happening with the club?" Tommy growled, breaking my reverie. "Bobby said you were supposed to have an opening, but you cancelled. That's why I'm down here. I was going to come. But I have to be back by next week."

I explained that we were having trouble getting the final clearance for the certificate of ownership, and that the opening would be pushed back a few weeks. I shrugged. Bobby escorted John over to our table.

"Tommy, what a pleasure it is to finally meet you," John began. More than you know, I thought. "I think it would be easier to meet the President, whatzisname?"

"How the fuck do I know the guy's name?" Tommy said. "Nice to meet you."

John took over the conversation. He had them all gawking as the talk ranged from the club to babonia to Caribbean smuggling routes. If that head of the FBI in Washington, William Webster, could have seen John Bonino that day, he would have been proud as hell of his undercover agent. You'd think these fucking gangsters, made guys at that, were talking to Don Johnson. Mobsters are always measuring themselves against images. Other guys. What they see in the movies. Books (for the few that could read). John measured up. They all wanted to think they were just like him. Crazy and handsome and living outside the law. What morons.

"So, like I was telling Joey, I want to fly back for the opening." T.A.'s forehead was watering his eyebrows again. "I told him I don't have my own plane. It costs money, you know."

"Tommy, don't blame Joe. It's all my fault." John was being solid. "I told him to tell you and Andy the date, but I fucked up. But, Tommy, it won't feel like an opening unless you're there. Please fly in when we do it, and I'll give Joe the money to give to you for your expenses."

That clinched John for Tommy, ever the greedy, egotistical fuck. "Thank you, John," he beamed. "See that, Joey. He got class. He's not like you."

We talked for a while and John gave Fat Andy his vig and Andy returned $200, saying he'd overpaid him. "See how honest we are, John." We stayed another half-hour before leaving.

On the drive back I complimented John on the plane-fare move. Very slick.

"Well, why not let the government bring him back," John joked. "How else we going to get him back here?"

Then John told me that Bobby had asked him for some names from his past, so he could check him out. "They're worried I might be an agent, Joe. Do I look like an agent to you?"

"So what did you tell Bobby?" I asked.

"I gave him a couple of names in Chicago and Indiana to check out. But he's not going to check anything. He's full of shit. And if he does, he'll find all my connections, all right. He'll find them in Boot Hill."

The words conjured an image of the body in the trunk of Little Dom Cataldo's car.

Back at the safe house I was introduced to the new undercover agent. His real name was Richard McKeen, but he was going to go by the name of Richard Bennett, or R.B. He was a tall, string-beany mick, with a head of full, frizzy hair. Our new bartender.

"I'm getting a lot of flak from Tommy and Fat Andy about the club not being open," I told Tony Amoroso. "Can't you push those empty suits in Washington, get them to lean on somebody?"

"It's not the agency holding things up." Amoroso sounded annoyed. "It's a judge. We got to get him to sign the wiretap orders. A Title Three. And stop calling the agents empty suits."

"Well, I'm sending out the invitations for a February seventh opening," John cut in. "I can't keep making excuses, Tony. If we don't have a Title Three by then, fuck it, we're opening anyway."

"Yeah!" I said. "How fuckin' long do we have to wait? You guys were in such a hurry before. For what? To sit with our thumbs up our asses? I did that in the army."

By now Larry had come to the conclusion that I was a hopeless case. "Hey, R.B.," he said. "I hope you enjoy working with Joe Dogs. He's been driving me up a wall. Look at the wrinkles in my face and the gray hair. I even smoke now."

"You do look different since the last time I seen ya." R.B. kind of reminded me of a woodchuck. There were dead ones all over the roads in South Florida. "In fact, you look better."

"Atta boy, R.B.," I said. "Listen, I know a gardener who will cut your hair and straighten it out for you. I'll take care of you, R.B. You look like a fag. But after I'm through with you, you'll be one of the boys.''

R.B. didn't say anything.

"So what did Agro say about that twenty large that Dominick is supposed to come up with to keep the Snake in New York?" Tony Amoroso was getting antsy.

"It's not Dominick, it's the Colombos," I said. "And Tommy said I'm supposed to get it in February."

"If we don't get it by February fifteenth, I'll have your pal moved out of that country club."

"Yeah, good." Fuck Dom. "I don't give a fuck. Then maybe the Colombos will finally do something. *Capisci?*"

R.B., sitting in a corner, didn't have a clue as to what we were talking about. John explained to him that I was currently the center of two major investigations for the Eye. The first, Operation Home Run, involved the Gambinos, soldiers like Agro, capos like Fat Andy, and all the way up to the Family's *consigliere*, Mr. Joe N. Gallo himself. The second, John went on, was the Favors Case. That centered on the Colombo Family and went even higher, right up to the head of the *Famiglia*, Carmine "the Snake" Persico.

The new undercover agent, laconic up to this point, allowed some emotion to show on his face. "And Joe Dogs is the key to all this?" he asked, with not a little surprise.

"Who do you think you're working with here, fucko?" I said. "Some gang of West Side micks?"

"Call Tommy tonight and tell him you're flying to Washington tomorrow," Tony interrupted. "Tell him your connection wants to talk to you about Gallo's kid."

"Oh yeah?" I was skeptical. "Suppose he wants to call me back? Then what? How do I give him a number with a two-oh-two area code?"

"Because you'll be there. Larry made arrangements for you to fly out in the morning. I'm flying up tonight, and I'll pick you up at the airport. From there, after Tommy calls, you fly to New York. I'll tell you tomorrow what to tell Tommy."

"*Gesù Cristo!*" I said. "How many fucking things do

you want me to do? I suppose you want me to wear the Nagra up there, too?"

"No, not this time, Joey," Tony answered. "But this *is* important. The New York office doesn't even know you're doing this, and I can't send Larry or Gunnar. So you're on your own."

I flew to Washington, D.C., the next day, January 12. Tony took me to a hotel and handed me a written sheet of instructions for my conversation with Tommy. He also gave me a portable tape recorder with a half-dozen tapes. I called Agro, gave him my number in the hotel, and had him call me back. When he did, I told him I was having dinner that evening with my Washington prison "connection," and that he should try me back around nine to find out what was going on with Joe Gallo, Jr. The phone rang at nine sharp.

"Tip, let's not take a chance on the phone. Meet me at the Skyway in Queens at nine tomorrow night. I'll grab the shuttle. You're buying dinner. I've got good news for you and your *compare*."

The shuttle landed the next morning and I hailed a cab to the Plaza. Hell, I figured, I may as well stay at the best hotel. The work I was doing for the Eye was dangerous enough to warrant a little luxury. Anyway, the room was only two seventy-five a night. After checking in I took a nap. The phone woke me up. It was Larry Doss.

"How did you know where I was?" I asked suspiciously. "I didn't tell anybody, and Tony told me the New York office wasn't even aware I was in town."

"Did you really think you could fly to New York without anyone knowing?" Larry asked. "Do you believe we'd do that to you? Listen, Joe, I was just worried about you."

I told the agent I was perfectly capable of taking care of myself. Then I gave him my agenda for the day. Larry made me promise to call him as soon as I returned from my meeting with Tommy A.

"Even if it's after midnight?" I asked.

"Joe, don't any of you Eye-talians unnerstand de Englisha? I said anytime at all, *capisci?* And if you need to reach an agent in an emergency, take this number down. It's the main number in New York. Ask for Andy, and they'll patch you into Agent Andris Kurins. Now go back to sleep."

That night I took a cab to the Skyway. It only cost forty-five bucks. T.A. had already ordered dinner for both of us by the time I arrived. I handed him a slip of paper. "Here's the list my connection told me to give you. He says that within two or three months Gallo's kid will be moved to a federal pen. Hopefully Allenwood. He'll stay there six months, and then he'll be moved somewhere here, to the city, wherever they can find a work-release program. He'll stay there for a year, and then be released altogether. No parole or nothing.

"That's the best my friend could do. These dates and times won't kick in until my friend gets the twenty large, up front. Do you understand this, Tommy?"

"Yeah, that's good, Joey! You know what I'll do? I'll give this to my *compare* and let him decide. He's sick over his kid being in with all them niggers. Now, your guy gave you this paper? This is his handwriting?"

"What, are you wacky, Tom? That's my handwriting. He thinks the same as you. He don't trust no one but me. He's paranoid. Listen, I thought you mentioned Joe Gallo might be here."

"He wanted to come, Joey," Tommy said. "But he's embarrassed because of that thing, you know."

"Oh, you mean a little thing like me getting whacked? Poor guy. I hate to embarrass him. By the way, Tommy, did you tell Gallo that you told me that it was his idea to make me dead?"

"You crazy, Joey? In fact, he just told me, 'Look at that Joe Dogs, doing all these good things for me after what we almost did to him.' You know, Joey, if this thing happens, you get your thing right away. Your button. You know?"

"Yeah, I hope I get something," I said. "These airplanes and hotels cost a lot of fuckin' money. I don't mind doing it for our *Famiglia*. But the little guy's *Fami-*

glia! I think the Colombos should come up with the expenses.''

We talked for another hour and I caught a cab back to Manhattan. It was midnight when I walked into one of the lounges and ran into one of Tommy's old girlfriends. She was a Penthouse beauty, and she showed me a wonderful time. She told me that Tommy was like Superman in bed. "Faster than a speeding bullet."

I flew back to Florida the next morning and went directly to the safe house, where Larry took a Form 302.

67
The Opening

THE FBI HAD SECURED THEIR TITLE THREE. OUR opening was set for February 7. I'd been pushing for January 19, the one-year anniversary of the day I was supposed to die. No one else appreciated the irony. John had hired a band and another bartender and a local caterer to lay out hors d'oeuvres. We were slipping into our tuxedos when the phone rang. It was Tony Amoroso.

"Joey, take this address. Meet me there tonight at seven. It's just a few miles west of Fat Andy's house."

"Tony! We're opening tonight at eight! This is all the way down south. What's going on?"

"Just be here, Joe. John can cover for you tonight. So you'll be a few minutes late. And wear a suit and tie. See you then."

What the fuck? I put on a suit and tie and drove south. I arrived at the address around 6:45 P.M. and wound my way through a dozen boxy American-made cars scattered about the driveway and lawn. Safe house, I figured. When I walked in, there were about fifteen agents gathered around a pool table. Tony Amoroso was briefing them. After introductions, Tony turned to me.

"You're just a precaution, Joe, we probably won't even need you. We're going in tonight to bug Fat Andy's house after he leaves for your opening."

The plan was for me and a female agent named Lucy to knock on Fat Andy's door in case he'd left any of his crew behind to guard the estate. If that was the case, I was to say that my date and I on our way up from Miami had run out of gas, and I needed to borrow twenty dollars to fill up my tank.

"And how many points should I agree to pay on this loan?" I asked Tony, who never seemed to appreciate my humor.

Agents staking out Fat Andy's house called in to say that the Gambino capo was leaving, and fifteen minutes later our federal wagon train rolled.

"No one answers the phone, and we think everyone's gone, but we're not one hundred percent sure." Tony had set up a mini command post in a vacant lot down the street. "So just go up there and knock on the door."

I pulled into Fat Andy's drive and Lucy popped open her purse to show me her thirty-eight. I opened my jacket and showed her mine.

"Joe, you're not supposed to be carrying."

"Honey, when I'm doing agent's work I carry a pistol. *Capisci?* Let's go."

The radio and television were blasting inside, an old Mafia trick. I knocked on the door. I punched the door. I screamed, "It's Joe Dogs," at the top of my lungs. No one was home. We returned to Tony's makeshift command post and I reported that the place was clean.

"Okay, Tony, Lucy here will be back around four in the morning," I said, not letting go of the female agent's hand. "I'll take her back myself."

"Get the fuck out of here, Joe. She ain't one of your bimbos. Come on now, you're already late. Lucy, get in my car."

"Goodbye, darling," I said.

"So long, Joe Dogs," she replied. "And good luck to you, too."

I blasted onto I-95 and sped north at a hundred miles per hour, thinking all the time of an excuse for being late to my own opening. My tux was in the trunk, but my blue suit would have to do. There just wasn't time to change. I looked at the knuckles on my right hand. They were bruised from pounding on Fat Andy's front door.

We named the joint "Suite 100." I arrived for the opening at nine-thirty, one and a half hours late. The club was packed, wall to wall, the smell of fresh paint and Moroccan leather mixing with booze and sweat. I loved that smell. I made my way through a sea of back pats and cheek pecks until I saw the players, the intellects, sitting at a table in a recessed foyer. Looking grim. They were surrounded by an invisible moat. They'd been waiting for me.

Tommy Agro, Fat Andy Ruggiano, Skinny Bobby DeSimone, and Gerry Alicino stared at me, looking like four bulldogs waiting to be fed.

"So, Joey, where ya been?" Tommy asked. The others stayed silent.

I made a big show of running my left hand over my right fist. John had sidled up beside me.

"Tommy, Tommy, you wouldn't believe what happened. I went to Miami to pick up this baby doll I met on the beach. Tommy, she's gorgeous, twenty-two with a fuckin' body, fuhgedaboudit. You remember, John? Jaclyn's her name. You met her at the Yacht Club two nights ago?"

John nodded.

"So where the fuck is she?" T.A.'s head swiveled. "Bring her in."

"That's why I'm late, Tip. Son of a bitch. Know what happened? I get to her apartment a little late anyway, and we're just getting into my car when her husband pulls in. He starts talking, this and that, yadda-yadda-yadda. Suddenly tears are running down the broad's face. Ruining her mascara. Then this mook jumps onto the hood of my car. So fuck him. I didn't care. I start speeding and he's holding on for dear life.

"So Jaclyn's screaming that I'm gonna kill him. So I slam on the brakes. He falls off. And I got out and hit him. Cut my fuckin' knuckles. She's still screaming bloody murder, so I gave her a boot in the ass, and here I am."

Smiles all around. They bought it. It was their kind of story. I was their kind of guy.

I began mingling. My daughter and son-in-law were there. I couldn't begin to name all the baby dolls who had come stag. I know I invited at least a dozen myself.

After a few drinks I sat down at Tommy's table and we began talking hush-hush about the favor I was doing for Gallo's kid. Tommy, like the rest of the crew, was drinking heavily. The normally taciturn Fat Andy was even bordering on glib.

"Did Freddie Campo show up?" he asked at one point. "Did you send him an invitation, Joey?"

"Yeah, I sent him one," I answered. "But he sent his right-hand man, the tall guy over there, Lee Lehman, to represent him."

"What is he, a fuckin' Jew?" Fat Andy sneered.

"Nah, he's an Arab, Andy. Nice guy."

"Arab, Jew, they're all the fuckin' same," said the amazing philosopher Fat Andy. "Go tell him we want to talk to him. Better yet, you got an office we could talk to him in?"

Fat Andy and Tommy A. unfolded in unison and headed toward the back room I'd pointed out—Tommy conspicuously ordering Bobby DeSimone to stay put—while I turned in the direction of Lee Lehman.

"What if he doesn't want to come?" I stopped.

Tommy Agro answered. "Then tell him I'll dismember him right here and take him in there chunk by chunk."

Lee Lehman, whose boss had aligned himself with the South Florida Colombos, didn't particularly care for the idea of an office visit to the Gambino delegation.

"Joey, what do they want with me?" he asked weakly. "I haven't done anything. I come here to have a nice time. I don't want to go in there and get hurt."

He's right, I thought. Lee was a nice guy. And he was involved in the simmering Colombo-Gambino dispute over control of South Florida only in the sense that his chicken-shit boss Freddie Campo had sent him here to take the heat.

I gave Lee my personal guarantee that no one would lay a hand on him in my club. It failed to raise Lee's confidence level. It was no secret to anyone what had happened to me at the hands of Tommy Agro. Lee wasn't in the office fifteen seconds before T.A. got right up in his face.

"Where's Freddie? How come he didn't come to my opening? He got an invitation. There's no fuckin' reason that he shouldn't be here."

Tommy's voice increased in volume as he went on.

"That fuckin' Freddie didn't help us with his cop friend. Who the fuck does he think he is? Does he think he owns this territory? Does he think the Colombos do? Where is the cocksucker? He told me to my face not to worry about the cop, who did us absolutely no good. Now where the fuck is he?"

Lee Lehman was ashen. He started to stammer out a reply. "Freddie," Lee said, "just couldn't make it." He meant no disrespect.

"He just couldn't make it," Tommy mimicked him in a high, sing-song voice. "Tell me something, Lee. Can Freddie get us some help in the county sheriff's department? He got an in there?"

Lee answered that Freddie knew no one there.

"Now hold it, Lee," I interrupted. "I promised you that you wouldn't get hurt in here. But if you lie, like you are now, you won't leave this room alive. Now tell them the fuckin' truth."

"Oh yeah." Lee made a big show of scratching his head. "I forgot. He's got a guy in the sheriff's department."

Tommy came around a desk and moved toward Lee. I could sense that he was about to pop him in the face, so I stepped between them. "No, Tommy, no. Don't hurt him. It's the opening. We'll take care of it later."

Tommy backed off. Now it was Fat Andy's turn.

"Listen, whatever the fuck your name is, I don't get as anxious as my friends here." It was the first time I'd ever seen the booze have an effect on the big man. "Freddie sent you here to represent him, so you bring him this message. You tell that cocksucker if he don't want to help us don't try and hurt us. And tell him to take this message wherever the fuck he wants. If he has people to go to, tell him to run to them. Don't walk! Run! Understand?"

"Yes! Yes, sir, Andy. Tommy. Thank you, Joe. Can I leave now?"

"Sure, Lee," Tommy said. "Go have a drink on me and Andy."

Lee left. The three of us talked for a few more minutes before John knocked on the door and walked in. "Everything all right?" We assured him it was and we all returned to the lounge. As we walked to our table, Tommy passed Lee Lehman holding up a wall.

"Lee, Lee, how are you, old buddy?" he said. "I'm glad to see you're still here."

When we got to our table a pretty broad named Cookie sat on my lap and asked for my phone number.

I gave it to her and chased her.

It was after 2 A.M. by the time people began clearing out. Tommy, showing the effects of the booze, put his arm around John and told him what happened in the office.

"I told Joe to hand Lee a roll of toilet paper so he wouldn't shit his pants all over your brand-new rug." He laughed as we showed him to the door.

The opening had been a success. In more ways than one. Tommy's intimate conversation with John had been a minor miracle and a major breakthrough.

"I just wish we'd had the video already set up," John said. We were hunched over Scotches in the empty lounge. "I know Tony would love to have that scene on tape. Well, soon enough anyway. We're scheduled to wire the room this week."

We opened the club Thursday to Sunday, with live entertainment Friday and Saturday nights. John found the acts. R.B., our kinky-haired undercover nerd, took care of the books as well as tended bar. He was good at both, despite the fact that he had a beer in his hand all the time. But playing a beer-rummy was part of his role.

Who would suspect that *this* guy was working for the Eye? R.B. was Larry Doss's protégé. They'd worked some cases together in Philadelphia. And when R.B. was first brought in on Operation Home Run, John and I were considering changing the name to Operation Fuck Up. But all in all, R.B. was all right. He'd give you two fives for a ten.

Aside from R.B., our staff consisted of Gary, our weekend bartender, and Greta and Terry, two foxy-looking waitresses who were friends of the guys in my old crew.

We usually opened the place for business sometime around 11 P.M., and if we had enough customers we'd go straight through till noon. Most nights John and I would both walk in around midnight, just to make an appearance. Then spend the rest of the night and wee hours cruising local joints looking to sign up Suite 100 members.

Aside from the gambling—our blackjack tables came from a local gyp joint the Eye had shut down in Tampa— I suggested to John that we start a little shylock operation on the side. "Just send them to the kitchen" I said, using the mob slang for a shylock's place of business. We had spots for weapons, in case of a stick-up. And we had spots to hide and bury money for the same reason.

The jukebox was loaded with Sinatra records and Italian music. R.B. hectored us for country-western. He spent most of his time fleecing the locals at backgammon while on the job as bartender, and then taking whatever they had left on the golf course. It occurred to me that if you were an FBI agent, golf must be part of your training. I was sure they had courses at Quantico in golfing, fishing, and drinking beer.

At one point I heard rumbles that the guys in my crew wanted to "take care" of R.B. because he was taking all their money. I laid down the law: R.B. was an "untouchable."

"Joey, why don't you get rid of that ugly Irisher bastard?" Don Ritz asked me. "Get an Italian guy in there. One of us."

When Tommy met R.B. he asked me, "Where did you

get this stupid-looking fuck? Fat Andy and Skinny Bobby looked at this guy, and they don't know what to think. I'll get you a good Italian guy to tend bar, if you want.''

But Tony Amoroso and Larry Doss wouldn't budge. "He stays," they told me in no uncertain terms. So my wiseguy friends were stuck with the hick-looking fed working in their midst.

68
Little Dom's Contract

"JOEY, I'M DOWN HERE. AT THE DIP. BOBBY'S WITH me. Meet me by the pool. I got to see you about my *compare*'s thing.''

It was the second-to-last day of February 1982. T.A. sounded calm.

I phoned Larry Doss, told him Agro was down south. My hunch, I explained, was that T.A. had the money to fix Gallo's kid's prison sentence.

"Well, if he wants to meet you by the pool, you better not wear the Nagra," Larry said. "Call me tonight when you get home, and I'll write out a three-oh-two.''

I hung up, but a thought nagged. I knew how important this conversation would be in open court. I decided in the shower that I'd take a chance on the Nagra, poolside or not. When I called back the Eye's offices, neither Larry nor Gunnar was there. John was in Chicago and Tony Amoroso was in Washington. That left only R.B. With some trepidation I called him, and he wired me up.

T.A. and DeSimone were drinking coffee at his cabana when I arrived. Tommy embraced me, and I said hello to Bobby.

"Did you bring the twenty thousand?" I asked.

"No, Joey. It's here, but here's what I want you to do." I smelled an Agro scam. "My *compare* says the same thing. In fact, it was his idea." Always hiding behind Joe Gallo's skirts. What ever made me think this guy was such a big man?

"Now, Bobby has the money, and he's going to take it and open an escrow account in your name, his name, and John's name. What's his last name anyway?"

"Marino."

"Okay, John Marino. Tell your friend in Washington that the money stays there until the kid is in the third phase of the arrangement. *Capisci?*"

"*Hai capito,*" I answered, ecstatic over how this moron's conversation was going to hang him in court. "Okay, Tip, I'm sure he'll go for that."

"So you just call him up and tell your connection you got the bread," Tommy said. "And everybody's happy."

I stayed there for over an hour with Tommy and Bobby, the Nagra rolling, the two thugs incriminating a lot of people.

"Tommy," I said at one point, "my friend in Washington is having Dominick shipped out any day now to someplace, in his words, 'far away.' There's nothing I can do. He's pissed about not being paid for the Snake staying in New York. He wanted to ship the Snake, too, but I told him it was all Little Dom's fault. That's what you told me to tell him, remember? But I still feel bad. Dominick's my friend."

"You feel bad, Joey? Did you hear that, Bobby? Joey feels bad about his *friend* Little Dom! Do you think I should tell him, Bobby?"

"Yeah, Tommy, I think you should tell him," DeSimone squeaked.

"What? What? Tell me what?"

Tommy started in on one of his slow-voiced rampages. He told me that Little Dom had not only taken credit within his *Famiglia* for his move to the country club, but that he'd also taken credit for the fact the Snake had remained in New York. He'd made it look like he had the connection, not me. Then T.A. stung me with the shocker.

"Little Dom even put a contract out on you, Joey," Tommy said. "The guy Dom got to whack you came to my people for the okay, and we put a squash on it at a sit-down. So how do you feel about your good friend Little Dom Cataldo now?''

I felt like I was glad that tape was running under my shorts, even though it was breaking my dick. I'd taken to wearing the Nagra in my crotch, because no wiseguy would ever grab you there. I also felt like I should have listened to Larry Doss from the beginning when he urged me to tape Little Dom's calls. I drove home that afternoon shaken. Larry called that night.

"Joey! Joey! How did it go?" Larry was starting to sound more and more like DeSimone every day.

"Okay, Larry. It went good.''

"Well, talk to me, so I can write it down.''

"Why write it down, Larry? Why not just come over tomorrow and listen to the tape?''

"You wore a Nagra to the pool!'' he cried. "Are you crazy?''

"Larry, wait till you hear this one. It's great. We needed this one! I called up that mayonnaise-faced R.B., and he wired me up. I met him at the club.''

"See you early tomorrow,'' Larry said and hung up.

John returned from Chicago in early March, and we set up a plan to lure Police Chief Boone Darden into our net. One night at the club I called Boone and asked him to stop by as John was wiring me up. At ten that night the chief stuck his nose through the door.

"Howya doing, Boone baby?''

"Fine, Joe, fine. I haven't heard from you in a while.''

"I know Boone, that's why I called. I got something for you, but let's take a walk in the parking lot where we can be alone.''

Outside, I slipped the chief $400 in cash. "This is just in case one of your officers gets overzealous about the gambling upstairs. We open the tables sometime next month. We can't give you no more than a hundred a week until the gambling starts up. Is that okay with you?''

"That's fine, Joe,'' Boone said. "I know how expensive it is to get a nice place like yours off the ground.''

We walked together to Boone's car and I escorted him off. Soon he, too, would be behind bars. A cop in jail has about as much of a social life as a guy with a fistful of fifties in the Women's House of Detention.

The next day John, Bobby, and I drove to Fort Lauderdale to open our escrow account. We did just as Tommy said, putting all three names on the account. T.A. had just buried Bobby along with himself and his *compare* Joe Gallo.

On March 12 Tony Amoroso called from Washington to inform me that Little Dom had just been moved to a tough federal prison in Ashland, Kentucky. I called Tommy A. and relayed the message.

"I expect a call anytime now," I laughed to T.A.

"So you play dumb, that's all," Tommy said. "Make like you don't know nothing. *Capisci?*"

I wasn't off for more than a minute when my phone rang. It was collect, from Dominick. Would I accept?

"Yeah! Dom! How are you? Geez, I haven't heard from you in the longest time."

"They shipped me out, Joey! I'm in fuckin' Kentucky! Your friend should never have did this, Joey. He should have shipped the other guy, not me. I didn't deserve this, Joey. You gotta do something for me quick. There's too many niggers here. I'll die over here, Joey! Please!"

"Hey, Dominick." I was stern. I was taping. "Number one, my friend waited since last November—last year!— and he still hasn't seen a quarter. Your own fuckin' people did this to you, not my friend. You challenged him, and now look where you are. I'm sorry, I can't do anything for you. You gave everyone in my *Famiglia* a bad taste in their mouth for you. *Capisci?*"

Our conversation went on for forty-five minutes. After Dom hung up, I immediately called Tommy to fill him in.

"Good, good, now maybe his people will come up with the bananas," Tommy gloated. "You didn't tell me nothing. *Capisci, Joey?*"

"Yeah, Tommy," I said. "I never even talked to you." I hung up and laid back in bed and thought about Dominick. So he put a contract out on me, huh? Now he wants a favor? Fuck the motherfucker!

69
This Joint Is Kosher

THE INVESTIGATION WAS NOW HURTLING FORWARD AT a frantic pace. On St. Patrick's Day, March 17, 1982, John and I again met with Boone Darden, who asked for an advance. He was in trouble with the Internal Revenue Service and owed $3,000 in back taxes. I told him I didn't think it would be a problem and gave him another $400 in "good faith." He thanked me profusely, sending Larry and Gunnar into convulsions of laughter when they played back the tape.

The following Friday Fat Andy came up to the club trailing his usual witless entourage of DeSimone, Joe Blaze, Fingers Abbandando, and Gerry Alicino. John and I, wired for sound, took them out to Bentley's in North Palm Beach for dinner. From there we all drove to Suite 100.

Despite our best intentions, it was obvious that neither John nor I would last long running a restaurant in the real world. At one point I ordered our weekend bartender, Gary, to buy the house a drink. He complained that John had just sent out three rounds on the house and that at the rate we were going we'd soon be owing our customers money.

I made a face, reminded him who was the boss, and he shrugged and bought the house again. Everyone toasted me. Ten or fifteen minutes later, John bought the house a drink. When we met the next day in the safe house with Tony, Larry, and Gunnar, R.B. was ordered to tot up the night's receipts.

"Let's see, the place was packed for a good eight hours." R.B. was making a big thing out of it. Drawing it out. "And we brought in a grand total of thirty-two dollars."

"Wow," said Gunnar, "you guys are doing great!"

"Yeah," agreed Larry, "maybe you should hire some more staff."

Tony Amoroso had called us in to inform us that a video camera and bugs were set to be installed in Suite 100's back office the following Monday.

"Make sure Boone Darden gets his three thousand 'advance' in that back room," Tony said. "And anytime any of the wiseguys have something important to discuss, it wouldn't hurt to suggest that they do it in the privacy of your office."

No sooner said than done. Early on the morning of April 3 we videotaped Police Chief Darden taking his payoff. John was there when the chief walked in, pretending he was sweeping the floor. I had just given him instructions on how to hold the broom, straw strands down. R.B. was doing his best to impersonate a guy who knew how to polish glasses.

To activate the video in our office, there was a switch next to the light switch, side by side, as many light switches looked. As I opened the door to the office I would reach in and flick both switches up. After a while it became second nature, like hitting the "record" button on my phone tape.

Boone looked right into the lens, hidden behind a mirror, as I counted out his $3,000.

Our transaction over, I went on to bait him about Freddie's contacts in the Palm Beach County sheriff's department. We went back and forth, long enough for Boone and I to star in a double feature. I was beginning to feel sorry for the dumb bastard.

"How did I look on the screen?" I asked R.B. after Boone had gone. It was R.B.'s duty to monitor the videotaping.

"No doubt about it, Joe," he said. "If they ever make another *Godfather* movie, you'll be able to play the horse's ass."

* * *

By April, I was running out of excuses for the club members who wanted to gamble. The Eye had kept the tables dark for reasons of their own. Personally, I think they were just too lazy to get into that whole area. So whenever the cry went up for gambling I produced a deck of cards.

One night Don Ritz and a friend named Carmine settled in for some high-stakes poker with a bent-nose crew from Utica, friends of Don Ritz. The game started getting a little out of hand.

Don's friends were losing heavily, about $5,000 apiece, and paying off in IOUs. Late in the game, Carmine pulled me aside and asked a favor.

"Mention something to these guys about the money they owe us," he said. "Because if they don't pay us, the word will get around that this joint isn't kosher. We'll give you ten percent for your troubles."

Carmine was right, too. You can't go to a gambling joint and not pay up the markers you owe people. So I stopped the game, bought the table a drink, and politely informed the two Utica gents that they were down about $7,000 each. "Boys, I gotta tell you something before you go any further. Whatever money you lose here, you pay. *Capisci?* This is my joint, and if I get a complaint that this money isn't paid, you will not only still have to pay it all, you will have to answer to me. I'm putting a ten-thousand limit on you two."

The two guys looked at me. This was my first call since I'd been "demoted" by T.A.'s beating. I could tell they were deciding whether to see my bluff. Finally they agreed to the terms. The game stopped after they'd both lost ten large. They promised to get the money to Don Ritz and Carmine within a week. And they did.

It felt good to be respected again.

"Joe, if I didn't know you were working with us in this operation, I'd have believed you," R.B. told me later. "Those two guys were scared shit of what you'd do to them. Good show! But I still think you're a horse's ass."

70
A Walking Dead Man

IN MID-APRIL TOMMY CALLED. "JOEY, THEY'RE COMING up with that."

"With what?"

"With the you-know, the money, you punchy fuck. Little Dom's people. You remember the twenty dollars?"

Obviously Dominick's sudden transfer to Kentucky had shaken Carmine "the Snake" Persico's money tree. "Yeah, good, that's good. It's also about time."

"Well, whatever, Joey, but let me tell you something, my friend," Tommy said, beginning in that patented low growl that would inevitably escalate into an ear-piercing scream. "You better be telling me the truth about this connection of yours. Everything you told the little guy about his you-know, and everything you told me about my *compare*'s you-know, it better be right. Because if I find out that you're making this all up, I'm coming down there to personally yank your tongue out of your mouth. Do you understand me?"

Tommy was screeching now at the top of his lungs. He was indeed so predictable. Although I did wonder from where this sudden distrust in my Washington prison "connection" came.

"Tip, would I lie to you?" I asked, smiling as the tape recorder rolled. "Honest, Tip. Everything I said is legit."

"It better be, Joey. Because I went to the top. Do you know what I'm talking about? Not my *compare*. Not the under. The top!"

"Yeah, I know, Paulie Castellano," I said.

"Don't mention names, you fuckin' moron! My people are going to wind up doing twenty years for all your bullshit. So anyway, fly in the day after tomorrow. You got to meet with the little guy's brother. He's got your bananas. You know who I mean?''

"Yeah, the little guy's brother Joe," I said. "Thanks a million, Tip. My connection will jump around like a jackrabbit he'll be so happy."

"He'll be happy, Joey?" Tommy said sarcastically. "That's good, he'll be happy. Because you tell that fuckin' idiot he fucks up with my *compare*'s kid, I'll make him so fuckin' happy he won't want to live anymore. Do you understand me?''

"Yeah, Tip. Yeah. Don't talk like that over the phone. It might be tapped. I'll see you in a couple of days."

I called Larry Doss and told him I had to go to New York. "Give me a couple of thousand," I added. "For the trip and expenses."

I flew into Kennedy Airport on April 16. Larry and Gunnar were stuck in Washington and couldn't make the trip, so FBI Agent Andris Kurins, who worked out of the Eye's Brooklyn office, met me in the terminal. Kurins and his partner, Joe O'Brien, were building an undercover case against Paul Castellano. Later the two resigned from the Bureau over a dispute involving their best-seller *Boss of Bosses*, detailing the private life of the Gambino Family Godfather. It was a book about a guy whose dick wouldn't work.

Andy Kurins asked me where I wanted to stay, and naturally I told him the Plaza. I had burnt a cigarette hole in the silk shirt I was wearing and Kurins bought me another for $140.

"Don't thank me," he said when I tried to. "Thank your uncle. The shirt was a casualty in the line of duty."

I met Tommy later that night at Regine's. He had arranged for two Penthouse models to join us for dinner. From Regine's I called Joe Cataldo and told him to deliver the twenty large to me at the Plaza the following morning.

"Don't disappoint me, Joe." I told Little Dom's brother. "Because I'm leaving for Washington on the afternoon shuttle to meet my connection. If I don't show up, he'll ship the Snake out pronto. *Capisci?*"

"Yeah, I'll be there, Joe, don't worry," Little Dom's brother assured me.

"I'm not worried," I said. "Frankly, I don't give a fuck whether you show up or not. This money was supposed to be paid last November."

I had a nice time that night. Tommy picked up the tab at Regine's. Why shouldn't he? He got the money returned to him later. They paid him rent from that place. Twenty cents on each drink sold.

The agents arrived in my hotel room early the next morning to wire me up. Joey Cataldo met me for breakfast, right on time. Dominick's brother was a legitimate guy. He'd been roped into this assignment through the Colombo mob, and I'm glad that the FBI in New York never indicted him. If it had been in Florida, the feds would have thrown the book at him. The Florida prosecutors would indict a guy for stealing a banana from a drunken monkey.

Joey Cataldo was all apologies over coffee and eggs. As far as he knew, it was Dom's capo, Donny Shacks, who was to blame for his brother getting transferred to some sump heap in Kentucky. "That guy Donny shoulda moved quicker on this," he told me.

"Did you count it, Joe?" I asked.

"No, but it should all be there," he answered. "They wouldn't fuck around at this point. The Snake'll kill 'em if he's shipped out."

The bribe money came in two stacks of $10,000. I counted quickly under the table for the benefit of the Nagra. Joe Cataldo and I talked for another half-hour before he left, the agents swooped down to change tapes, and I was off to Lanza's restaurant, in midtown Manhattan, where T.A. and his capo, Joe "Piney" Armone, were waiting for me.

I opened my jacket and flashed the money to Agro, who smiled. Joe Piney said hello to me, and for saying that he got fifteen years in prison. I'll bet he'll never say hello to anyone again for as long as he lives.

Tommy bragged about how Paul Castellano himself, not to mention his underboss, Neil Dellacroce, had gone to bat for me and my alleged connection against the cheapskate Colombos. "C'mon, Joe, who is he, a senator?" Tommy wheedled.

"I can't tell you, Tip. I can't give him up to you no more than I'd give you up to him."

Tommy always had a way of turning his bullying around into some fractured test of loyalty. Today was no exception.

"Good, Joey, good. That's just what I wanted to hear," he said. "If you would have told me I would have been disappointed."

I stayed and chatted for another twenty minutes. I flew back to Florida the next morning. Andy Kurins kept the Nagra and tape. Larry Doss took the $20,000 and marked the serial numbers after he debriefed me.

Two weeks later Tommy woke me up with a phone call. He needed, he said, to see me in New York right away.

"Jesus, Tommy. For what? I was just up there."

"I know, Pip, I know. But I have to talk to you. Get up here right away."

They were onto me. Don't ask me how I knew. I just did. I was, I had been told all my adult life, now a walking dead man. I called Larry, who tried to calm me down. I told him I wouldn't go unless he and Gunnar were right behind me. He argued that there was no way Tony Amoroso would spring for the expense. Hadn't Andris Kurins watched my back just fine last trip? he asked.

It didn't matter. My mind was made up. I wasn't going without the two guys who got me into this whole mess.

The next morning I boarded a flight for New York City. First class, naturally. After takeoff I lit a cigarette, called over the flight attendant, and ordered drinks for the two gentlemen sitting together back in coach.

"They're two FBI agents," I told the stewardess, "and they're following me to New York. Tell them Joe Dogs sends them a drink and ask them to please stop following me."

I looked back a moment later and Larry was shaking his fist at me.

Andy Kurins picked us all up at the airport in a van.

They wired me up right away. I was going straight to Lanza's. Then they handed me a little instrument that looked like a miniature transistor radio.

"It's called a T-four," Kurins said. "It's a precision mike that sends back voices to a machine we have here in the van. If you see a problem coming, or if you sense something's wrong, you say the words 'Home Run' and our guys will be on you like white on rice. In seconds, Joe, with guns drawn."

I stuck the T-4 into the front of my cigarette pack. I was admittedly nervous, and the thought of the cavalry being only a "Home Run" away eased my mind.

Inside Lanza's I said hello to T.A. and Piney Armone.

"Joey, how ya doing? You're ten minutes late," Tommy replied.

I hadn't sat down before Tommy decided we should go next door for ice cream. Piney went his own way, Tommy and I headed for the ice cream parlor, and I was hoping this fucking T-4 was working. From my booth I kept one eye on everyone who walked in or out. I was wondering which one of them was going to grab me and whack me. I kept the other eye on Tommy, who had moved to the back of the store and was talking to someone in the shadows.

A waitress brought over ice cream. I thanked her, but I wouldn't touch it. I was sure it was laced with knockout drops. It just sat there and melted.

Tommy came back and sat down. His friend followed. This is it, I thought. I should yell "Home Run" right now! But the guy with Tommy turned out to be an older man, and I calculated hurriedly that I could handle the both of them and still yell "Home Run" should things get out of hand.

Tommy introduced me to his friend "Frank" and asked why I hadn't eaten my ice cream. When I told him I didn't like chocolate, which was actually my favorite, he made me order something else. The closest bin was butterscotch, so I ordered that and watched carefully as the dessert moved from spoon to bowl to table. No one had touched it. I ate it and didn't gag.

Tommy and I conversed for a while about the same-old, same-old, Gallo's kid this and Gallo's kid that. And though our taped conversation turned out to be a coffin nail in the subsequent prosecution of the Gambino *Famiglia*, there was nothing about it that couldn't have been handled pay phone to pay phone, Florida to New York. They were onto me, all right. And I wondered why I wasn't dead.

After we split up I walked downtown, took out that T-4, and yelled "Home Run" into the receiver as loud as I could without attracting attention. Nothing happened. Those motherfuckers! I stood on a corner and yelled "Home Run" for a fuckin' half-hour before they came driving around and spotted me. My cavalry turned out to be F-Troop.

"How did it go, Joey?" Larry Doss asked.

"Fine, fine, but I'm sure glad you guys taped it in there with this little T-four," I answered. I was in the mood to break some balls.

"Why?" Larry asked.

"Because I forgot to turn the Nagra on. But I don't feel so bad, seeing as how you had all this spy equipment in the van."

Everyone in the van panicked, except Larry Doss, who examined my Nagra. When he saw that I had indeed activated the machine, I sat back and laughed as the New York feds had agita.

71
The Homestretch

JOHN AND I INVITED FAT ANDY AND HIS CREW UP IN late April. Tony Amoroso wanted to get him on videotape. We had been faithfully paying him $500 weekly— or two points—on the $25,000 he shyed out to John, and now we had a business proposition to make him.

After dinner in Palm Beach we all went to the club, and I maneuvered the capo into Suite 100's private office. The videotape began rolling when I switched on the lights.

"Andy, John wanted me to ask you if we could deduct the nine thousand that we put out for you here from the principal we owe?" I began.

"Deduct what from what?" Fat Andy replied. "What nine thousand are you talking about?"

"John's figured his expenses for the upstairs gambling come to something like twenty-seven large. The tables, the carpentry, the rugs, cards, chips, even the thirty-eight hundred we've laid out to Boone Darden. It's all written down in our books. Anyway, since he don't have a piece of the upstairs, he divided that three ways between me, you, and T.A. I talked to Tommy, and he told me to ask you to leave John's juice at two points a week, and to ask you to deduct your nine-grand share of the expenses from the twenty-five principal he owes."

Trying to get money out of a Gambino is like trying to draw blood from a stone. Fat Andy looked like I had insulted his sainted mother.

"I can't do that," he said finally. "The shyed-out money isn't technically mine, it's Sal's, although I'm the one in charge of it. What I can do, Joe, is make sure John's juice stays at two points. And we'll give him a piece of the upstairs. He deserves it. He works hard, that John. So tell Tommy A. that's what we'll do. And let's go outside now. I need a drink."

Fat Andy headed straight for John to tell him the "good news." And R.B. stopped me before I could join them.

"How'd I look on tape?" I whispered. "Did I look like a horse's ass again?"

"No, Joe," R.B. replied. "You looked good with your suit on. You looked like a jackass this time."

By mid-May Tommy had been convicted of extortion in New York, but he was out pending appeal. He was like a maniac over the phone. He wanted money and he wanted it yesterday. He ordered me to send him the $20,000 the Colombos had forked over to keep Snake Persico imprisoned in New York. Since I couldn't tell him that the FBI had the money, I just refused him outright. I think he threatened to kill me ten times over the next week.

Meanwhile, Tony Amoroso told the undercover team that he felt the feds had gotten all that they were going to get out of Suite 100.

"We'll keep the downstairs bottle club open for a while, but to start in with gambling now is more than it's worth," he said at a meeting at our safe house. Before I could object that the wiseguys were getting suspicious, Amoroso came up with a plan to keep them from squawking.

"Tell Fat Andy and his crew that the FBI has been snooping around asking questions about Suite One Hundred," he said.

And that's just what John and I did at a meeting with Fat Andy and DeSimone at Dano's restaurant in Miami.

"Well then, don't open now, don't take the chance" was the Gambino capo's suggestion. "They'll come in there with axes and chop up the place and plant something there and then you're fucked.

"They might have gotten wind of this through that fucking Freddie," Fat Andy fumed. "That cocksucking rat bastard might have to disappear for good."

John paid Fat Andy four weeks' worth of juice, and then went into a big song and dance about how disgusted he was that our club had run into so many problems.

"I've put close to a hundred grand into that joint, I'm paying five hundred a week juice, and I still owe twenty-five thousand," John raged. "That fucking Freddie has caused me these problems. That fucking *cornuto* prick."

John's outrage was so well done that the thought occurred to me that the FBI agent's acting may have just signed Freddie Campo's death warrant. No matter. We stayed for another forty-five minutes, drinking and eating and bragging about how much money Suite 100 was going to take in once the heat was off.

"Hello?"

"Joey, wake up, you punchy fuck! It's only four

o'clock in the morning." It was the lovely voice of Tommy Agro.

"Yeah, Tip. I'm awake. I was waiting for your call."

"Joey, what's your friend doing with my *compare*'s kid? When's it going to happen?"

"In about three weeks. I talked to him today. He said everything is on schedule. Tell your *compare* to tell his kid *niente*, nothing at all with his mouth. *Capisci?* Now let me make love to Lori."

"Who's Lori? Is she nice, Joey? How old is she?"

"Lori, how old are you? Wait, don't tell me, say hello to Tommy."

"Hi, Tommy," my little baby doll purred into the phone. "Oh, thank you. . . . I'm nineteen . . . blond. . . . Oh, I don't know about that. You'd have to ask Joey. . . . Hee-hee."

Lori handed me back the phone.

"You should be ashamed of yourself, Joey. She's too young for you. Send her to me. That's an order, Joey. You hear me, you punchy fuck?"

"You won't like her, Tom. She's white. I'll talk to you tomorrow."

I threw Lori another fuck and sent her home. Told her to come back when she turned twenty.

On June 3 Tony Amoroso ordered me to call Tommy and tell him Gallo's kid would be moved in two weeks. I followed orders.

"That's great, Joey," Tommy said. "I'm on my way to see my *compare* now. I'll tell him. Send me some money, you hump."

That night over drinks at the Yacht Club I asked John when he thought he'd be leaving. We both sensed that after eighteen months Operation Home Run was winding down. It saddened me a little. I was going to miss John. The guy was a true pro, a straight shooter, and he'd become my friend. I know he felt the same way about me. John had taught me something. There was something inside him that all the wiseguys and all the sluggers in the world didn't possess. I wondered if I was going soft.

"I won't be out of here until sometime next month,"

John said. "We still got seven or eight weeks to break each other's balls. Listen, Joey, who's that girl that's talking to those other two girls, the one that keeps pointing over here? The redhead, the pretty one?"

"She's a ball buster, John. Her name is Annabelle. I don't know her last name. She don't like me. She smashed me once in Lord's restaurant, back when it was open."

"She smacked you? Why?"

"Well, Freddie Campo told me she was rated in the top ten for giving head. So when she came over to our table to have a drink with us, I asked her if every guy's sperm tasted the same. The fuckin' sorehead slapped me and called me a filthy pig. Can you imagine that? The bitch!"

"Yeah, Joe, I see no reason why she should have smacked you for that. She should have shot you. Come on, let's get the fuck out of here. I'm sick of these joints. Let's go to the club, get a bottle, and go home and drink it."

"Okay," I said. "Whose locker are we going to steal it out of this time?"

"What's the difference, Joey? It's all our booze anyway. R.B. just puts them in lockers in case a liquor inspector comes nosing around. Very few of our members have a bottle in their locker that we didn't give them."

We went to my apartment, talked all night, and finished the booze.

A week later John was in Chicago for a short weekend visit when Bobby DeSimone dropped by the club. He started asking when John planned on paying off Fat Andy's loan.

"I don't know, Bobby, ask him." I said. "If Andy's not worried about it, why should you be? Did Andy tell you to come in here and ask me that?"

"No, I'm asking on my own, Joey. You know we don't know much about John, and the only reason we gave him the loan was because of you."

"Wait a minute, Bobby," I said. "You're saying we. Is some of that loan money yours?"

"No, Joey, no. None of it's mine. I just use that term 'we.' I meant to say 'them.' "

"Well, Bobby, you do more talking and worrying than they do. So if you're not part of the 'we' or 'they,' then mind your own business. You're sticking your nose around where it don't belong."

"Yeah, well, I worry about it, Joey," Bobby said. "I hope nothing goes wrong. We—I mean they—can't find out nothing about John's background. He comes back blank."

"That's because he's not like us, Bobby. He's legitimate. I'm the only fucking flaw in his life, and I bet he'd love to get rid of me. Even Tommy trusts him. Tommy's the one who wanted John's name on the escrow account for Gallo's kid, remember? So it looks to me like you're the only one talking."

"I guess you're right, Joey." Bobby was backing off. "I like John a lot. I just hope nothing is wrong. What do you have on him, Joey, that he's so loyal to you?"

"Good night, Bobby. I don't know who sent you here, and I don't care either. I'll let Tommy know how you're talking."

They definitely knew.

72
"Kill It"

"HELLO?" AFTER PICKING UP THE RECEIVER I'D AUTOmatically punched the "record" button. The ritual had long since become second nature.

"Joey, go outside and call me right away. I don't trust your fuckin' telephone. I'm home." Tommy Agro hung up.

I reached into a desk drawer and lifted out my portable tape recorder. I opened a fresh tape, inserted new batteries, and wondered if T.A. had ever heard of this invention, the moron.

There was a pay phone just across the street from my condo apartment. It was early in the morning, and there was very little foot traffic. I suctioned the rubber nipple of the recorder onto the back of the receiver and dialed Tommy's number.

"Yeah, Tip. What's up?"

"That thing with my *compare,* kill it."

"What?"

"I said kill it, Joey! Kill it! Don't you understand English? My *compare* is sick over this whole fuckin' thing. I never should have started it. I should have minded my own business. Son of a bitch. He's scared. So kill it."

It was June 10. The Eye was scheduled to move Joe Gallo, Jr., in four days.

"Jesus Christ, Tip, I don't know if I can stop it. He's supposed to go on the fourteenth of this month. You fucking don't know what you want, and then when it's just about to happen, you call and say 'kill it.' Tommy?"

"I know, Joey. But it ain't me. It's him. He's afraid something is going to happen, that something's wrong. Go get the money out of the escrow account right away. Bobby's calling John right now."

I told Tommy that DeSimone wouldn't find John at home. He was still in Chicago. "He called me last night and said he'll be back in maybe ten days."

"No good, Joey." There was an unfamiliar tone to T.A.'s voice, and it took me a moment to figure it out. Then it hit me. It was desperation. "No good at all. Get in touch with him and tell him to fly back today. He needs to sign out that money. I'll reimburse him for the trip. Better yet, give me his number out there."

"No, Tip, that's all right. I'll call him. He'll fly in if I tell him to. But I'm telling you up front, I don't know if I can stop the kid's move."

"Try, Joey! Try hard! The kid is going crazy in the can. He knows something is up, and he's nervous. Kill it, Joey. Kill it."

I promised Tommy I'd call him back as soon as I knew anything. When I returned to my apartment, I called

Tony Amoroso and played him the recorded conversation.

"Something's wrong." I said it softly after the reel had spun out.

John flew back that day. He arrived at the club at midnight, meeting me in the office to go over the next day's scenario.

"Let's bring Bobby back here and make him count the money," John said.

That was a good enough scenario for me. The next morning at eleven Bobby met John and me at Suite 100. We were both wired, naturally. We drove to the bank together. There were no problems. The three of us signed off on the escrow account. We'd even made $181.04 in interest. I was carrying the dough.

We returned to the club, had R.B. mix us three cocktails, and went into the office. I flicked on the videotape. We talked, I handed Bobby the money, and he counted it.

"You know, Junior Abbandando don't like you," Bobby told me out of nowhere.

"Who? Fingers don't like me?"

"That's one of the reasons he don't like you," Bobby said. "All them manicure jokes about him having nine fingers. He thinks you're a smart-ass."

R.B. videotaped us for an hour before Bobby left. R.B. made his regular horse's ass joke. Today it didn't seem so funny. I couldn't help wondering exactly whose neck this noose was tightening around. Mine or theirs.

John didn't go back to Chicago. In fact he threw me a birthday party. On June 14, 1982, I was fifty-one years old and washed up in the mob. It started out at Joey's Disco, but we soon gathered a bunch of people and went bouncing around Palm Beach. The usual crowd showered me with gifts. Unfortunately, they were all the same. I got twelve cigarette lighters.

Tommy called three of the joints we were in. I told him the thing with Gallo's kid had been fixed. I'd killed it. But that didn't seem to make him happy. He kept asking when John was going to pay back Fat Andy's loan. These conversations kept up for the next week. Fat Andy himself never called. He was afraid of talking over the phone.

In early July we sent a juice payment of $3,000 to Fat Andy. We never did pay him back the principal.

Each call from Tommy was more shrill. I was enjoying seeing him sweat. I was also enjoying making him crazy. Or crazier, I should say.

"So anyway, like I said, Tom, I was driving up to the club minding my own business, and two FBI agents stop me. They tell me they want to talk to me about John, and you, and Fat Andy."

"So what did you tell them? What did you tell them?"

"I told them to fuck off, what do you think I told them? I told them that if they wanted to talk to me, they could do it in front of my lawyer."

"Yeah, that's good, that's good, Joey. What did they do? Do you have a good lawyer?"

"They didn't do nothing," I said. "They turned around and left. And yeah, sure, I got a good lawyer. I got sentenced to a month one time and he got me out in thirty days."

"Yeah, yeah, that's good, Joey. Hey, wait a minute, a month is— Stop fuckin' around, you punchy fuck. If I had my hands on your throat right now, I'd choke the shit out of you, you cocksucker! What do they want to know about this fucker John? You and your fuckin' club. I didn't earn a fuckin' quarter from this fuckin' club. You brought this fuckin' guy around for what? Tell me, you motherfucker! For what? Did you hear me, you deaf fuck?"

"Yeah, yeah, I hear you, Tom," I said as I lay back in my bed, a Scotch in one hand, a cigarette in the other, and the phone cradled in the crook of my neck. His tirade brought a smile to my face.

"Tommy, I brought John in to start the club," I told him. "So we all could earn. Don't you remember our conversation a year ago March? When you and Andy told me to start a club? It was your idea, not mine. I just found somebody with money, Tip. *Capisci?*"

"Don't blame me, you motherfucker! Why do they want to talk to him? He's liable to tell the Eye everything he knows."

"What does he know, Tip? He don't know nothin' from me. Did you ever tell him anything?" I was really trying to aggravate him now.

"Did I tell him anything? Is that what you said? Joey, when I get you, you see that tongue of yours, I'm gonna rip it out of your fuckin' mouth and shove it up your ass, you motherfucker! Did you hear me, cocksucker!"

"Yeah, you said you were going to—"

"I know what I said, you rotten bastard. You're going to kill me with all this talk, you motherfucker."

"Tip, take it easy, buddy. Relax, don't get excited. Have a drink. Take an aspirin. Be calm. I don't want you to get sick over this. Let me see John, and I'll call you back, okay? Tip, be calm, buddy. Go lay down."

"Okay, Joey." He was gasping as I hung up.

John was packing to leave when I reached him at his apartment. I invited him up for a drink. He told me he was hoping I'd say that. We were always there for each other. Don't misunderstand me. We had arguments about what was right and what was wrong. But never anything serious. I was teaching John how to be a hood and he was teaching me how to be an honest, law-abiding citizen, which was a lost cause. He learned. I didn't.

I called Tommy back the next day.

"What did you tell John to do, Joey? And don't start with me again. I'll fuckin' come down there and kill you, you motherfucker." Today T.A. was half calm and half his normal apoplectic self. I took that as a good sign.

"I told him like this. I said the club is a bust. I told him the Eye and guys from the State Liquor Authority have been around, looking to ask him a bunch of questions. I told him to go back to Chicago and leave R.B. down here to sell the place. Only thing though, I told him, he still had to pay his juice every week until Fat Andy got his loan back."

"Yeah, that sounds good, Joey," Tommy said. "What did he say? Can you trust that mick bartender? He looks like a cop. Even Andy and Bobby told me that if he wasn't a friend of John's, they would have made him for a cop all the way."

"Nah, R.B. ain't no cop," I lied. "The guy did eight years in Atlanta. What the fuck's wrong with you guys? Don't you think I check anything? *Marrone!*"

"He was in Atlanta?" Tommy seemed relieved. "Oh good, Joey. You should have told that to me and Andy."

"Well, what's the difference now anyway?" I said. "Everybody will be splitting up after the club is sold. R.B. will be going back to Chicago with John. Anyway, I didn't think I had to prove myself to anyone."

"You don't, Joey," Tommy said. "I didn't mean that. Call me if anything develops."

I reached over to turn off the recorder and found that I'd forgotten to put in a tape.

John was off the case, back home in Chicago. The club was closed. I was alone. Tony Amoroso ordered me to leave town with R.B. We skirted the north end of the Everglades and drove to Fort Myers on the west coast, where we hid out for a week. But all we did was play golf and get on each other's nerves. Even when we played golf, we rode in separate carts. The caddy masters never understood. I told them we were playing grudge matches.

I had to get back. Even in Fort Myers I was calling Tommy every day. It's like I was addicted to Agro, which I thought was a good name for a drug. He never even knew I was gone. And when I returned to my condo on Singer Island his was the first number I rang.

"Joey, Bobby's been trying to reach you," he said. "He says you never answer your phone."

"I ain't answering my phone because I think it's the feds trying to reach me," I told him. "What the fuck does that motormouth want? All he talks about is the loan John's got out. Tell him not to call me no more, that fuckin' jerk. He's going to get me pinched."

"Yeah, you're right," Tommy said. "He does worry about Andy's money a lot. That skinny fuck. Andy's the only one there that's made money from John. That two points a week was good. I'm going to call that skinny cocksucker right now and tell him not to bother you no more."

73
The Last Whack—Me

THE REST OF JULY RAN SMOOTHLY. TOMMY CHECKED IN daily, asking about the sale of the club. I told him these things take time. In August I was called to a probation hearing regarding a two-year-old beef where I'd pled to aggravated assault. The prosecutor argued that I'd gotten off easy to begin with, and wanted to extend the probation. The judge ruled in my favor. I had been a good boy, I told him. I was off.

I fell in love again, with a girl named Francie. This was really it.

Around mid-August Tommy called with an urgent message. Carmine "the Snake" Persico had been transferred to somewhere in California, and my "connection" had to get him back to New York. I told Tommy I'd see what I could do, and then forgot about the whole thing while I spent time with Francie.

Finally, a week later, I called T.A. back and told him my "connection" was doing everything he could to get the Snake back to the city, but it might take a little time. Meanwhile, Tony Amoroso was worried for my safety. There were rumors on the street that the Colombo capo Victor "Little Vic" Orena—with whom I'd done B and Es back in the early 1970s—had a source in the Eye. And his source, so the rumors went, had leaked word that Joe Dogs was cooperating with the feds.

Amoroso ordered Gunnar and Larry to baby-sit me back in Fort Myers while the Eye found me another apartment. I was fuming. I had a date with Francie the day they kidnapped me. But a phone conversation with Tommy, where he threatened to kill me without raising

307

his voice—very unlike Crazy Tommy Agro—convinced me that the feds had the right idea.

The Bureau found me a little one-bedroom place in out-of-the-way Cape Coral, and just in time. On August 16 Larry and Gunnar reported that a couple of Agro's sluggers had been nosing around asking for me at my old Singer Island condo. Agro was looking again to whack me.

Cape Coral had to be the hickest town in western Florida. Five miles up the Caloosahatchee River—and that about says it all—from the "metropolis" of Fort Myers, I was stuck in a town with not one good joint to hang out in. Christ, they even passed off macaroni as pasta. I had no phone, no car, and probably no future. My first day in town I went to the bank and got five hundred quarters, and spent the next five days on the pay phone across the street talking to Francie.

I also had to call the Eye's offices every day to assure Larry I was all right. And then I got to walk around and see the sights. I think I would have rather faced Tommy A. Tony Amoroso had taken my rental car back. He had a plan to shoot the car full of holes and spread some of my blood over the front seat. These guys, I figured, watched too many television shows. Luckily, Tony's plan never got implemented.

When I called the Eye's Palm Beach headquarters on my sixth day in the ghost town, a secretary told me Larry Doss had flown to Washington, D.C., and I was to call him collect immediately. When I reached him he told me to pack four or five days' worth of clothes and fly up to meet him. It was even an ordeal getting to the airport from the spot I was in, and when Larry met me later that night in D.C. I begged him to let me go home.

"You guys aren't gonna leave me in that place?" I whined. "I hate it there. The people are all rednecks."

"Joey, stop your complaining," Larry said. "Once we get you a new car and you meet a few new fiancées you'll grow to love the place."

"Are you kidding?" I asked him. "Fiancées! I asked this broad that lives next door for a ride to the airport.

Offered her twenty dollars. She said for that kind of money she'd cook me dinner, too. That's your kind of broad, Larry, not mine. You know, no teeth. You got to get me out of there.''

In a Washington hotel they had a big meeting of the minds. Tony Amoroso was there, along with Larry and Gunnar. Agent Andris Kurins had flown down from New York. And a federal prosecutor from Florida, Roma Theus, had come in from Miami. He was the black guy who would prosecute the Operation Home Run case, the same black guy Larry had warned me about embarrassing with my frequent telephone references to "niggers."

They left me in the lounge while they met, which was the wrong place to leave me. Because by the time they were through, I was bombed and in no way able to figure out exactly what they wanted me to do. I had been out of circulation for over a week, and the drinks had a strong effect.

When the agents woke me for breakfast the next morning, Tony explained everything again. The general feeling within the Bureau, he said, was that Operation Home Run was over and that my cover was blown. But no one could be 100 percent sure of that, and Tony had a gut instinct that the investigation could last a little longer. After all, he said, they'd once tried to kill me and taken me back. What was that against a few whispers on the street?

The plan was for me to call Tommy, Tony said, "and act like you just talked to him yesterday. If he starts blowing his top, which we both know he will, then make up some excuse why you haven't called him for a while. Just get it straight in your mind what you're going to tell Agro. This call is important! We have to see what he says, what he sounds like, before we make a decision whether to send you to New York or not."

"Oh, you mean I'm coming back from the dead after the fatal shoot-out in my car?" I said. "I guess it's a good thing you guys didn't do the trick with my blood. My poor daughters would be heartbroken. They don't even know I'm alive as it is."

"Are you telling me the truth?" Tony asked. "You didn't speak to your kids from Cape Coral?"

"The only person I've talked to is Francie," I said. "And I told her some big fucking lie and she believed it. You told me not to call my kids, Tony. Don't you remember?"

They hooked up the tape recorder to the phone and I dialed Tommy's number. All the agents in my room watched intently.

"Hey, Tip. How you doing, buddy? Listen, Tip, I didn't— Tip? . . . Tommy? . . . Are you there?"

"Joey! You're alive! You're fuckin' alive! I don't believe it." T.A.'s voice was surprisingly calm. I was worried. But I felt better in a moment when he started to scream.

"Where the fuck you been, you cocksucker? You know that you got everybody that knows you thinking you're dead? Did you call your daughter? She's crying. She thinks John killed you. I got a mob of guys. We were going to Chicago to look for John and whack him for whacking you, you dopey fuck."

"My God, Tip, hold your fire," I said. "Why would you think I was dead? And why would you think John would have something to do with it? He's a nice guy. But, shit, my poor daughter. I better call her. I don't know why you would think someone killed me, Tom. Everybody likes me. I'm a nice guy. Ain't I?"

"Yeah, but Joey, this ain't like you," Tommy answered. "You call all the time, then you just disappear. What happened?"

"Oh, Tommy. I'm in love with the cutest little baby doll you ever did see. She wanted to take me to Costa Rica. But I told her first I had business in Washington— that's where I'm calling you from—and that I had to wire you five thousand, and then the two of us would go off to Costa Rica together."

The thought of collecting free money would always, I knew, throw Tommy Agro off any suspicious scent. It didn't fail this time either.

"Oh, you got five thousand for me Joey?" he said.

"Yeah, Tip, but wait, let me finish what I'm saying

here. So she's got her tongue in my ear, telling me to forget about business for a few days, and, well, you know how it is, Tommy. I ended up in Costa Rica. You would have done the same thing. So that's how I got lost.''

I smiled and looked up at the admiring agents. Tony flashed me the thumbs-up sign.

"No, Joey, I wouldn't have done the same thing," Tommy said. "We were all set to head for Chicago and whack a few people over there. My *compare* even gave me the okay. Listen, Pip, don't ever do this again. *Capisci?* Now, the little guy's main guy, Mr. *Serpente*, is still out there on the West Coast. What's going on with that thing?''

"That's what I'm doing in Washington," I told Tommy A. "I'll find out this afternoon, sometime before two. Here, take my number and give me a call after that. I'll know everything by then.''

Tommy took the number and hung up. The agents took the tape and left. They ordered me to stay put. I'd find out soon what to tell Tommy when he called back.

While they were gone I called my daughter Sheryl, who told me that Bobby DeSimone had been calling her every day and telling her John had had me killed.

"He said they were flying to Chicago to kill John for revenge," Sheryl said. "Gee, Daddy, you almost got that nice guy killed. And he's the best friend you ever had.''

I wished then I could tell my daughter that I was working with the FBI, but I just couldn't risk it.

Tommy called right on the dot, at 2:05 P.M.

"Okay, Tom, he could do it," I began. "It'll happen a week from tomorrow. So you can go to the guys and tell them I did it. But you have to call me back and tell me where they want me to ship him.''

"Joey, send him to where the little guy was," Tommy said, meaning the Allenwood federal facility in Pennsylvania. "Don't send him back to New York.''

"Okay, Allenwood it is," I said. "But just to be sure, call me back at nine tonight and let me know for certain that's what they want.''

Tommy indeed called back at nine and complimented

me on my thoroughness. "You were right, Joey. Nobody's positively sure where he wants to go. Give me a day on this before we decide."

"Well, Tip, I guess I have no choice. But get somebody to make a decision fast. I want to get back to my girl. It's love this time, Tom. I think I want to get married."

"Good, Joey, I'm glad to hear that. I can't wait to meet her. When you come in, bring her with you."

Exactly twenty-four hours later, at 9 P.M. on August 26, 1982, Tommy Agro called my Washington hotel room. He and the Colombo capo Donny Shacks were partying at the Skyway Lounge. The Snake, they informed me, had decided on Allenwood.

"Joey, these guys thank you from the bottom of their heart," T.A. said. "There ain't a fuckin' thing you can't have in the city. Believe, Joey. They are so happy. Their boss is coming back home!"

Tony had instructed me to try to get some kind of commitment from T.A. about becoming a full-fledged wiseguy. That's why Amoroso was a fed. Never say die, and all that shit. Personally, I thought the idea was ludicrous. These guys planned on whacking me, not handing me a button. The feds may have been blind to the leak in their outfit, but I knew otherwise. Or at least I smelled a rat. I had lived too long with the mob—and thought like them and fought like them and schemed like them—not to realize when my number was up, even if Tony and the other agents thought different. Nonetheless, with everybody so full of gratitude, I figured now was the time to score some brownie points with the people who would soon be protecting me. It couldn't hurt, when they listened to the tape, to see that I was still following orders.

But first I wanted to find out why Tommy had sent his sluggers nosing around my old apartment. I had to give him credit, he thought quick on his feet. He explained that they'd merely been trying to find out why I disappeared, looking for "clues" that John had had me whacked. I pretended to buy it and pressed him about my button.

"Yeah, that's good, Tip. But what about me and this *Serpente* thing? What about my thing? What do I have to do to get it? Kill a dozen guys? Then I can get it when I'm going to the chair? Is that the way this is gonna work?"

"Joey, Joey, not over the phone," T.A. said. "Don't worry. Right now there's nobody bigger than you. There's no one more respected than you. So don't worry, and don't ask. *Capisci?*"

"Yeah, I'm not asking for nothing financially."

"I know exactly what you're talking about," Tommy said. "Patience, Joey. Patience."

Tony listened to the tape and liked it. A decision had been made. John and I were to be reunited in New York to work undercover. That was fine by me. I wasn't afraid of anything as long as I knew John was watching my back. But first we'd fly back to Florida to give John a chance to make his travel arrangements and then detour through Chicago and say goodbye to his family.

But then our team got stung. Gunnar Askeland quit the FBI. One of his sources told him there was a leak on the streets about Operation Home Run. Gunnar reported it to his supervisor, and when his supervisor ordered him to give up his source's name, Gunnar refused. They lost a good agent. I lost more confidence. Apparently I wasn't alone.

The plan, Tony told me, was on hold. John and I would eventually get to New York, but for now, he said, "Let's move more cautiously."

"Why don't you feel out Tommy," Tony suggested. "See what he thinks about you moving back."

On August 30 I called T.A. from my room at the Hyatt Hotel in West Palm Beach. After guaranteeing him that the Snake was set to be moved within the week, I popped the big question.

"Listen, Tip, I been thinking about moving back to New York. I want to come there with my girlfriend and start a chemical business. She knows all about the business. What do you think?"

"Sure, Joey," he said, a little too eagerly. "I'll be glad

to have you here. What kind of business is chemicals? I never heard of that.''

"Restaurants use them in the kitchen," I told him. "You know, soap and polish and all that shit. Do you think you could help us get into a couple of joints and hotels?''

"Are you kidding? I'll put you in a hundred places the first week. Will I help you, Joey! You talk like an asshole. Joey, right now you're the biggest guy in New York. You have so much prestige that I don't even have as much as you. You're a five-star general. I'm only a three-star.''

Soon we would see. This soldier was moving out.

74
Still Watching My Back

I DROVE TO CAPE CORAL THE NEXT DAY TO PACK UP MY clothes. When I returned, I called Francie and told her about our new chemical business. "You'll have all the big hotels and restaurants you want," I said. "You'll have a hundred people working for you.''

She became all excited and asked how I planned to get all these places and customers. I told her the mayor of New York was a friend of mine. She asked me the mayor's name. I was at a loss for words.

"Don't you know?" I asked her.

"No.''

"His name's Carlo Gambino," I said.

She didn't blink an eye.

On September 14 Francie and I flew to New York. I had plans to meet Tommy at the Skyway Lounge in Queens. The FBI didn't like me taking Francie along. In fact they hated it. They thought there might be trouble. But Tommy insisted on meeting her.

After landing, Francie and I checked into the Holiday Inn in Manhattan. Agents Larry Doss and Andris Kurins checked in down the hall. While Francie was showering I made an excuse to go out, and I walked to their room to get wired. We took a cab to the Skyway that night, and as we exited the taxi I noticed the place was surrounded by agents. Off in a shadowed corner of the parking lot I even saw Kurins and Doss.

The lounge was busy. Agro was sitting at a table with Paulie Principe. Fat Andy was at another table with Sal Reale, Ronnie "Stone" Pearlman, and two or three others from his crew. Not a good sign. The Ravenite Social Club in Manhattan was Fat Andy's usual New York hangout. The Skyway had about seventy-five people in it. Forty of them had to be feds.

After introductions, we sat down and ordered a drink. Tommy was calm, although talking a mile a minute. There was a guy at the table next to us that had to be a fed. No one wore white socks and wingtip shoes to the Skyway Lounge. At one point Francie had to go to the ladies' room. I walked her to the door and three guys walked up to me and asked if I was "Bob Jackson," their old master sergeant from basic training.

If I wasn't so scared I would have laughed out loud.

I walked to the bar for a drink, and the bartender complained that, considering the crowd, he'd never been stiffed so much in his life.

"These fuckin' people aren't tipping tonight," he complained. "That's when I know the joint is crawling with cops."

Christ, I thought, even the bartender knows!

Fat Andy hadn't received his juice from John for close to nine weeks. He was owed $4,500. That definitely was a problem that needed to be solved. If it hadn't been for me taking Francie along, there was no way all those agents would have been present. To this day I feel I was supposed to be killed that night.

When I went to the men's room an hour later, two guys followed me in to ask if I was "Bob Jackson." I told them no and asked how many guys they had covering the joint. "Too many," one of them said.

Francie and I were getting ready to leave when I stopped by Fat Andy's table to tell him John would be back in Florida next week. "Not only to make good on his back juice payments but to settle up on the principal." I knew he didn't believe me when he patted my stomach, just missing the Nagra stuffed into my pants.

"Gettin' a little fat there, eh, Joey," he said. It wasn't a question.

We left and I knew they were onto me. If all those agents hadn't been there I would have been history. I found out later they even thought Francie was a fed.

Francie and I went into Manhattan for the night and walked through Central Park the next afternoon. It would turn out to be the last time I'd ever walk through my home town. Larry, as disheartened as I was, mentioned that we could still fall back on the blood and bullet-riddled car trick. I declined. I couldn't cause that kind of grief to my family.

When I got back to Florida, Tony closed down the investigation. I was being careful and cautious, taking no calls from New York. Larry moved me out of the Hyatt and holed me up among the hicks of Cape Coral. If it wasn't for Francie's Friday night visits—against all FBI rules—I would have blown my fucking head off.

My agenda was set for the rest of my life. I'd spend the next decade testifying against my old friends, co-workers, and *compares*. Then I could look forward to a change of identity and growing old with grace (I hoped) under the aegis of the Federal Witness Protection Program.

But there was something inside me that still pulled me back to my old way of life. Call it the residue of a bad seed or the love of the easy life. Attribute it to the memories of the thrill I felt being a wiseguy, the power that surged around a mobster like some kind of electrical field. It was this natural force that led me to pick up the phone and dial Tommy Agro's number one last time.

"Tip," I began softly. "You shouldn't have never beaten me. You shouldn't have never fucked me all up."

"What's done is done, Joey. Eh, Joey, did you get followed here the other night? There were agents all over the fucking place." Tommy was speaking calm and slow.

I felt like he was only making conversation. Like he already knew the answer. Like he was playing my game back with me, just for old times' sake.

"What do you mean?" I felt weak.

"What do *you* mean what do *I* mean?" T.A. laughed. "I'm telling you, there were agents all over the fucking place. You brought them down with you. They were even spotted going into my fucking car."

"There was nobody following me," I said half-heartedly, and for a moment I thought he'd hung up.

Then T.A. said slowly and softly, without a lick of heat, "Hey, Joey, let me tell you something here and now. If you're working with those fuckers I'll get you. And if I don't get you, my *Famiglia* will. You better watch your back for the rest of your fucking life, my friend. Because I'll bury you, Pip. I won't miss you next time. And I'll take this promise to the fuckin' grave."

For once Tommy Agro was as good as his word. Based almost solely on my testimony, Tommy Agro was convicted in 1986 on charges of loan-sharking, extortion, and attempted murder. He was sentenced to fifteen years to life, but the verdict was overturned on a technicality. Rather than repeat the ordeal of trial, T.A. pled out and was given twenty years in the Florida State Penitentiary. In 1987 he was granted a medical parole in order to die at home, which he did that June, of brain cancer. I'm still watching my back.

Postscript

I TESTIFIED IN TWELVE TRIALS OVER THE NEXT TEN years, putting away just about everybody I ever worked with. I got my revenge, all right. Some of it sweet, some of it bitter. Thirteen days on the witness stand during the Agro trial was my personal record. But I came close to that with Joe N. Gallo, spending eleven long days pointing my finger at the seventy-four-year-old *consigliere* who dozed through much of his trial—though not my testimony—and who was sentenced to ten years in December of 1987, almost two years to the day that his former boss Paul "Big Paulie" Castellano got whacked. But I felt real bad for Little Dom Cataldo, who got thirty-five years, largely based on what I had to say, and then ended up dying in prison.

And though I became more or less a professional prosecution witness, shuttling between Florida and New York, playing a very serious game, it is the absurd little moments I remember the best. How Tommy A., for instance, who'd been a fugitive for almost a year in Canada, showed up in court in 1986 in a wheelchair, the typical Mafia "sympathy wagon." And how the judge kept yelling at me for smiling at him throughout the whole trial.

Or the way Fat Andy Ruggiano, who had also dodged his indictment and was hiding out with a Miami motorcycle gang, tried to blend in with his new pals by growing a scruffy beard and putting on even more tonnage—so much so that the feds had to handcuff him in front, as opposed to the traditional rear position, because his arms wouldn't fold backward.

Or Skinny Bobby DeSimone's reaction when agents showed up at his front door with warrants containing my name. "That fuckin' Joey," he raged. "I knew it. I knew it. I told Tommy that it was too fishy that Joey came up with all that money right after the beatin'. I told him it didn't look right. I bet you that John Marino was in on it, too."

The agents nodded, and explained that "John Marino" was actually Agent Jack Bonino.

"And R.B.?" DeSimone asked.

The agents nodded again.

"That fuckin' Joey," DeSimone muttered again. "I'm gonna get a million years in the can for this. I told Tommy we should have killed the motherfucker."

I put them all behind bars. T.A., Skinny Bobby, Little Dom, and Joe N. Gallo. Andrew "Fat Andy" Ruggiano and Ronnie "Stone" Pearlman. Carmine "the Snake" Persico and Dominic "Donny Shacks" Montemarano. Chief Boone Darden and Frank "Fingers" Abbandando. Gerry Alicino, the gentlemanly Joe "Piney" Armone and Sal "the Shylock" Reale.

The jury acquitted Paulie Principe. And Frank Russo, who along with Principe had used my head for batting practice, was indicted but never arrested. The feds eventually dismissed the indictment against him. Out of all the characters I ran with, Freddie Campo came out ahead in that he was never charged in connection with any of our schemes. As far as I know, he is still walking around South Florida. I hear that Freddie's pal Robbie—who told me he put three or four in Stanley Gerstenfeld's head and one in his heart to stop the bleeding—is also still hanging out in South Florida. Apparently, the authorities never went after him—maybe it was just a good story. Who knows?

After we shut down Operation Home Run, Francie and her lovely daughter Danielle came to live with me in Cape Coral. That lasted about a year, or until she got wind of the full scope of the work I'd been doing for the Eye. Who could blame her for being scared? But to this day I still think about her and still love her. If I knew where she was right now, I'd go running after her.

During the last frenzied days of the undercover operation I received a "Dear John" letter from Nena. How she could have the audacity to do something like that to such a nice, loving, monogamous person such as myself is beyond me. I wish her all the happiness, health, and wealth in the world. She was a fantastic lady.

Case Agent Larry Doss, who received some kind of an in-house FBI award for all his hard labor on Operation Home Run, swore to me that he'd never accept another organized crime assignment again. In fact he said he was so sick of Eye-talians, that he'd stopped eating pizza. Larry's wife divorced him, and he said it was because of the operation. I get blamed for everything.

Agent Gunnar Askeland rejoined the Bureau in 1984, and the feeling here is that the government is fortunate that Gunnar came back. He returned at the time of Skinny Bobby's racketeering trial, and we both got a kick out of the motormouth's courtroom attire. A neck brace. The jury may have gotten a kick out of it, too. But they didn't buy it. After a short stint in the Seattle office, Gunnar was transferred back to West Palm Beach.

The supervising agent of Operation Home Run, Anthony "Tony" Amoroso, retired shortly afterward at the age of fifty. I believe he was annoyed because Judge William Webster gave him the shaft. Tony had applied for the position of FBI legal attaché in Rome and walked around all day listening to Italian tapes and practicing the language. He was led to believe that the post was his up until the last minute, when a non-Italian guy got the job. Tony's wife divorced him, also because of the long investigation. *Marrone*, that's two they're blaming on me.

Agent Richard "R.B." McKeen was transferred from the West Palm Beach office down the road to Fort Lauderdale, where he vowed to memorize every word of the song "Ninety-nine Bottles of Beer on the Wall." The last time I saw him he was dancing to "The Beer Barrel Polka." R.B. didn't get a divorce. He was never married, to my knowledge.

After more than a year of dangerous undercover work,

Agent John "Jack" Bonino returned to his family in Chicago. He had infiltrated the mob using intelligence, charisma, and courage, befriending both a capo as well as a strong, if not maniacal, soldier in the Gambino Crime Family, which had embraced him as one of their own. The $25,000 juice loan he received from Fat Andy was the largest ever received by an undercover operative from La Cosa Nostra.

John received an award from FBI headquarters that in no way truly reflected the danger in which he had placed himself. He did an outstanding job and made me feel safe and secure throughout our investigation. John continues to specialize in organized crime out of the Chicago area. Sarah Bonino, the toughest of all wives, did not divorce her husband.

I have been asked by several people, mostly feds, if, knowing what I know now, I'd ever do it again. It's a tough question. Some nights, after sitting in that witness stand putting my old pals away, I went back to my room and cried. It was never my intention to break everybody, to fuck everything up.

I got into the whole thing for one reason. I wanted revenge on Tommy Agro. Burned with it. Later, when I found out all the circumstances surrounding the beating I got, I wanted Gallo, too. So the answer to that question —Would I do it all over again?—is no. Under the same set of circumstances, I wouldn't have worked with the feds, I wouldn't have turned on all my friends.

I would have just grabbed a gun, killed that fuckin' T.A. myself, and been done with it.

You live and learn. *Capisci?*

Acknowledgments

I never thought I'd write a book, much less a list of acknowledgments. I mean, fuhgedaboudit. Where do you start? There are people in life you can't live without. How do you tell them? I guess you just do. So, first of all, I'd like to thank Bunny and my four children for respecting me, for sticking by me, and for giving me the support and encouragement that allowed me to come through—in one piece—the ordeals of the past ten years.

My thanks and appreciation also go out to Special Agent John Bonino of the Federal Bureau of Investigation. Working undercover, hand in hand with someone in difficult and dangerous situations, allows you to take the measure of a man. I know of no one who measured up as John did during Operation "Home Run." Here I must also mention Robin Marie Stienbach Bonino, recently killed in an automobile accident. I know you're in heaven, Robin, and my prayers go out to you and your parents, John and Sarah.

I'd also like to thank my best female friend, Loretta, for helping me with the typing of the first ten chapters of this book. Loretta's husband Bob deserves my gratitude for his understanding and friendship. (For that, Bob, I won't accept any payment for the fishing tackle and angling secrets I taught you in Florida.)

My sincerest thanks also goes out to two dear friends, Ruggero Miti and Nicoletta Jacabacci, of Rome, Italy's RAI television network. Their technical assistance and support was invaluable.

I would be remiss without making mention of the several lovely ladies who nourished me with their kindness and friendship during my wild ride through the Mafia and beyond. Jewel Mason, Janet Scavone, Libby Proctor, Stephanie Lamy, Linda Carter, Cindra Ridge, and Tina Windsor, I thank you. And Bridgid from Naples, I'll never forget you.

I would like to extend my devoted thanks to Michael Korda of Simon & Schuster, who gave me the opportunity to get started on a new life and (I hope) career. God bless you, Michael. Also, thanks to Nick Pileggi for jumpstarting that career by introducing me to Sterling Lord and his wonderful staff, especially Jody Lee and Jacob Hoye. All three showed extreme patience in the face of my ignorance of the literary world.

Thanks also to Bob Drury and Carolyn Beauchamp for their friendship, knowledge, and expertise. (Without Drury, this book would have contained a lot more four-letter words.)

Much thought and gratitude goes to the following FBI agents who helped me with dates, esoteric information, and plain old facts: Supervising Agent Anthony "Tony" Amoroso, Case Agent Larry Doss and Assistant Case Agent Gunnar Askeland of Operation "Home Run"; Agents Al Sadowski, Richard "Dickie" Gentelcore, Dennis "Tricks" Tierney and Don Dowd of the FBI's Florida office; Bruce Mouw, Supervising Agent of Operation "Castaway" in Brooklyn, and Agents Kenny Brown, Charlie Beaudion, Richard Tofani and Ralph "Ralphie" Hilborn, who all worked under the supervision of Agent Christopher Mattiace who deserves special thanks during the Manhattan phase of Operation "Starquest." And, of course, I thank the prosecutors who put the bad guys away, including Roma Theus, Aaron Marcu, Peter Lieb, Laura Ward and Peter Outerbridge.